I Paid My $209,000 Student Loan Debt in Less than Five Years!

Richard Holzmuller

DEDICATION

This book is dedicated to free thinkers that listen to what people say; consider their worldview, and use what they learn to make decisions that help make them better versions of themselves.

Dedicated to You! 11-1-2021
I thank you for picking up
my book here at the
Gazebo in Little Falls!
I write about my experience
here on page 224
of this book! I
hope you enjoy
reading it, like I
enjoyed writing it!
— RH

P.S. All of my Social media
is at RichardHolzmuller.com

CONTENTS

ACKNOWLEDGMENTS

I am thankful for my friends that reject the status quo, and have the courage to try something different. I am appreciative of the supportive teachers I had, that helped me get acclimated to a trade I knew nothing about. I am grateful for the hiring managers I had as a contractor, and shortly thereafter as a company man—who also rejected conventional wisdom and took a chance on me, an academic, to do a trades job with no trades experience.

1

Paterson

Song Suggestions:
Corey Hart—Sun Glasses At Night
The Pointer Sisters—I'm So Excited

My mother is originally from Macedonia, and came to the United States of America when she was 29. My father was born and raised in the Riverside neighborhood of Paterson, New Jersey. Both of his parents were immigrants; his mother was from Scotland, and his father was from Germany. My parents met one summer evening in passing on Market Street in Paterson, New Jersey. After a few months of dating, they married each other in the Macedonian Orthodox Church "St. Kiril and Metodi" in Passaic, NJ. I was delivered via cesarean section at General Hospital in Wayne, NJ, and subsequently baptized in the same Independent Macedonian Orthodox Church my parents were married in. The church in Passaic burned down by arson; but a couple years later the church community rebuilt the church in Cedar Grove, NJ. For the first year of my parent's marriage, we all lived in my mother's apartment on Ward Street in Paterson, and then my father bought a house for us on Sherman Ave., in the Totowa section of Paterson.

Our house on Sherman Ave. was surrounded by rich cultural diversity. Jamaican's lived in the house to our left, Puerto Ricans lived in the house to our right, and across the street from us was a Russian Orthodox Church. A block away from us, still on Sherman Ave., was the Roman Catholic private school St. Mary's School.

A good education was really important to my parents, so they

3

enrolled me in the parochial St. Mary's School. As an indelible baptismal right, I was an independent child, and didn't like to do what the nuns in school told me to do. When I got into arguments with other children, I would end those arguments by beating up the kid I was arguing with.

One kid at school I hadn't fought yet was Billy. Conveniently, he lived down the street from me on the same block. He had toy cars that you could get in and pedal around like you were driving. Billy used to push the cars up the street to my house, and then we would pedal down the street to his house to play with his toys. I was a bit of a rabble-rouser, was loud, and Billy's parents yelled at him because of me. After one too many warnings to be quiet because his dad was sleeping, Billy's parents told him that he couldn't play with me anymore. I liked playing with Billy's toys, and knew I wasn't going to see Billy for a while, so I asked him nicely if I could take his fire engine pedal car to play with at my house. When I asked him, he made a mean face, and puckered his lips as he assertively said: "No." I tried to do the right thing and ask; but he didn't want to work with me, so I decided I was going to steal that pedal car.

As I was leaving his house, I quietly grabbed his fire engine pedal car, and slowly walked down his walkway to the sidewalk. I was halfway between their house and the sidewalk, and I looked back at their house, because I knew they could see the street from the second story. When I looked back at the house, Billy's grandmother was sitting on the front porch, watching me. I looked at her, looking at me, and shyly told her: "it's mine," and kept walking. I didn't want to say too much to her because I knew she would start asking questions. After my succinct statement, she didn't say anything, so I kept slowly walking with the pedal car to the sidewalk. When I got to the sidewalk, I knew I was safe, and kept leisurely strolling up the sidewalk to my house with Billy's pedal car. I didn't know what to do with it, so I left it in front of my house. I felt good that I got away with it, and Billy had a couple other toys that I liked, so I went back to his house to get them.

I casually glanced at Billy's grandmother when I walked past her to the back of Billy's house. She was staring at me with a confused look on her face, but I looked away and kept walking. I found the other toys I wanted, grabbed them, and started walking out front again. This time, Billy's grandmother asked me with a concerned tone in her voice: "are those yours too?" I meekly replied: "yes," and continued to carry Billy's toys with me down their walkway. Either she believed me, or she didn't care, but she left me alone, and let me finish stealing those toys too.

I knew my parents would recognize the toys weren't mine. I needed a ruse to keep Billy's toys, and just my luck, the Puerto Ricans had a pile of garbage in black bags at the curb in front of their house. I put the toys I stole on top and beside the bags, so my parents could easily see them from our house. I went inside our house, called my parents to the front window, and showed them the toys our neighbors were throwing away. I asked them if I could have the toys, and of course they said I could have them. My scheme to steal Billy's toys worked!

I enjoyed playing with Billy's toys, until he came over to my house one day. I was already in my room, in trouble for something, when I saw through my bedroom window that Billy just walked up our walkway into our backyard. I thought my mother would let me play with Billy since he came over to our house, but I could see he didn't come over to play.

He was asking my mother about his toys, and then he pointed at his toys in our yard, and told my mother they were his. She asked me if what he was saying was true. I wanted to lie, but Billy was standing right there, and I knew I wasn't going to be able to get away with that. Disappointed, I nodded my little head that Billy was telling the truth. My mother pursed her face with fury as she yelled at me.

She came inside, grabbed my arm, and tried to beat me with my own leather belt. But my mother is a small woman, and I was a tough boy. I wriggled my little body so she had to struggle to keep a grip on me, and then she couldn't get a good hit on me with her hand or the belt. After a minute of that she was frustrated, started angrily laughing, and said she was going to tell my father. Things weren't right with Billy and I after that. I would see him in the hall at school, say hi to him, and he would just stick his tongue out at me.

When I wasn't getting into trouble, I loved watching cartoons after school. Our television was right next to our backyard living room window. While I was watching cartoons, I always looked forward to my Jamaican friends yelling for me to come outside and play with them. Like the pope, I made them wait for me, and listened to them yell my name a few times as I continued to watch cartoons.

Before they gave up, I acknowledged their calls, and told them to give me a few minutes. Instead of going out front and walking around, I always went to our backyard, and hopped the fence between our yards. Their parents always yelled at me when they caught me doing that, and I would always say: "okay, I'll stop," hoping they wouldn't catch me the next time. I loved playing outside with my Jamaican friends; we played marbles, hide and seek, tag, rode our bicycles around, and even did sedentary stuff sometimes like talking, and board games. Their grandparents lived in the house behind me. Occasionally we would go over to their house to play too.

Their grandfather didn't have any top teeth. Well, he had false top teeth. Sometimes he would pull his dentures out in one hand, raise his arms above his head, and growl at me like a monster! I would scream in terror and run away as my Jamaican friends laughed and yelled for me to come back. But I refused to come back until I knew for sure their grandfather put his teeth back in his mouth. Usually when he left them, and was inside his house, I knew it was safe for me to come back. It was soo scary for me, and really interesting for me at the same time. When he had his teeth in his mouth, I would walk by him and stare at his mouth, trying to figure out how he could do that.

Other than the teeth thing, he was nice to me, and I enjoyed going to his house. He grew grapes, and made wine with his grapes. I liked walking through his vineyard, and seeing the wooden barrel full of grapes and grape juice in his backyard. He said I could play back there, but he sternly warned me to never play with his wine barrel, or the grapes inside the barrel. I respected the man, so I just stood next to the barrel admiring it, or I would just scratch the ground with a stick near it.

One night after playing with my Jamaican friends at their house, I did what their parents told me, and I didn't hop the fence to go back to my house. It was dark, but I wasn't scared or in a hurry to get home, so I was shuffling my feet up the sidewalk in front of my house. All-of-a-sudden, some teenager threw me against the wall of the porch in front of my own house! He put his hands on the wall at opposite sides of my head, and used his arms to block me in on both sides. I looked in fear in his eyes, and he just stared at me, breathing heavy from his chest. I was surprised he hadn't done anything yet, so I ducked under his arm, and started running away.

I wanted to look back, but I knew I was in trouble, so I just kept running. I ran around the corner and down the block to my Jamaican friends grandparent's house. Nobody was outside, but as soon as I was in their driveway, I knew I was safe. I figured, worst case scenario, I could just run into their house and yell for help. Even if the door was locked I was going to beat on the door, yell for help, and ring their doorbell.

Hiding between a wall at the side of their driveway and their car, I looked down the street I just ran down to see where the teenager was. I was hoping I could see him so that I could be sure I was safe. After a few seconds, I saw him under the streetlight on the corner across the street. The lower half of his body was behind the corner, his arm wrapped around the corner with his hand on the wall, and his face was at the edge of the building looking in my direction with a look of loathing on his face. I wasn't sure if he could see me or not, and I didn't want to wait to find out, so I ran down the driveway toward the vineyard.

As I was running, I started to think the teenager would come back across the street to find me in front of my house again. When I turned into my Jamaican friends backyard, I wanted to do the right thing and not climb over the fence. I tried to imagine that the teenager was gone, and that I could walk up the street without any problem. But, I really didn't want something to happen to me worse than being yelled at, so I climbed over their fence to get into my yard. I didn't tell my parents about the teenager, because I didn't want them to put any restrictions on my playtime, but I also tried not to stay out past dark again.

A few nights later, I was in my room, getting ready for sleep. My bedroom light was out, but the backyard light was on, and I was standing at my window looking into the backyard. I saw someone with a black hood over his head jump over the Puerto Rican's fence into our backyard. The guy pulled some newspapers from his jacket, and lit them on fire on the side of our house. My mother was in the living room right next to my room watching television. I wanted to tell her right away before our house burned down, but I didn't want her to get hurt, and I knew our house wouldn't burn too much. So I stood at my window, motionless behind my curtain, watching the guy. After he knew the fire was lit, he climbed over the Puerto Rican's fence again, and was gone.

I knew it was safe at that point, so I let my mother know our house was on fire. She ran out to the backyard, got a bucket of water, and put the fire out. As my mother was finishing putting the fire out, my father was coming up the sidewalk, just getting back from work. He asked what happened, and if I knew who did it, but I had no idea. My parents discussed the situation a little more, and I went to sleep, knowing I was safe because my dad was home.

My father was a machinist at Marcal Paper Mills Inc. (now burned down) in Elmwood Park. One summer, while most of the rest of the machinists were on vacation, my father needed help. Marcal contracted Sam Stout of D & S Machine Repair Inc. in Hastings, Michigan, to come to the paper company to help fix one of their machines. While Sam and his team were at Marcal, Sam met my father, got along well with him, and invited him to come to Hastings.

My mother, father, and I, took a trip to Hastings to visit Sam. My parents liked that there was soo much space, everything was clean, and there wasn't any graffiti on anything. Sam even took us out in his boat on Lake Michigan; which was awesome, until my mother got motion sickness.

Sam turned his boat around, and headed back to the dock. I was hoping we would just drop my mother off at the dock. But when we got back to the dock, my mother got off of the boat, and my father wanted me to go with her. I really wanted to stay on the boat with the guys, because it was a lot of fun being in the boat as the waves rocked the boat on the water. I pouted at the edge of the boat until my father told me I needed to take care of my mother. With that charge, I saw it as a good thing for me to get off of the boat. So, I got off of the boat, and Sam and my father went back out on the lake.

As Sam and my father were fishing, my mother and I slowly walked around on the sidewalk. There wasn't anything to see or anyplace to go, but being on-shore made my mother feel better. When Sam and my father returned, my father was soo happy, and showed off the big fish he caught.

All things considered, we had a good time on the trip. Sam offered my father a job, and even knew a guy who had a rental available near his house. My parents weren't ready to accept his offer, but it was nice to have that option.

Because of my lack of consideration for others, rejection of their attempts at teaching me socialization skills, and general disobedience to authority figures, leaders at my school thought there was something wrong with me. After school one day, my parents came to the psychiatrist's office at my school. They calmly sat next to each other in the office, and the psychiatrist authoritatively sat behind his desk. There wasn't another chair, so I sat on the floor at my mother's feet as he spoke with them.

After a while, the doctor asked me to draw a picture of my family. That was an easy one; insulted, I wanted to take the big black crayon and draw heavy sharp zigzags diagonally on the manila construction paper. But as I was sitting on the floor, looking up into my mother's face, she gave me this look of pleading. I could tell this was really important. I knew I needed to use a nice color, so I grabbed the thin green crayon. I drew a picture of our house, the tree in front of our house, and stick figures of my father, my mother, and me. The psychiatrist looked at my drawing, and told my parents I was very smart.

He suggested to my parents that some medication might do me a lot of good. My father wasn't interested in medicating me, or appeasing the school, so he rejected the doctor's suggestion. I was grateful for that, because I didn't trust that psychiatrist at all.

But, the psychiatrist did give me good advice. I often used to say mean things to my mother at home. He told me when I wanted to say something mean to her to just stop, try to think of something nice to say, and say that instead.

I did what he told me because I didn't like to see the sad looks on my mother's face. The only nice thing I could think to say to her was: "I love you." So I said that; a lot, usually with a mischievous grin on my face. Hearing me say that always made my mother happy, and she would respond with something in kind.

After a year of frustration on the school's side, and on my parent's side, my father decided to accept Sam's offer. So when I was six years old, my father sold our house, and we started our move to Michigan. Our UHAUL moving truck was parked, loaded, and locked with all of our stuff in front of our house. My father and uncle Ricky left mid-morning so they could drive straight through, and get to Hastings that night.

My mother and I stayed back, and waited for my aunt Evelyn to finish her shift at work, so she could drive with us to Michigan. Late afternoon, we finally left Paterson, and started our drive in our newly purchased 1985 Chevrolet Chevette. My aunt drove our car because my mother isn't a confident driver. After driving for what felt like forever, it was late, and I was tired. I decided I was going to sleep in the back.

Cleverly, I folded the back seat down, so I could lie flat like I was sleeping in my bed. Unlike my bed, the back of the seat was hard, and a little uncomfortable. As I lied there, I looked up through the back window at the stars while we drove. After a few minutes, I closed my eyes, and fell sound asleep. My mother and aunt also started sleeping soundly.

When we all woke up, I was sitting in-between my aunt and my mother, loudly crying with my foot stuck in the steering wheel. A paramedic helped me free my foot, and get me out of the car. There were no lights anywhere except for the headlights and flashing red and blue lights of the emergency services vehicles that lit up the area. As I was standing next to our car at the bottom of the hill next to an emergency services worker, I looked up the hill, and I could see we had driven through the guard rail at the side of the interstate. My aunt and mother were wearing their seatbelts, but my aunt was a little heavyset, so she needed help getting out of the car from the emergency services workers. My mother was fine, and got out of the car on her own.

We all rode in the ambulance to go to the hospital together so we could get checked-out. While my aunt was being looked-at in another room, my mother was with me in my room, and I was sitting on the examination table. A nurse treated, and put a little bandage on a cut behind my ear. That was where my mother and I learned from my nurse that we were in Ohio. In the morning, my aunt rented a car, and continued driving.

When we finally made it to Michigan, my aunt drove straight to the car rental place to drop the car off. Except, the car rental place was in Grand Rapids. After we dropped the car off, we took a taxi to Hastings.

Our taxi driver didn't know where the motel was, so he just dropped us off at the edge of town, and we started walking. While we walked, my aunt and my mother weren't sure we were going the right direction, but I recognized the area from the year before. I told my aunt and my mother we needed to turn left at the light, and the motel would be there. They weren't soo sure about that, but they followed my direction anyway. We turned left, walked down a block, and I saw our UHAUL parked in front of one of the motel rooms. I excitedly pointed it out to my mother, and she was soo surprised and impressed with me. My aunt Evelyn and uncle Ricky spent the night in the motel with us, and went back to New Jersey the next day, leaving us to start our new lives in Hastings.

2
Hastings
Song Suggestions:
Social Distortion—I Was Wrong
The Chemical Brothers—Dig Your Own Hole

We left a culturally diverse big city to live in this culturally insulated small town, and we didn't even live in the city. The house we were renting was in the country, a few miles North of Hastings on Broadway. It was a small, white, two-story home with a few trees on the property. Behind the house was a pasture with a couple horses on it, and behind the pasture was our landlord's house. Our landlord had children older than me, but they still accepted me as their playmate.

Nearby was Sam's neighborhood with a few more children that were older than me, and a country school with a playground that nobody used anymore. The area wasn't bad. We had neighbors with children I could play with; it's just that the neighbors were far away, so I had to learn how to use the telephone pretty quick.

In Paterson, my mother met me outside school at the end of the day, and we walked home together. I saw the busses outside of the school, and I really wanted to ride those busses, even though we lived a block and a half away from my school. Now that we lived in the country, I was riding the bus to school every day, and I really didn't like riding the bus.

I was going to Northeastern public school, and it was more of the same for me. I tried to make friends, but the people I wanted to be friends-with didn't want to be friends with me, and said mean things to me. During lunch recess, I was by myself, leaning against the side of the school.

Three boys walked up to me as I was standing there. At first, I thought maybe they wanted to be friends with me. But they surrounded me, and started picking on me. The kid in the middle was doing most of the talking, and the boy to his left just chimed-in a little behind him. I didn't know how to get out of there, I just wanted them to stop. A tear streamed down the side of my face, but I didn't want them to see me cry. I needed to get away from them quick. My frustration became desperation, and I swung.

I punched the kid in front of me right in his nose. All-of-a-sudden, the two boys broke up the circle around me, and huddled around the kid I just hit. I slowly walked away from them, and began crying. When I looked back, I saw the group of boys still huddled around the kid I hit, and they were walking to go into the school. I thought they were going in to tell on me. Another boy standing nearby saw me hit the kid, and told me I gave the kid a bloody nose. I thought the boy talking to me was going to tell on me too since he saw what happened, but he was cool, and tried to calm me down. Shortly thereafter, my parents met with my teacher after school to have a conference about me. While they were inside talking, I got to go outside, and enjoy the playground equipment all by myself.

It was my mother's childhood dream to own a house on a hill, overlooking a lake, and to have a big yard filled with flowers. Before the end of the school year, my father was able to fulfill my mother's dream. He found and bought my mother's dream house on a hill, across the street from a lake. The property didn't have any flowers in it, but the yard was large enough that my mother could plant as many flowers as she wanted, and she was okay with that. The house was in a rural residential community, so the houses were next to each other, but the houses weren't as close together as they were in Paterson. The neighborhood wasn't designed as a retirement community, but it might as well have been.

Most of our neighbors were retirees, and the rest of the neighborhood was middle-aged commuter workers who didn't have any children, or whose children were already grown. The retirees really didn't come out of their houses, except to check the mail. Sometimes I would see them drive down the street in their big old cars, and they would wave at me as they drove by. On an even rarer occasion, their grand children would come to see them, but that was it, there were no other children in the neighborhood.

I rode my bicycle around the neighborhood exploring, and found a private drive along the lake where there were a few empty vacation houses, a few more commuters, and a few more old people. Riding my bicycle the other direction, I found a bridge over the stream that flowed from the lake, and led into a wooded area. I really liked to go to the bridge over the river, and listen to the water as it flowed over the rocks.

One day I was riding my bicycle back from the river, and one of the old people two houses down from us had a table set-up in his driveway to sell some little things he didn't need any more. I didn't have anyone to talk to, so I rode up to him, and started talking to him. He asked me personal questions my parents told me not to answer, so I was vague when I answered his questions.

His name was Mr. Lee; and he shared his ranch style brick house on a basement with his wife, Mrs. Lee. I made friends with them fast, and they invited me to come over to their house whenever I wanted to. I don't know why, but I didn't tell my parents about Mr. and Mrs. Lee for a long time. I was able to get away with that because I would just tell my parents that I was going for a bike ride, and then I would go over to Mr. and Mrs. Lee's house. I had fun visiting them because Mrs. Lee enjoyed baking sweets, and she liked sharing her baked goods with me. They also played games with me like Triominos, Dominos, and Checkers. But, all of that good stuff came at a price.

Mr. Lee was very religious, loved reading the bible, and went to a Baptist church a couple times a week. Once in a while we would all sit around the kitchen table, take turns reading from the bible, and then talk about it. I really didn't enjoy reading the bible or talking about what we read, but Mr. Lee still gave me a bible, and told me to read it when I was home. I kept the bible in the bottom drawer of my dresser with a few of my toys, but I never read it.

When I went back over to his house, he always asked me if I had been reading my bible. I really enjoyed eating Mrs. Lee's sweets, and playing games with them, and I didn't want my "no" answer to ruin that for me. So when Mr. Lee asked me if I had been reading my bible, I shyly told him: "yes." I considered it to be an honest answer because when I shoved the book out of my way, the book sometimes briefly opened, and I saw that there were words on the pages as it was open. Mr. Lee didn't accuse me of lying, but he usually replied to my shy answer with a little lecture about the importance of reading the bible, and sincerely encouraged me to continue to read my bible. I just listened to him, and nodded my head in agreement.

Right next door to us lived another religious person, Thelma. Thelma was a classic old lady. She liked going to church every Sunday morning, and she liked cooking stews with red wine. When she went to church, she wore a plain solid colored dress, chunky heeled black shoes, a few simple pieces of jewelry, and carried a classy little clutch.

One day after church, my father was outside, and Thelma started talking to my father about the local parochial school. She recommend to my father that he enroll me in that school. My father talked to my mother about it, and they saw it as a good thing for me. My mother liked the idea because the parochial school had a religion class, a music program, and they assigned homework. So my parents decided to enroll me to start second grade in that Roman Catholic school called St. Rose of Lima, and Thelma even went to the school with us to vouch for us.

That summer, before I began attending classes at my third school in two years, my father had a talk with me at the back porch of our house. He told me to avoid fights, and only to fight someone if I had no other option. It was a really serious conversation. I didn't like hearing what he was saying because I thought I was already doing that. But I really didn't want to get in trouble anymore, and I didn't want my dad to get mad at me, so I kept reminding myself about what he said.

When school started again, I repeated in my head the words my father said to me. Whenever a kid said something I didn't like, I asked myself: "Is there no other option?" As mad as I got at the boys, every time I answered myself: "no." It was a huge playground, and the kids never backed me against the wall, so there were plenty of places for me to run. Listening and doing what my father said changed me from assaulting my peers when they were being mean to me, to just taking the verbal abuse, and not doing anything about it. Their unkind words and actions didn't feel good, but at least I wasn't getting into trouble anymore.

I did get along okay with one of my classmates, and we spent the night at each other's houses on occasion. His father owned a business in-town, they had a big two-story house with a pool, and a driveway filled with luxury cars. That was where I got my initial inspiration to start my own business. I wasn't sure how I was going to do that, but it seemed like something I needed to get into.

My parents weren't religious, so we didn't go to church together, and my mother worked most weekends anyway. Church was important to our neighbor Thelma, and she knew I wasn't going, so she offered to take me with her when she went. My parents trusted her, thought it was a good idea, and so Thelma started taking me to the Catholic church with her every Sunday.

There was soo much stuff we were supposed to say and do at church. From the moment we entered the church, we had to do certain stuff at certain times. And during the church service, there was a lot of standing, sitting, kneeling, and other gestures we needed to make with our hands at specific times during the mass. I didn't know what to do or when to do it. I felt so inept; I really didn't like that everyone around me knew what to do, and I did not. Because I didn't know what was going on, I just followed Thelma's lead, until I was able to say the words and do the gestures by rote.

Church was became routine for me, so I was getting bored at church. I would listen to the priest, say the words, and sing the songs along with everyone else, but I would also start to daydream. I tried to pay attention in church because I wanted to learn. But we would say something, the priest would say something, or I would just see something, and my mind would begin to wander along a delightful little daydream until something else caught my attention.

We always sat on the same side of the church as the song leaders. I was a little envious of the song leaders. They were at church, but they really weren't at church. They got to sit off to the side, and share witty little quips with each other, while everyone else in the church had to listen to what the priest was saying. And then there were our car rides to and from church.

Thelma looked nice going to church, but she wore some cheap stinky perfume that filled the car with her odór. That made riding with her in her big old car really unpleasant for me to breathe, but I was nice, and never said anything about it. It was only a 10-minute car ride to church, so I didn't have to suffer much, and on the way home most of the smell was already evaporated off of her.

Our car rides were respectfully quiet. Thelma didn't say much to me, and I didn't say much to her. She interacted with me only as needed, like a teacher. One morning, the sun was pouring into the car through the windshield, and I sneezed. Thelma said the sun made me sneeze. It really didn't make sense to me, but I just went along with it. She was always really serious with me, but I'm sure she joked around with her grown-up friends.

Thelma was active in the church community, and liked socializing with practitioners in the local religious orders. One evening, she was driving home after one of her wine and stew dinners. She fell asleep at the wheel, smashed her car into a tree, and died in the wreck. It was unfortunate that she died, but it didn't bother me. We really didn't have much of a relationship outside of our obligatory church trips. She liked to swim in the lake, and tried to teach me to swim, but that was about it. So, that ended our Sunday morning ritual, and my swimming lessons.

My father asked me if I still wanted to go to church. This was my opportunity to sleep-in on Sundays, and never go to church again. I liked that idea, and was really tempted to passively answer him: "not really." But, we had religious education class at school. I hated when my teacher would mention something that the priest said during his homily on Sunday; ask for participation from the class, and I wasn't able to contribute because I didn't know what she was talking about because I wasn't there. Even though I mostly daydreamed during the homilies, I didn't want to cheat myself of the chance to be able to answer the teacher's question when she asked. So when my father asked me if I still wanted to go to church, even though I really didn't want to go to church, I quietly told him: "yes." He was disappointed by my response, because he didn't want to go to church, but he agreed to do it.

The following Sunday, we went to church together. My father put-on his baby blue suit, he had his hair laser parted to his left, and he looked sharp. After mass, one of the small town guys sitting behind us recognized that my father was new to the church, and decided to introduce himself. He was also wearing a suit, but not nearly as stylish as my father's. Trying to be witty, the small town man followed-up his introduction with some stereotypical small talk about my father being from New Jersey. Playing along with the guy, my father said something that made the man feel very uncomfortable.

All-the-while my father was pleasant, and kept a smile on his face, but they were both very off-put by their exchanges.

My father is a very mind his own business, don't stick your nose where it doesn't belong kinda guy. The nosiness of the small town man rubbed him the wrong way, even though he was just jesting with my father to be friendly. I don't appreciate that kind of humor either, so that was the end of our trips to church, and the beginning of my trips to church.

I still needed to go to church for school, but after that unpleasant interaction with the small town man, my father just dropped me off at church on his way to breakfast at a local restaurant. After church, he picked-me-up where he dropped-me-off, and we would go home. I was only nine years old at the time. Clearly my father trusted the people in and around that church.

I always sat by myself in the pew; unless it was one of those busy holidays, then I had to slide over and let other people sit with me. I didn't feel awkward about the experience at all. I could do as much or as little as I wanted. Before mass, I liked looking at the local small business advertisements on the back page of the church bulletin, and often daydreamed about advertising my own business there. Eventually I got bored, so I became an altar server, and did that for a few years.

They had two mass times on Sunday; 8am and 11am. My father preferred to drop me off at the 8am mass to get it out of the way; but they needed someone to fill-in as an alter server at the 11am mass, so one week I went to that mass instead. I normally didn't have time to do anything before church, but because I was going to the late mass, I had time to kill. It was a perfect sunny day, so I went for a leisurely little bike ride toward the bridge. Past the bridge is the highway. When I made it to the highway, I turned around to go back to my house.

On my way home I saw a water diversion dip that looked big enough that I could jump-it with my bicycle if I had enough speed. But it was right on the edge of a river rocked driveway, so I had to pedal on the grass half of the way to get to it. It wasn't completely undoable, so I went for it. I built up as much speed as I could on the road, and kept pedaling hard on the grass trying to keep-up my speed. Then I hit something, flipped forward, and caught my fall with my gaping mouth in the river rock. The first thought I had was that I just broke all of the teeth at the front of my mouth, and it was going to cost my parents a lot of money that we didn't have to fix all the teeth I just broke.

When I picked myself up, and my bicycle, I was surprised I didn't see any blood on the river rock. That made me feel a little better, so I looked to see what I hit. There was some tall grass in front of my jump. When I moved the grass to the side a little, I saw a railroad tie under the grass. All of the grass was cut except for that one little area. I felt soo dumb for not checking what was in the tall grass before I tried to hit the jump. I knew I busted-up my teeth, I just didn't know how much, so I had to get home and see.

As I rode my bicycle home, slowly, I imagined how mad my parents were going to be that I hurt myself. I also imagined us making an emergency trip to the dentist to get my teeth fixed; me in the dentist chair, and my parents in the room watching the dentist work. When I got home, my parents didn't greet me as they did in my imagination, so I just walked over to the mirror. I was surprised to see all of my teeth were still there, they weren't broken, and there wasn't any blood in my mouth! All I had was a little cut at the side of my mouth that I cleaned-up with a some hydrogen peroxide, and that was it. I still went to church, and still fulfilled my alter server duty. Of course, I had to explain to everyone what happened to my mouth, but that was nothing in comparison to what I imagined.

I used to think my parents didn't have any money because they didn't buy me all the stuff I wanted, we never went out to eat, and they never really gave me any money. But, they didn't buy me all the stuff I wanted because they wanted me to learn to be satisfied with what I had. We only went out to eat on special occasions because the food was expensive, and wasn't the food we preferred to eat. And my parents didn't freely give me money because they wanted me to understand money has to be earned.

My mother did give me five dollars every Friday for taking out the garbage, getting the mail, and keeping my room clean, but I usually spent that as quick as she gave it to me. I always wanted more money, and I was really impatient to get it. I tried to get money any way I could.

I started with picking-up empty bottles and cans from the sides of the roads. In Michigan, store clerks gave me 10¢ for every refundable empty I brought back to the store. I even brought-in flattened cans, and they still gave me money for them.

Then I was doing yard work, and other miscellaneous work. I mowed a few lawns regularly, raked leaves, and planted-plants. One guy needed a little helping hand, so he paid me to help him do his siding, insulation, and drywall. Another guy didn't like housework, and never washed his dishes, so he paid me to wash his dishes for him. I really didn't like most of the work I was doing, but the cash incentive kept me interested in doing the work.

I was doing good earning an honest living; but I wanted to get rich quick, so I fell into money making schemes. A few of the things I did was stuffing envelopes, printing and selling self-improvement booklets, door-to-door selling motor oil additives, making dangly beaded earrings, and becoming a distributer for a jewelry wholesaler. I even joined Amway, and tried selling their products. By sixth grade, a family with children around my age finally moved-in across the street, and I made friends with them. My new neighbor friend David wanted to get rich quick too, so I bought the kit, and talked him into making dollhouse furniture with me. With all of the get rich quick schemes I tried; I ended up spending more money getting into the scheme, than I was able to make selling the products.

Likewise, David and I weren't able to earn any money selling dollhouse furniture, and eventually gave up on the get rich quick idea. Regardless, it was really nice to finally have people in my neighborhood to hang out with again. We did biking, boxing, boating, swimming, running, laser tag, ice skating, ice hockey, listened to music, spent a lot of time on their trampoline, and even watched movies and played video games sometimes.

The private parochial school I was going to didn't have classes past the sixth grade, so for seventh grade, I was back in the public school. Things went a lot better for me in the public school this time. Curricularly, I was ahead of my peers, so classes were really easy for me. And there were more children, so for the first time since I had been going to school, I actually had some classmates that wanted to be friends with me.

During summer break between seventh and eighth grade, I had my first official taxable income wage earner job. The job was walking through cornfields detasseling corn. No matter the weather, we were out there detasseling the corn. I didn't enjoy that work, but I liked earning the money.

In eighth grade, in an effort to grow the little bit of money I had, I bought candy from Sam's Club, and sold it out of my locker before school, in-between classes, and after school. I liked the money I was earning with my candy business, but I didn't like the thin profit margins. So I started stealing my candy from the local big-box store. Business was good, but I was getting a lot of activity around my locker, and that started raising suspicions of the teachers in that hallway. One afternoon, I was called down to the principal's office, because the principal thought I was selling drugs out of my locker. They searched my locker, and didn't find any drugs in my locker, but that was the end of my candy business.

I loved the whole experience of stealing; cleverly going into the store, getting what I wanted, and getting out of the store without getting caught. Since I couldn't sell candy anymore, I switched to stealing and selling portable cassette players. I sold the cassette players for half the price they would have to pay in the store, so it worked-out good for both of us.

One weekend I was at a Meijer store in Battle Creek, and decided to steal a couple cassettes and compact discs (CD)s for myself. While my parents and I were walking toward the exit door, security stopped me at the door. My mother started crying right away, so she stayed outside with our cart of stuff that they bought, and my father went back with me into the security room.

My father sat across the room from me, and we both just sat in our chairs with our heads hung, silently staring at the floor. As they were filling-out the police report, I looked up at my father, and I saw a sly little smile come across his face as he shook his head. That gave me a little hope, until he looked up at me, and his face quickly turned disapprovingly stern again.

Now that I had been caught, the fun was gone, and I was done stealing. When I went to court, the judge said he went to church with me, and watched me as I grew up. He said he respected me, and was surprised that I would do such as thing. He made me do a research paper about stealing, and then I had to go to court again to give him a ten minute speech about what I learned. After that, he took me out to lunch a few times to check-in on me.

The following year, my father told me he fell in love with a young woman when he was young, and they had a daughter together. But, because they were young, they were too poor and immature to raise their baby girl, so they gave her up for adoption. She was adopted when she was a baby, 16 years before I was born. Now that she was an adult, and had a family of her own, she wanted to get to know her biological parents.

Her name was Sue, she lived in Vermont, and my father was first to visit her. Things went well on his visit, he told Sue about me, and Sue was interested to meet me too. My father made the arrangements for me, and I flew to Vermont. The first time I flew to Vermont to meet her, I wasn't sure anyone would pick me up at the airport. When I arrived there, I saw a man, woman, and child walking together toward me. I didn't know what my sister looked like, but I figured it was them, so I walked toward them and we did the awkward first-time introductions. We all got along well during my time there, and Sue invited me to come back to visit. After that first trip, I went to Vermont a couple more times to see my sister and her family, and everyone was always so kind to me, leading me to believe we were cool. I wanted to fly and visit her more often, but I needed a job.

I wanted a legitimate job to start earning money as soon as I could get one. At 15, I took a driver's education class, passed my exam, and earned my learner's permit. On my 16th birthday, my mother went with me to get my driver's license, and they actually gave me one! That was so nice to have, and made it a lot easier for me to get a job.

One of my business teachers knew the owner of our local J.C. Penney store. My teacher knew J.C. Penney was looking for a part-time stock boy toward the end of the school year, trusted that I wouldn't make him look bad, and referred me to the owner for the job. I met the owner, he liked me, and he hired me.

During the summer I would drop my mother off at work in her 1991 Mercury Topaz, go to football practice, and then work in the J.C. Penny stockroom unpacking boxes and delivering merchandise to the floor for a few hours. When my mother got off work I picked her up at work, dropped her off at home, and then I went back to work in the stockroom. When school started in the fall, I didn't have time to pick my mother up and drop her off, so she helped my buy a car.

We went to a used car dealer, and I picked out a 1991 Geo Tracker. I liked that it had 4-wheel drive so I could get around easily in the snow. I also liked that it had a soft-top, so I could take the top down in the summer. My mother co-signed a $5,600 loan with me to buy the car, and I was responsible for the car payments, so that was my first debt. I was barely earning enough money to make the payments and put gas in it, so my father paid the insurance on the car for me. And, because I couldn't afford to pay for oil changes, my father taught me how to change the oil and filter on my car myself. Changing the oil in my car was easy; my drive to work was smooth, and I always stayed busy in the stock room. But, the small town of 7,000 people must have been shopping somewhere else other than their local J.C. Penny.

A year after I started working there, they were preparing to close the store. I enjoyed the job, and was disappointed that I was soon to be jobless, so I started reading the help wanted advertisements in the local newspaper. A couple cities up from me, Showcase Cinemas movie theater in Cascade, MI was hiring.

I applied at the theater (which was later bulldozed and turned into a strip mall), and they hired me. It was about a half-hour drive to get there, so I only worked there on the weekends. I usually didn't finish work until midnight, so trying to stay awake while driving in the country was always a challenge. There wasn't anything like businesses, billboards, or cars on the road to catch my attention or keep me interested.

One night, I was driving on this long stretch of straight road, and fell asleep at the wheel. I knew I fell asleep at the wheel because when I opened my eyes and looked around, I had no idea where I was. My heart was racing with fear, I was soo scared. I slowed down, turned around, and began driving the other direction. I didn't recognize anything for a couple minutes, and that freaked me out too. As I kept driving, the scenery started to look familiar, and then I finally saw the sign for Hastings Road where I needed to turn. I couldn't believe I fell asleep at the wheel, and didn't drive off the road! After that, I went to the grocery store when I finished my shifts, and bought bakery items like chocolate éclairs to get some sugar in me to help me stay awake.

Another night, I was driving home in the middle of winter, close to the same area where I fell asleep and missed the turn. The sky was perfectly clear with a full moon lighting the night. I had just driven 20 minutes at highway speeds with no problem; and when I turned onto Hastings Road, I continued to drive at highway speeds. But, the road had snow packed onto it. I was driving up a hill, and was approaching a farmer's house at the top of the hill. I must have nudged the steering wheel a little, because all-of-a-sudden I started drifting to-and-through the on-coming lane and kept going. I hit the farmer's mailbox, and I kept driving diagonally off the road. I ended-up off the road, stopped on the side of the hill, next to the farmer's field. The steep embankment I was on ran all-along the side of the road so I couldn't just turn back onto the road. I really wasn't sure how I was going to get myself out of this mess because the snow was up-to the bottom of my door. I thought about going to the farmers house and asking for help, but I thought he was probably asleep, and I didn't want him to make a big deal out of it. I decided to try to get myself out of there.

In the deep snow, I was surprised I could open my door. I trudged through the snow in my sneakers to lock the hubs of my car, then I put it in 4-wheel drive, and tried to drive. I was soo surprised my car was moving forward! I could hear the leafless branches of a thicket of bushes scraping the side of my car but I didn't even care how scratched-up my car was getting as long as my car kept moving forward.

I turned off of the steep embankment, and began driving on the edge of the field. I thought about driving deeper into the field and trying to turn around, but then I thought I might just get stuck in the field, so I just kept driving on the edge of the field, next to the embankment, parallel to the road. I wasn't sure where I was going, or how I was going to get out of the field, I just kept going. The steep embankment finally turned into a ditch once the hill plateaued. I considered trying to drive through the ditch, but I didn't know how deep the snow was, and I didn't want to risk getting stuck by stopping to check it out, so I drove straight some more. After driving for about a-third of a mile, I finally saw a farmer access point to the field that connected to the road. I felt soo lucky! I safely drove through the field access spot, and stopped in the middle of the road.

When I stepped out of my car onto the highway I nearly slipped and fell because the road was soo icy. I understood now how I lost control of the car, and wondered how I hadn't driven off the road much sooner than I did. I breathed a deep sigh of relief, enjoyed looking at the stars in the moonlit sky for a minute, and then surveyed the damage on my car.

There was a large scratch on the hood of the car where the mailbox was sliding along my car, and my driver side mirror was knocked-off when the mailbox finally hit it. All things considered, it wasn't that bad. I got back in my car, kept the 4-wheel drive on, and cautiously drove home without further incidents. After that, I was much more wary about snow-packed roads. We didn't do an insurance claim on it, because it was a hassle that was just going to cost us more money, and it was mostly cosmetic damage anyway. I had a lot to learn in regard to driving, but I was doing really well in school.

With the idea of becoming a businessman burned in my brain, I enrolled and excelled in all of the classes the business department offered at my High School. I was also active in anything else I could find that was business related. There was a day long securities management competition at Davenport University, and I lead my team to take the most awards at that competition. I was involved with Business Professionals of America; competed at the state level, and won ninth place for my business plan for a new fitness center. One summer I led another team in a three-day business management competition at Hope College; there too, my team won the most awards. I was soo active in anything business related in High School, that I even received a little trophy from the heads of the business department, for being one of the few students in the history of the department to complete all of the offered business classes. I wanted to go to college to continue to study business. I had decent enough grades to get into most colleges, but my parents couldn't afford to pay for college for me.

One morning, I was sitting in my chemistry class in High School, and there was a large postcard for the Marines on my table. The picture on the postcard was of camouflage-covered Marines holding rifles, in an inflatable boat, floating on a river in some jungle. I briefly thought about joining the Marines; my father was very proud to be a Marine, but that picture seemed a little too hardcore for me.

Kellogg Community College was hosting a College Night, and I met with an Air Force recruiter there. The recruiter told me they would give me a salary, food, a place to live, uniforms to wear, money for college, and they would even pay for some of the tuition for classes I took while I was in the military. That seemed like a pretty good offer to me, I didn't see how I could lose at all in that deal. I talked to both of my parents about me joining the military; and they were both supportive, so I signed-up through the delayed enlistment program.

My guidance counselor knew I was planning to enlist in the military; so he told me about the National Youth Leadership Forum. I talked to my father about it, and he paid for me to go to the National Youth Leadership Forum on Defense Intelligence and Diplomacy in Washington D.C. The forum was almost a full week.

Through the forum, we toured the national monuments, went to the Smithsonian National Air and Space Museum, met with officers at the National War College, saw the changing of the guard at Arlington National Cemetery, toured the capitol building, I got to meet an aide for one of Michigan's political representatives, and I watched part of a vote from the gallery. At our hotel, we listened to speeches from high ranking officials, and met daily in small groups to learn how and why our government uses defense, intelligence, and diplomacy. All through the forum, we worked through a mock scenario to reduce the severity of a developing crisis, and our group of 14-ish people elected me to be President of the United States. Positively influenced by the experience, I ran for election in our student government, and my peers elected me to be our senior class president. I liked learning from my classmates, and learning in general.

Things that interested me most were diet and physical fitness. My mother read books about natural healing and homeopathic remedies; she loved sharing with me what she learned, and I loved to learn what she told me. We learned that nitrites in pork were bad, so I stopped eating pork.

A few months later, I was in one of my business classes. We were watching an investigative journalism video about a food chain that sprayed their ground beef with red dye to make the meat look fresh when it was at the end of its original shelf-life date. That weekend, I was preparing some ground beef to make hamburgers for us to grill. When I opened the meat mound to pour some spices in the middle of it, I saw the outside of the meat was red, and the inside of the meat pile was brown. A few days before that, my mother was talking about artificial colors being bad. When I saw the color difference in the ground beef, I was shocked and angered, so that is when I started excluding beef from my diet.

Another good thing I learned in my business classes was investing. One of my business teachers was explaining the time value of money, and told me I would be very wealthy if I started saving for retirement while I was still in High School. I was interested in becoming wealthy, so I did what he told me. He told me to call an investment management company, order a prospectus for a low load mutual fund, and start putting money into the fund monthly. I chose an international growth stock fund that had a $100 minimum investment, and setup the account to withdraw $50 per month from my checking account the day after I received my paycheck. I felt really good doing something now, to help me prepare myself for my future.

I was only working weekends at the movie theater, so most of the little money I was earning was going to my car payment. Although I had a car, I couldn't go very far because I didn't have enough money to do anything other than drive to and from work. When I turned 18, I wasn't restricted on the number of hours I could work in a day, or week, so I got another job.

Hungry Howies was opening in Hastings. I wanted more money, so I thought about working there after school during the week. I applied, and they hired me. Actually, they hired a dozen of us high schoolers. Opening night we were shoulder-to-shoulder in that kitchen learning how to fold the boxes, cut the pizzas, take telephone orders, wash the pans, and read the wall map to see where to deliver the pizzas to. They rotated us into different positions throughout the night so we could learn all of the roles, and there were soo many people in the kitchen that you had to actively look for something to do, otherwise you could end up uselessly standing around.

When the owners saw people just standing around, instead of asking them to sweep or do something else, they politically just said: "Thanks for coming-in, we're good for the night, we'll call you when we need you." And guess what, I never saw those people again. I was one of the few people that actively looked for something to do, always asked the owners how I could help, and they were really pleased with my work ethic. They complimented me how well I did that night, and asked me to come-in a couple days later because they were doing another make-or-break night the following night.

When I went back to the restaurant, I picked up where I left off, and continued to help however I could. I really wanted to be a delivery diver, and I actually had to work up to pizza delivery. It was competitive to get into a delivery driver spot because it was the most lucrative part of working at the pizza franchise, so everyone wanted to do it.

As a delivery driver, they wanted us to jog out to our cars in an effort to get the orders to our patrons a little quicker. Some of the drivers refused to do that, so when the owners saw me jogging out to my car, it made them very happy to see that I was a team player. I had a lot of fun doing that job, and some of the homeowners I delivered-to were really cool. With the money I was earning in wages and tips from the pizzeria and working at the movie theater, I was starting to get a little more breathing room economically.

All-the-while I was going to school and working, I was also working-through the application process to get into the Air Force Academy at Colorado Springs, Colorado. I'm not sure where I originally got the idea; it may have been from the first Air Force recruiter I spoke with at College Night, but I was interested to get into the Academy and become an officer. It was a lengthy application process; and I met most of the requirements such as grade point average, participation in extracurricular activities, a personal essay, civic engagement, reference letters, and a nomination from the governor, but I fell short on my ACT and SAT scores. I retook each of those tests a couple times, but my scores were still a little too low for me to meet the minimum requirements to earn acceptance into the Academy. I've never been great at standardized tests, but it also could have been bad karma from all of the stuff I stole. Regardless of my bad karma or poor aptitude for standardized tests, a couple months after I graduated High School, I told my employers at Showcase Cinemas and Hungry Howie's I was going into the military.

The day I was scheduled to leave for the military I was at a Military Entrance Processing Station. One of the guys there was reviewing my file, and saw that I had a stealing conviction in my background report that I hadn't mentioned anything about. It was a close-call. Because of the age I was during the crime, I was a few months under the cutoff, and just barely allowed to enter the military.

With no other drama, I went to the airport, and joined my peers for dinner at a restaurant. There were about eight of us around the table. One guy was a little nervous and revelrous, but the rest of us were cool. When the plane landed in San Antonio, they bussed us to Lackland Air Force Base, and we began basic training.

3
Texas

Song Suggestions:
Underworld—Born Slippy (Nuxx)
Goldie—Inner City Life (Radio Edit)

Basic training wasn't that bad in the Air Force. At the time, it was only 6-weeks long, and basic training was literally basic training. We spent a lot of time marching, or waiting in line. We waited in-line outside in the morning so we could wait in line at breakfast. We marched to appointments on base for shots and haircuts, and waited in line when we got there. Then we marched to lunch and waited in-line. We marched to trainings in the classroom to study military history and codes of conduct, marched to trainings in the field to shoot the M-16, and then we marched back to the dormitory (dorm) to wait in line for the dinner line. Every other morning we did a little physical conditioning, and when we were in our dorm we spent our time cleaning, or ironing our underwear to make our wall-lockers look perfect. Because of all of that, I started earning college credit right away through the Community College of the Air Force (CCAF).

I didn't have any intention to continue to go to church when I went into the military. I figured I was in the military, and I was just going to do whatever they told me. But our training instructors told us that we could go to church on Sundays. I was really surprised by that. So when they offered church, and a lot of people went to church, I decided to go to church too.

Church was interesting in the military. Air Force people that were acting as ushers at the church wore white ropes around their shoulders that looked very distinguished. Church was in a large auditorium, and there were a couple hundred of us basic trainees there. Other than that, the mass was essentially the same as what I grew up with.

While I was in basic training, we filled-out a dream sheet of all of the places in the world we were interested to be stationed. I wanted to go to almost anyplace overseas, or to the East or West Coast of the United States. At the end of basic training, they gave me orders to my next training station. I was disappointed to learn I was going to Medina Air Force Base, which is only a 10 minute bus ride away from Lackland Air Force Base.

In the technical training school at Medina, I continued to earn credits toward my CCAF Associate Degree. Our military instructors taught our class of 12 people electronics principles, how to read electrical schematics, and crimping and soldering. I wanted to be successful in the military as I was in High School, and I wanted the time to go fast, so I started volunteering for extra-curricular activities.

I liked the way the chapel ropes looked in basic training, so I volunteered to be a chapel rope, and usher-in the little basic trainees. Another thing I did to help pass the time was read. Just like in basic training, there was a lot of time we were standing in line waiting to go somewhere or do something. I hated doing nothing, so I read books about nutrition and food, because I was new to vegetarianism, and I wanted to open a vegetarian restaurant. I regularly went to the library on-base and checked-out books to read.

After we successfully completed our electronics principles training at Medina, we received orders to go to our next training stations. My next training station was Sheppard Air Force Base near Wichita Falls in Texas. At Sheppard, I continued to learn the basics I needed to do my Air Force job, Avionics Test Station. To help prepare me for my job, I trained on test station simulators in the classroom that were similar to the test stations I would be working with at my eventual duty station. At Sheppard too, I read and volunteered, but instead of ushering at church as a chapel rope, I joined the color guard, and still got to wear a rope on my uniforms.

Even though I wasn't volunteering in the church, I decided to continue to go to church. It was a little weird sitting in the pews of the church with everyone else instead of working at the church in some capacity during the mass. At the end of the mass, they usually had announcements of what was going-on in the church community.

During the announcements one-day, they said they were going to have a bible study. I had never been to a Catholic bible study, so I decided to go. Instead of a bible study, it was more of a get-to-know-Catholicism study.

A couple dozen of us technical training students showed-up to the Catholic course. I was asking the group leader, Brett, a lot of basic questions about what we were supposed to believe and why. One of the questions I asked led into a discussion about conscientious objection. Brett appreciated my questions because he also recently asked himself the same questions. Even after our group meeting, a couple people approached me and mentioned they liked the questions I asked because they were wondering the same things. I even started hanging out with one of the girls I met at our little bible study which was also very nice. After that first meeting we had, the meetings became more fun, and we talked a little more about the bible. We had a good group; I enjoyed the experience, and considered starting a Catholic bible study at my next duty station if they didn't already have one.

After 10 months of training at three bases, I finally received orders for my first duty station. We were all hanging around the day room in the dormitory when we received our orders. Instead of sending me to any of the bases I listed on my dream sheet, I received orders to go to Ellsworth AFB, SD.

I had no idea where Ellsworth AFB, SD was. At first I thought SD was the initials of some tiny island nation in the South Pacific; it wasn't, it's not. SD stood for South Dakota. I didn't even know where South Dakota was. After asking a couple guys in the day room, and checking the large wall-map we had there, I learned that South Dakota is a landlocked state in the heartland of America. I was really surprised by that, and found it hard to believe that our government was sending me to serve our country somewhere in the middle of the United States. Regardless of that presumed misfortune, I wanted to continue to do well in the military.

4

Ellsworth Air Force Base

Song Suggestions:
The Exploited—Alternative
Roni Size & Reprazent—Share The Fall (Full Vocal Mix)

I had about a week before I needed to report to my first duty station, so I went to Michigan to visit my parents. My father told me he had another daughter, and it was the same story as with Sue. They were young, fell in love, had a child, were too young, and lacked the resources to properly raise her, so they gave her up for adoption, and a nice family adopted her. Again, she started her own family, and wanted to know who her biological parents were.

Her name was Kathy, she lived in New Jersey, and she invited me to meet her and her family. Kathy and I were both a little nervous to meet each other, but we worked through it, and enjoyed starting to get to know each other. What stood-out about my visit with her is that she drove a Mercedes. I was happy to see she was doing well, and that inspired me to work hard so that I too could afford a Mercedes one day.

After visiting my sister Kathy and my niece and nephew for a few days, I drove back to Michigan. I packed my Tracker with a few things, and left my parents to go to Ellsworth. The girl I met in the Catholic bible study was already stationed at a base near Omaha.

On my way to South Dakota, I made it a point to drive to Nebraska to see her. We walked around downtown, and checked out a few local shops. I enjoyed Omaha with her, and she let me spend the night at her place while she worked her night shift. In the morning I continued my drive, and after driving all day, I finally made it to my base on-time. I intended to go back to see her again, but Omaha to Rapid City was a lot longer of a drive than was reasonable for me to do in a weekend.

In the morning, the first thing I did was report to my boss at the shop where I was supposed to work. Because I didn't have a place to live yet, my boss told me to find the dorm manager, and get a room in one of the dormitory buildings on base. They assigned me a room in the Roosevlet dorm building, and I moved the few things I had into my room. It was like a studio apartment; it was just one room with a sink, mini-refrigerator, and a bathroom that was shared with the room next door.

I didn't think they would still give me free food at the dining facility on base because I wasn't in training anymore; so my first night in my dorm room I went to Dan's supermarket on Omaha Street, (this place was also bulldozed and turned into a strip mall). At Dan's I bought a loaf of French bread, and a block of mozzarella cheese to eat. So that was my breakfast, a handful of bread, and a little wedge of cheese. When I went to work after breakfast, I was delighted to learn Airmen that lived in the dorms still got to eat for free in the dining facility.

The first week in my dorm room I didn't go anywhere. I looked out of my dorm-room window, saw the black hills in the background, saw my tracker parked underneath my window, and daydreamed about exploring the area. But my gas tank was empty, and I couldn't afford to fill it, so I stayed on base. I passed the time writing hand-written letters to friends and family, writing poems, reading papal encyclicals, walking around the dormitories reading the bulletin boards, and keeping my room clean and organized. I also went to the library on base, and checked-out music CDs to listen to, because I couldn't afford to buy any music.

When I finally got phone service, I started calling friends and family. One of my friends I called was Heather. We used to work together at Showcase Cinemas, and hung-out after work playing billiards at the Anazeh Sands pool hall. When I went into the military, she moved to California with her boyfriend. In one of our conversations, she recommended to me that I buy a computer, so we could keep in-touch online.

I thought it was great idea, even though I wasn't really sure what I would do with the computer the rest of the time. This was 1998, the internet was relatively new, and America On Line (AOL) was still mailing free trial CDs. Gateway computers was also heavily marketing. I didn't have the money to buy one of their computers outright. Unfortunately for me, they were offering a financing option. Missing some critical life experiences, I naively ordered a Gateway computer, and fell for the finance trap.

My computer was financed through MBNA America, and I was approved for $2,500. I financed $1,800 for what I thought was a good computer, but four months later they were selling computers that were twice as fast for the same price. I was a little disappointed by that, but I still enjoyed my dial-up modem computer. I started surfing the internet, and found some electronic music to listen-to that I desperately wanted to hear more of. I really liked the music, but I lived in a rural community, so I couldn't just turn on the radio to listen to the music. And I was poor, so I couldn't afford to buy a lot of CDs. The internet was finally a way I could affordably listen to more of the music I really wanted to hear. I didn't want to spend all of my time on my computer, and so-far in the military I was having good church experiences, so I decided to continue to go to church.

The Catholic church on base didn't have their own bible study; and I briefly considered starting one, until I saw a flyer hanging on the bulletin board in my dorm. The flyer advertised a bible study in a vacant room at one of the other dorm buildings on base. I went to the protestant bible study; it was a Friday night, and about a half-dozen of us showed up. After our bible studies, we would all go out to a local restaurant and get some desert, tea, or something light like that.

One of the guys I met there, Quilian, was from Miami. Quilian was about my age, was a part-time carnivore, and he too was a first generation American. Quilian and I got along well, so we hung-out often. We did driving tours of the Black Hills, went to plays, tried yoga, sometimes went to Calvary Baptist Church and their youth group bible studies, went to science based bible studies at the School of Mines, often ate at the Seventh-day Adventist vegan restaurant, and regularly hung-out at the local book store, desperately trying to expose ourselves to cultures we weren't seeing in our local community.

Another guy I met at the bible study was fittingly named Peter. I was hanging out with Peter in his room, and he was on his Gateway computer that was twice as fast as mine, and some AOL instant messenger message popped-up on his screen. I asked him about it, and he said it was some Christian girl he was talking to. She wanted to talk, he was folding his clothes or something, and I asked him if he was cool with me talking to her.

He didn't care, so I started instant messaging the girl. We had fun instant messaging back-and-forth, so we exchanged emails, and started talking via email. After a few weeks of this, we became pretty good online friends. And then our weeks turned into months, and it kinda turned into an online relationship. We were online dating before online dating was even a thing! Our relationship didn't work-out, but around the same time my cousin Tracy met someone online, and her relationship did work! She ended-up moving to Colorado, marrying the guy, and 20 years later they are still married! Being active online, and in my local communities, helped me learn about myself.

One day after mass, there was an announcement they were looking for volunteers to lead youth bible studies. I wanted to be active in the church community, and was still developing my relationship with God. I thought this would be a great way for me to get involved, be a positive influence, and help others learn and grow too.

Soon thereafter, a young officer volunteered to lead the youths with me. We had some great group meetings at church, and fun group outings skiing and going to a religious retreat. I wasn't too focused on the religiosity of it all, I was more-so interested in fostering understanding of self, and connection with God. Everything was cool, until one of the youths in the church got pregnant. She wasn't even in our youth group. Relax, it wasn't me, it was from her High School boyfriend. But the older adults in the church still got nervous, and didn't want me to participate in the youth groups anymore, because I was too close in age to their children. The older adults had the young officer leading the group with me break the news to me. The young officer bought me dinner at the Pizza Hut (now closed down) off base, and broke the news to me. This hit me hard because I enjoyed working with the youths.

I was soo disappointed and frustrated, I told one of our priests I wanted to excommunicate myself. He of course discouraged that decision, and told me it's better to not burn any bridges. I understood that, agreed with him, but told him I was going to take a break from the church. He didn't argue with me about that. The spiritual thing was still important to me, so Sundays became spiritual development days for me, and a day to deepen my connections with others around me. The rest of the week I was doing my test station job.

My test station job was scheduled like a civilian job; I worked Monday through Friday 7 a.m. to 4 p.m., and had an hour lunch. When I started working in the shop on base, I was surprised to learn I had to study more electronics for career progression. So for most of the first year I was at Ellsworth, I was studying for my Career Development Courses (CDCs) tests. I was disappointed about that too because I thought I would be able to take college classes right away; but, I needed to complete my CDCs before I could enroll in college. The good thing was, as I was working on the career development courses to progress in my military career, I continued to earn college credit toward my CCAF degree. I studied in my off-time, and during my work-day I was learning my job.

My job was to fix the defensive electronics of the B-1 bomber. Because we worked with electronics, and because those electronics all had classified data on them, we worked in a windowless, climate controlled, combination-locked-room. The electronic test stations and the electronic units we tested generated a lot of heat, so the air conditioning was always on to keep the rooms cold.

There were four different rooms like this in the building that I worked-in. Each room had a different team that specialized in some of the other types of defensive electronics of the B-1. There wasn't much interaction between the different teams most of the time, so there weren't many opportunities to get to know the members of the other teams, unless we were getting together for something like a squadron picnic or volunteer event.

Other than my protestant bible study group, I didn't have a group of friends that I regularly hung-out with, so I hung out with everyone. One of my co-workers the next shop down from me had a Jeep. He liked to drive his Jeep on the trails in the Black Hills, and invited me to come along since I also owned a 4-wheel drive vehicle. I was talking with the guy who worked supply across the hall, Rob Buss, and he was interested to go 4-wheeling too. Rob didn't have a

4-wheel drive vehicle, so he rode with me, and we went trail riding. We had a lot of fun that day, and Rob became one of my good friends in the military.

Rob (now deceased) thought it was a shame that my Tracker was damaged from the mailbox I hit in Michigan, and suggested that I get it fixed. He didn't think it would cost that much money, and it would look great for years to come. I agreed with him, and took my little car to an auto body shop to get fixed. It was about $800 to fix the damage. I asked them if I could make payments to them; they rejected my offer, and wanted full payment before they would release my car.

I didn't have that much money, but MBNA America always sent me cash advance checks to use when I needed money. This was one of those times I needed money, so I used one of those checks. The great thing was, I was able to pay for the repair-work for my car, and get my car back. The bad thing was, they didn't do that great of a job color-matching the new paint with the old paint, so it was obvious that I had body work done to the car. Also, the cash advance interest rate was 24%. I didn't have much understanding about interest, so 24% didn't mean anything to me.

All I knew was, all of a sudden, I was having a very difficult time making even my minimum payments. I think it had something to do with my car payment, MBNA America payment, home phone bill, cell phone, internet bill, visa payment, and DPP Military Star Card payment. I had much more debt than I could comfortably manage, and I was spending all of the money I was earning. Needless to say, I was a little uncomfortable. I couldn't go anywhere, do anything, or buy anything because I didn't have any money, and my credit was maxed-out.

In order to give myself a little more economic breathing room, I went to one of those cash advance lenders. They gave me $350 for a $50 fee, and if I was late on my payment, I was charged another $25. Working with the cash advance lender gave me the money I needed to get caught-up on my payments; but I thought the service charges were exorbitant, and I really didn't like that I put myself in that situation.

One day, as I was making my payment to the manager at the cash advance lender, I told her that I hated the place. I thought she would be empathetic with me. Instead, she was surprised and offended, and that made me feel awkward. I paid-back the cash advance lender in-full, on-time, and tried to not put myself in that desperate position of need again.

Had I known a little more about money, I never would have financed the computer. It would have been much better to save my money, and pay cash for a computer. In the time it would have taken me to save enough money to buy a computer, technology would have improved, prices would have come down, and I would have been able to get a much better computer at a much lower price.

After joy riding in the hills, and driving back and forth to the payday lender, it was time for me to change the oil in my Tracker. I didn't know there was a place on base where I could change my own oil, so when I got to Ellsworth AFB, I stopped doing my own oil changes. I had a decent paying job in the Air Force, so it wasn't that big of a deal to go downtown and pay someone to do my oil change for me.

I went to one of those quick oil-change places, the service was pretty good, and they gave me a free car wash. I did that a couple times, and everything was cool, until one day I was driving my car, and the low oil light suddenly came on. I thought that was really weird. I pulled over to a gas station that was closed, and didn't know what to do, so I called one of my coworkers to help me out. My gut instinct told me to buy a drain plug, fill it with oil, and try to run it. I kinda didn't want the hassle of trying to find a drain plug, and was thinking my engine was already destroyed from running on no-oil for a few minutes. So I left my car at the gas station, called the quick oil change place, explained the situation, and they made arrangements to have my car towed and repaired.

I wanted the repair shop to see if my engine was salvageable. I asked the guy in the shop if he confirmed that the engine was actually seized, and he gave me a quick response like: "oh yeah, we checked it, that engine was gone." I didn't trust that he actually verified the engine was ruined but it was too late; they already had the engine out, and a replacement engine from the scrap yard to put in it. When the work was done, they called me to come get the car.

I was happy to get my Tracker back, but a little skeptical about the work. I drove away from the shop, and it didn't drive the same or sound the same as before. I thought about taking it back to the shop, but I still wasn't sure what the problem was, or even if there really was a problem. I drove it a few more minutes. It seemed to lose power, and sounded progressively worse. I knew for sure there was something wrong when it all of a sudden it made this awful sound like I was driving around without an exhaust pipe. I took it back to the garage, and they said they forgot to install a gasket on the exhaust pipe where it connects to the engine.

I was soo frustrated; and not happy, especially considering how many problems I was creating for myself with the car. I was barely keeping up with all of the debt payments I had to make; I really didn't need the car because I lived and worked on-base, so I thought I would do myself a favor and get rid of the Tracker. I was able to sell the car for what I owed on it, and that helped me put myself in a position so I wasn't suffocating from my debt anymore.

At work, one of the things our squadron leaders told us to do was volunteer. I volunteered for stuff in our local communities in high school, mostly because I knew colleges looked for involvement in some selfless activity in their applicants, but also because I liked meeting new people and having new experiences. I was successful in High School, and I wanted to be successful in the military, so I volunteered.

They were looking for people to volunteer for a day to play with the children at the Black Hills Children's Home. I was a little reluctant to go there; because I didn't know anything about children, but we were encouraged to go, so I did. While I was volunteering at the Black Hills Children's Home, I met a guy from one of the other teams, his name was Mike.

Mike had a strong sense of adventure like me, so we got along well. On the weekends, we went on hikes in the Black Hills. After our hikes, we ate at China Buffet, or something like that. Mike wasn't religious, so while we hiked, we talked a lot about our differing beliefs. I really enjoyed our conversations because they helped me open my mind about what I believed and why.

Because I did what they told me, and didn't complain, I was starting to have a lot of the successes in the military that I had in High School. After only a year at Ellsworth, I earned recognition as Maintenance Professional of the Month, Airman of the Quarter, and even Airman of the Year for our Squadron. Professionally I was successful, economically I had a long way to go.

Selling the Tracker motivated me to continue to pay-off my debts.

I like living openly, honestly, and transparently, so I naturally told my friends where I was economically, and what I was trying to do. Quilian heard my economic story as a plea for help, and bought my $1,800 computer from me for $800. Quilian really helped me out; I appreciated what he did for me, and I continued to consider how I could begin to pay-off the rest of my debt. I had $3,000 in my mutual fund that I started in High School. The money I was earning from my mutual fund was a lot less than what I was paying in interest on my debt, so I sold all of my shares in the mutual fund, and used that money to finish paying-off my MBNA America account. I still had $2,000 on my Visa, $1,700 on my DPP Military Star Card credit account, and I was too impatient to slowly pay-down those debts.

I went to Sentinel Federal Credit Union to get a car loan to buy an old Mazda RX7 for $700 from a guy on-base. The lady at the credit union wouldn't give me a loan for the car, so she increased the limit on the Visa credit card I held with them. I took that money, bought the RX7, and got a part-time job off-base working as a convenience store clerk at Common Cents. Going into more debt so I could earn more money made sense to me at the time. But, I had to work two months just to pay-off the car. At the same time, I was exploring cooking my own meals in my dorm room, so I spent all of the extra money I was earning on cooking appliances. Getting my part-time job was quick and easy, so leaving the job wasn't a big deal for me.

I told my boss at Common Cents I was quitting because the job was too stressful. In reality, I was quitting because my hiking buddy Mike was talking about a road trip. I should have been honest with my boss at Common Cents, and told him to not schedule me for a couple weeks because I was going on a road trip. Instead, I confused him, so when I wanted my job back, he reminded me why I quit in the first place.

My grand plan to pull myself out of debt quicker failed because I didn't stick with the plan. I saw I had extra money, so I spent it, and ended up with more stuff and more debt. Adding insult to injury, my RX7 needed a new radiator that I couldn't afford because I already spent all of the money I was earning, so I just signed-over the title of my car to the mechanic. Obviously, my debt repayment mode was short lived. And, since I got rid of my car, we had to take Mike's car on our road trip.

It was 1999. There was a lot of concern about computers

crashing and causing huge disruptions because of the Y2K bug. Mike and I had never been to New York City for New Years Eve, and we really wanted that experience, regardless of the risk of the world ending. Ready for anything, we took some leave from the military, and started our road trip.

After driving 16 hours from Rapid City, we spent the night at my parent's house in Hastings, Michigan. The next day we drove another 12 hours to New Jersey, and spent the night at my uncle Ricky's apartment in Paterson. My cousin Eric (now deceased) lived in up-state New York, so we drove to his house, and partied with him the eve of New Years Eve, drinking shots of Sambuca Black. The following morning we drove back to New Jersey, and took the train over to Manhattan. We got there early afternoon, and the streets were already filling with people. We kept pushing our way forward toward Times Square until police put-up a metal barricade, and we couldn't go any further. Then, we just stood there.

There really wasn't much to do while we were standing there. We didn't even drink; and I was glad for that, because the police didn't want to let you back into the crowd once you left it. And the restaurant owners didn't want to let people from the crowd use their bathrooms either. For the restaurants that did let the public use their bathrooms, I think they were charging people to use them. Not drinking prevented some problems for us, but it also made the time pass a little slower. Although, we did have a few other things to look forward to.

Once per hour we all counted down to the top of the hour, getting ready for the midnight countdown. Occasionally, women would sit on their boyfriend's shoulders and flash their boobs, which was always a pleasant surprise. I even saw some people crowd surfing, and that looked really cool, but I was nervous for them about how they were going to get back to their friends. Regardless of the problem of getting separated from my friends, I saw this as a rare opportunity to crowd surf, and I had to do it.

I told Mike to pick me up. He said he needed some help, so I tapped people on their shoulders around us, and gestured with my thumbs up as I mouthed the words: "pick me up." Mike interlocked his fingers, I stepped into his hands with my boot, and everyone around us lifted me up over the crowd. It felt soo awesome to have people moving me above them. I really didn't know where they would carry me, or how far I was going to get from my hiking buddy Mike, so I looked over the crowd as they were carrying me, trying to keep track of where I was so I could find Mike again. The crowd carried me a little over 50', and then dropped me. I scraped my elbow a little, and stained the seat of my off-white jeans with grime from the street, but overall I was good.

The crowd was shoulder-to-shoulder, I wasn't even going to try to make it back to where I came from. So, I just stood there for a few minutes, and looked around. There wasn't much difference between my new standing spot and my old standing spot. Everybody at my new standing spot was doing what we were doing at my old standing spot. The fall to the ground hurt a little, but at least the crowd dropped me next to a cute college girl from Canada, so I started talking to her.

I ended-up talking to her the rest of the night. She, unlike me, was dressed for the cold weather. Endearingly she nestled me in her arms to help keep me warm. It worked-out really well for both of us, and at midnight, we did the traditional New Year's kiss. At 20 years old, she was the first girl I french-kissed! After midnight, the crowd quickly dispersed, and the streets opened-up. We exchanged e-mail addresses, had a goodbye kiss, and I walked toward where I thought Mike would be.

After a couple minutes of walking and looking, I actually found him! I don't know if he was drunk, or just excited that we found each other again, but he was really happy to see me and gave me big bear hug! Somehow, we even saw one of the guys we worked with at that intersection. Our coworker was meeting some other friends, so we didn't hang out, but it was still really cool to see him. After our farewells, Mike and I walked to the closest bar.

I didn't think they would let me in because I was underage, but all the bars were packed, and nobody was checking identification cards (IDs). We met a couple girls from Iowa at the bar, and drank Goldschläger shots with them. After a couple hours of that, we were all ready to go. Mike and I wanted to spend the night with the girls in their hotel, but they were more responsible than us, and politely rejected our request. Drunk and exhausted, Mike and I made our way back to New Jersey to spend the night at my uncle Ricky's (now deceased) apartment.

The next day, Mike and I drove down to Philadelphia. We found a parking spot, and parked the car on one of the main streets downtown. Just as we were getting out of Mike's car, a guy was walking by, and we started talking to him.

We told him we were looking for a bar, but I was underage. He said there was a place he usually goes, he knew the bartender, and said if we all went-in together the bartender wouldn't ask to see our IDs. So that is what we did, and the bartender was cool! He made sidecars, and other mixed drinks for us all-night, and we drank with a couple girls we met at the bar. After the bar closed, we went out to eat, and all spent the night at the guy's apartment that we met on the street.

The morning after, Mike and I drove down to Pensacola, Florida to spend the night with his family there. I got to meet Mike's little brother, we talked about electronica, and he gave me a Bad Boy Bill & Richard "Humpty" Vission—House Connection 2 CD. Mike and I listened to that CD on the car drive back to South Dakota, and I still listen to that CD on occasion! Although it was winter, it was still nice to go to the beach, and it was cool to meet Mike's family.

For spring break, Mike and I flew down to Cancun. We tanned on the beach in the day, and drank all night in the electronica clubs. The electronica clubs were $20 to get in, and then it was free drinks the rest of the night. They played great music in the night clubs, and one club had aerial acrobatics!

Once we were in the nightclub, we went our separate ways. Mike usually just stood around drinking while I went out to the middle of the dance floor to dance. I love the lights, sound, smoke machine, and being in the center of the action. Early morning, as the bar-crowd thinned-out, we usually found each other, and made our way back to the hotel.

One night, I couldn't find Mike. It was early morning, and the only people left in the bar were the cleaners, so I knew he wasn't in there anywhere. I wasn't really sure where the hotel was, but I hopped onto a bus to take me to the general area where I thought it might be.

On the bus, a guy was drinking a beer, and offered me a drink and a pill. I had no idea what he was offering me, I think it was ecstasy, but I kindly rejected his offer. I'm glad I'm not into drugs, I'm sure that wouldn't have ended well for me. As the bus was driving, I closely watched the side streets, desperately looking for some landmark that seemed familiar. I got off the bus at an area that I thought I remembered, and began walking.

It was daybreak as I was walking, so everything was dimly lit, but somehow I found the hotel! Once I was in the hotel it was easy for me to find our hotel room, but the door was locked, and I didn't have the key. I knocked on the door; trying to knock loud enough to be heard, but not too loud to cause a disturbance. When I knocked, I didn't hear anyone in the room.

After a few minutes of knocking, I was relieved to hear Mike groan, and shuffle his feet toward the door. When I walked into the room, he muttered to me that he got thrown out of the nightclub we went to. He said literally, the guys picked him up, and threw him into the street, just like they do in the movies. I'm not really sure why they threw him out, and I'm not so sure Mike knew either. Cancun was a lot of fun, but it was really exhausting partying every night. We left there broke, and tired, but it was important to us to go there and have that experience.

At one of our shop picnics we had that summer, I met a couple of my coworkers, Mat (spelled with one-t) and Gabe. Mat and Gabe worked in a shop a couple doors down from me, and we learned we had a mutual friend, so we all started hanging-out together on our days off. Mat, Gabe, and I had some fun adventures with the guys we worked with. We spent most of our days off-of-work hiking the trails through the Black Hills, and hiking the trails around the lakes and reservoirs there. We all lived in the dormitory on base, so it was easy for us to find each other, and get together on the weekends.

When the dorm managers started running out of dorm rooms for new airmen coming to the base, they gave us offers to live off-base because we had been there a while, and had enough rank. If we moved off-base, then they would give us a little extra money in our paychecks to pay for our food and housing, since we would not be using the dining facility on base, or living in the dorms anymore. Mat had the brilliant idea that if a group of us shared a house off-base, and split the rent and utilities, then we could cover our living expenses, and still have a little money left-over at the end of the month. Mat knew two other guys who were interested to do that, so after a couple quick strategy sessions, we executed our plan to move off-base.

Four of us rented a 3-bedroom house on East Indiana Street in

Rapid City. It was Mark, Jason, Mat, and I. Originally, Mat and I were going to share one of the bedrooms, and Mark and Jason would get their own rooms. But as Mat and I stood in the bedroom, in a house with no air conditioning, Mat threw his dirty socks onto the bedroom floor where I would be sleeping. I really didn't want to sleep on the floor next to Mat's stinky socks, so I moved into the living room.

We had two hand-me-down couches in the living room. I used to sleep on a couch, behind a couch, or wherever was comfortable for me that night. We even had a couch on our back porch that I slept-on in the summer sometimes, because it was nice and cool in the evenings.

Living off-base was a good time. When we weren't exploring the hills, we would ride our bicycles around town and on the bike path, or play video games in the house. When we had 3-day weekends, we occasionally went on road-trips. Essentially, we were just kids, growing-up together.

I didn't own a car when we decided to move into the house off-base. At the time, it wasn't a big deal because we were all on different shifts, and there was always someone available to carpool with. A few months after we moved-in, that all changed. Jason was about to separate from the military, Mark moved to another base, and Mat moved to swing-shift while I was still on day-shift. My solution to this impending problem was to ride my bicycle to-and-from base.

Ellsworth was about 10 miles away, so it wasn't that bad of a ride. Even with the wind against me, I could get to-and-from base in about an hour. I would shower at the gym on-base, and kept my uniform in a locker in the parts room at the shop. After a couple of months of bicycle commuting, summer was coming to an end, and I was thinking that riding my bicycle in the winter was probably not going to work well for me. I had just finished my shower in the gym one morning, and I heard a radio commercial advertising low payments on new cars at a local dealer. The timing was perfect, my judgment was not. After work that day, I rode my bicycle to the car dealer to test drive a 2001 Mitsubishi Eclipse GS.

Since I had a full-time job in the Air Force, and I had been in the Air Force a couple of years, I easily qualified for a loan to buy the brand new car. I justified the purchase because I knew I needed a reliable car to get to-and-from work. I knew I was getting out of the Air Force soon, but I arrogantly thought I was easily going to find a job that paid as good, if not better, than my Air Force job. I was already in debt for another computer that I bought with my DPP Military Star Card; and my credit cards were maxed-out from buying name-brand clothes, shoes, entertainment, and travel. I was pretty-much living paycheck-to-paycheck. But, because I didn't have much life experience, and took the money I was earning for granted, I bought that Eclipse.

On the radio, the car payments sounded like something I could easily afford. In real life, I had a hard time making those car payments. After paying for the registration, insurance, and gas, I didn't have money for anything else. When my next car insurance payment was due, I didn't pay, because I couldn't afford it. I was already economically crippled, but my new car payment kicked the crutches out from underneath me.

To make matters worse, it was soo easy to buy the car, that I didn't appreciate the car. I got bored with the car after a few months, and wanted to trade it in for something else. I was looking at the Subaru WRX. It was a nice sporty little car, and I thought by trading-in my car, maybe I could get a little lower payment. But because I had just bought my Eclipse, and owed soo much on it, the Subaru dealer was not able to work with me at all. I even tried selling my Eclipse. I received soo many compliments for it, I thought for sure I could sell it, but no. I owed soo much on the car, essentially a buyer was paying new for a used car. So, I was stuck with my car.

Gabe would come downtown to visit us, and sometimes asked me about my debt. I've always been open about talking about my personal finances, and in most of those conversations, I was talking about how much debt I had. With the car and credit card debt I had, Gabe usually just shook his head at me with a look of pity, and gave a sigh that he was grateful it wasn't him in that position. Occasionally he'd try to give me a little advice or words of encouragement, but I was always able to just skate by, so I didn't see my problem as something that required me to make a drastic change. I just thought I needed to earn a little more money, and that would solve my problems.

Until then, whatever I needed, I used my credit cards. When we moved off base, I thought I would use the extra money I was getting to put me in a better economic position. I didn't, I wasn't focused, and just used the little extra money I had to have more experiences.

One week, there was a three-day weekend. I took five days of leave after that weekend so I wouldn't have to work my work week, and then I got the following normal weekend off, so that gave me 10 days-off in-a-row. At the beginning of those 10 days-off, I dyed my hair green. The next day, we drove-up to Regina, Saskatchewan, Canada.

I don't think the Canadian border guards appreciated my green hair, and they must have thought we were all on drugs because they patted-us-all-down, searched our bags, and searched our cars. This was even before 9/11, when it was supposed to be a lot easier to get into Canada. When we finally made it to Regina, there was more drama for us.

There was a big football game that weekend. Most of the people that saw me thought I had the green hair because I was rooting for the rival team, so a few of the locals were yelling at us as we walked around the city. Other than all of the hecklers, Regina was a good time!

One nightclub we went to, a group of cheerleaders formed a circle on the dance-floor, and were just dancing with themselves. They weren't wearing their cheer uniforms, they were just out for the night before the game. Anyway, I saw the dance circle, and I thought it was a good idea to jump in the middle of the circle and start dancing, so I did. I had fun dancing by myself in the middle of their circle, and tried to get some of the girls to dance with me, but I couldn't get any takers. It could have been my green hair, or they could have had boyfriends, or maybe it was just group politics. In any case, I didn't care, I was just there to have fun dancing to the music.

We went to another nightclub, and I met a local girl who drove a combine. She was cool, and real, and had fun talking to me with my green hair. The rest of the Regina trip was relatively eventless. We went to a local bar, took-up the backroom, and watched some American football while we had lunch.

When we got back to Rapid City, I still had seven-more days off-of-work. I was close to finishing my Associate degree, so the time-off allowed me to study-for and take a few College Level Examination Program (CLEP) exams. I had to take the exams on-base, and I knew my green hair did not meet Air Force regulations, so I wore civilian clothes to the testing center, and tucked my green hair under my white UMASS cap. I saw Quilian at the testing center, and he was doing the same thing as me. I knew he hadn't seen me since I dyed my hair, so I lifted up my cap to show him. Quilian smiled with surprise and mouthed the words: "oh man" as he looked away presumably thinking: "oh man, you could get in a lot of trouble for that." But, he didn't say that because we were about to take our tests.

The proctor must have seen my green hair too, because after the exam, he told me the flight chiefs wanted to see me in their office. I was getting a little nervous, and quickly considered what I could do about my hair. But I lived off-base, and the sergeants wanted to see me now, so I didn't have time to do anything. Knowing this wasn't going to be good, I went to the flight chiefs office, and they told me to remove my cap. I removed my cap, and my green hair tumbled-out like clowns out of a clown-car. The sergeants weren't happy about the situation, but they were mostly dumfounded by it, and they wanted me to take care of it.

Before I returned my hair to military regulation, I had to go see Quilian, and tell him what happened. Quilian worked in the contracting office on-base. I walked up the stairs at his office, taking them two-at-a-time as I normally do, and started looking for him when I got to the landing. I found him in his cubicle area, and told him I got caught. We did a little small talk about dying my hair, and my meeting with the sergeants, and then I told him I wanted to get a photo of us.

Quilian zig-zagd through the cubicles to his boss's office to ask him to take a picture of us. I wanted the photos because I liked the contrast of him in his uniform, and me in shorts and a t-shirt on-base. Also; I was wearing his old clothes, Quilian gave me his clothes because they were too big for him. After a couple minutes of waiting, I was surprised when Quilian returned with his boss, and he was cool taking a photo of us.

After his boss took a few photos of us, I went out to my car, and drove off-base. I was going down the commercial gate road, and took one last photo of myself as I was driving under the interstate overpass. When I finally got home, I shaved my head over the toilet.

I only had about a year left of my enlistment in the Air Force, but I had to take care of something that was eating away at my conscience. I met with a Judge Advocate General (JAG) officer on-base. Her office was in the same building where Quilian worked. When I met with her, I told her I thought I might be a conscientious objector. She gave me a packet about conscientious objection, and I couldn't wait to start reading it.

I tepidly walked down the stairs from her office to the main floor lobby, and I saw a seating area in the middle of the large unoccupied room. It was a grey, rainy, day. The naturally lit two-story lobby with floor-to-ceiling windows shone gloom into the room. I walked across the slate-tiled floor toward the couches in the seating area. The seating area was bordered by a couple dwarf trees, and there were potted green-leafy plants on the end-tables. There was a table and a rug in the middle of the two-leather couches, and two-leather chairs. The leather chairs had their backs to the doors. I wanted to see whomever walked-in from outside, but I didn't want to be seen, so I sat at the arm of the couch closest to the entryway to the building. Decorative foliage on the end-tables hid me from direct view, but I could still see who was coming-into and going-out of the building.

Solitarily I sat in the corner of the couch; the supple deep-brown leather was consoling to me. I felt warmth and security as I read my conscientious objector packet that cold-rainy-afternoon. Each paragraph I read resonated with me, and I nodded my head in agreement as I progressed through the pages. The packet described what conscientious objection was, and the process to separate from the military as a conscientious objector. Like the application to get into the Air Force Academy, the application process to get out of the military was similarly complicated.

To establish credibility, and build the case for my separation, I had to take a personality exam, meet with a clergyman and get a written recommendation from him, write a personal essay, and complete a formal application. I'm sure there were a few other steps in there, but it didn't matter. Whatever it was they wanted me to do, I did it with fervency, and submitted my packet for separation as a conscientious objector. After I submitted my packet to separations, all I had to do was wait for my application to be reviewed and approved, or rejected.

While I was waiting for the decision from separations, I had another great idea. Fall 2000 there was a homecoming football game at the South Dakota School of Mines and Technology. Gabe knew some people that lived nearby, so we went to their house. I wanted someone to write: "STOP EATING ANIMALS" on my back. They didn't have a marker, so one of the guys there grabbed a can of black shoe polish, and used that. After he drew my message onto my back, I left their house.

I strolled down the street toward the School of Mines stadium, shirtless, in my tear-away pants. I walked around the outside of the stadium to the far end of the football field, farthest from the University. The gate to the field was open, and a paramedic team was sitting in their ambulance outside of the track at the corner of the field. It was toward the end of the fourth quarter of the game, the home team had no chance to win, and a lot of the spectators were leaving or had already left the game. While the teams were lined-up for the next play near the end-zone closest to me, I leisurely walked onto the track, ripped-off my tear-away pants, and started running naked over the track and onto the football field.

As I ran from that end-zone to the other end-zone down the middle of the field, I was thinking: "I can't believe they haven't tackled me yet." I didn't want to look behind me to see who was chasing me, and I didn't want to see how close they were to catching me, I just wanted to keep running. One of the people in the band even played the first part of the *Charge Cheer* on his trumpet as I was running. It wasn't until I was through the opposite end-zone, over-the-track, and crossing the top of the fence that I looked back.

When I looked back, I was surprised to see that nobody was chasing me. I was almost disappointed about that. Regardless, I still had to get to my car, because I was naked.

In my hurry to get over the fence, I cut my scrotum a little on the jagged part at top of the fence. It was a little painful, but not bad enough that I had to stop, so I kept running. I was going to run through the center of campus, but there was a family of four or five walking up the stairs, so I ran on the edge of campus alongside the four-lane road to-and-from downtown.

I made it to my car in the parking lot on-campus and got inside; but as I was looking for the key that I had hidden in there, I saw someone approach my driver-side window. I hid my crotch as I talked to him, and tried to play-off the situation. While I was talking to him, I looked in my rearview mirror to see if I could just back-up and get out of there, but it was too late. He had me blocked into my parking space, and already called the police. He was a volunteer deputy, peace officer, or something like that, and said he saw me running naked along the road. When the police arrived, they asked me to get out of my car, and wrapped a blanket around me as I stood up.

I was arrested, booked, and charged with public indecency. They gave me prison-orange pants and a shirt to wear. I was only in jail a few hours when Mat and Gabe scraped-up the cash to bail me out. They also brought some clothes for me to wear, so I didn't get to keep my prison pants or shirt. Our housemate Mark was home watching the news on a local broadcast channel, and recorded the newscast with one of the VCRs we had at the house. Later that night, we watched the recording of me on the news. I couldn't believe what I did was actually newsworthy. I went to court, pled guilty to public indecency, paid my fine, and it was over.

They talked about my streaking event a little bit in the shop on-base. One hardcore guy was raising hell about it saying his wife saw my bare ass on television (TV); she didn't, they had my butt blurred-out. The media was kind and reported me as a member of the student body; so there was no connection back to the military, and the sergeants in my shop didn't see any reason for further recourse for me.

I really didn't have any other incidents while I was in the military. I used to wear my UMASS cap in my car while I was in-uniform driving to-and-from work on-base. I bought that cap when Mike and I went on a road-trip to the Mall of America, so the cap reminded me of better days. One day I forgot to take the UMASS cap off and put my battle dress uniform cap on, and I was walking up to the shop from the parking lot. One of the officers in my building saw me in the white cap, told my boss, and I was admonished for not wearing my military cover while I was in uniform.

The shop-chiefs didn't feel comfortable with me fixing the electronic units for the bombers anymore, so they had me do in-processing and out-processing of parts and electronic units for the shop. I played it cool over the winter, and just did my job. It was a difficult time for me, mostly because I was doing a job I didn't want to do, and I had to keep doing it, until my conscientious objector application was approved or denied.

I was miserable; it got soo bad I was doing a couple double shots of Jägermeister before I went to work to numb the pain a little. When I got home, I backed my car into the garage at our house downtown and just sat there, with the motor off, listening to Moby— My Weakness playing on repeat. I still feel a sense of calm and reassurance when I listen to that track.

The following spring my spirit lifted a little. Sometimes after work I looked for a job I could do when my Air Force career was over. I liked the in-processing and out-processing administrative job I was doing; so I looked for work as an expeditor using job services like Monster, Hot Jobs, and Indeed. But, I'm pretty sure I screwed-up the application processes of the jobs I was applying for, because I didn't get any replies to the resumes and letters of interest I sent out.

One night, after getting drunk at the bar, I was hungry. I went to Hardee's, and drove through the drive-through because they always locked the lobby at night. The only thing I ate at Hardee's was their curly fries, and I usually got two large orders of their curly fries because I love them, especially with ketchup and Vegenaise. There were only a couple cars ahead of me in line, so I didn't have to wait long to place my order. I really didn't mind sitting in the drive-through line, because I knew I wouldn't get stopped by the police. I felt smug as I idled in-line, and saw police cars pass-by on the street. But I was most comfortable when at least one other car pulled-in behind me.

After I placed my order and pulled forward, I saw a line of cars forming behind me that was almost completely around the building. When it was finally my turn to pay and get my curly fries, I looked through the drive-through window into the restaurant, and the workers looked soo frantic trying to fill all of the orders as fast as they could. I watched them for a minute as I calmly sat in my vehicle; and thought, I want to do that.

A few days later, I went to Hardee's after work, and I told them I wanted to work there. I filled-out an application, met with the general manager, and he told me to bring-in my proof of citizenship to complete my new-hire paperwork the next day. I liked that it was easy to get the job there. I started working evenings and overnight shifts as much as I could; because I was bored, but also because I needed the money. I had a lot of fun working there, and most of the people I worked with were cool. What made it nice was that it was a really low responsibility job compared to what I was doing in the Air Force, and it wouldn't have been a big deal if they wanted to fire me. I worked in the kitchen grilling burgers, running the fryer, and making sandwiches. I really liked the job when it was busy because the time passed quickly.

One bright, balmy, summer afternoon in 2001, I was at my desk in our windowless work room, and I heard the phone ring in the main area of the shop. One of the guys on the floor answered the phone, came back to my area, and emotionlessly told me someone was on the phone for me from separations. I had a glimmer of hope in me, but I really thought this guy was just messing with me. I picked-up the phone, and with a tone of disbelief, I answered the call: "Airman Holzmuller." I heard the young lady on-the-phone say she was from separations, my application to separate as a conscientious objector was approved, and she told me I could separate that day if I wanted to. I was elated! As much as I wanted to leave that day, I knew there was a lot of out-processing paperwork that needed to be completed on-base, so I told her to give me a week.

My last appointment, at the end of that week, was in the same building where I originally started the conscientious objection separation process a year earlier. I was meeting with an Air Force Reserve recruiter to discuss joining the Air Force Reserves. It was a formality, I was not interested in joining the reserves, and he saw that my DD-214 was coded so that I would not be let back into the military even if I changed my mind. He signed-off on my separations form, and I was on my way.

I actually did finish my CCAF degree while I was in the military, and earned an Associate of Applied Science Avionic Systems. While I was in the military I was young, and I was still getting to know myself. I learned that life in the military was not the life for me, and I wanted to get out early. I always felt like I could do better, or do more, and after all of that, I only separated one-month earlier than my original enlisted agreement discharge date. I should have given myself positive self-talk, and justified why I should stay-in and complete my original enlistment agreement, instead of looking for reasons to be a sad sap and get out early. Looking back, I don't regret serving in the military. I appreciate what our active duty service members do, and what our veterans have done for us. I think dying my hair green and streaking were my youthful rebellion against a system that wasn't right for me; childish acts for sure, but I wasn't much more than a child at the time anyway.

I drove away from that building, where I started and finished my separations process, with a sense of bewilderment. I was at the intersection next to the building, about to turn onto the commercial gate road where I took a photo of myself with my green hair driving off-base a year or so earlier. I had the windows down in my car, and I started listening to Modest Mouse—Styrofoam Boots/It's All Nice on Ice, Alright turned-up a little on my car stereo. I spent soo much time anticipating getting out of the Air Force; but I ended-up being surprised when it actually happened, and wasn't really sure what to do next.

With my newfound freedom, I started partying a little. I partied for a couple weeks when I got out, but I couldn't keep doing that. I wasn't earning enough at Hardee's to party, pay rent, pay for my car, and make my credit card payments. I was kinda broke, and I needed to find a higher paying job. I didn't have any place else to go, so I left from South Dakota in my car, and drove to my parent's house in Michigan to move-in with them again.

5

Michigan

Song Suggestions:
Delerium—Heavens Earth (Key South Remix)
Nude Dimensions: Naked Music, Vol. 1—The Petalpusher
Session Mixed by Miguel 'Migs'

I honorably discharged from the Air force July 2001, and by August, I was in Michigan. There was a company near Grand Rapids looking for a forklift driver. The job paid really well, so I applied in-person for the job. I told the lady I didn't know how to drive a forklift, but she said they could train me. I asked them if they drug tested, and she said they did. At the time, I was still on my high of living on my principles, and I didn't want to work for a company that dictated to me how I should live. It was a fantastic opportunity, their drug policy shouldn't have been a big deal to me. I really wasn't into drugs, but I chose not to make it work. I think we were both disappointed by my decision, but I left, and kept looking.

I signed-up with Adecco staffing agency to find a temp-to-hire job. The girls at Adecco found a position for me at a warehouse loading trucks, but I needed to pass a drug test. I really needed money, didn't have a lot of options, so I compromised my values, and submitted to the drug test. Like I said, I wasn't a regular drug user. I passed my drug test, and I was ready to work in the warehouse.

I had never worked in a warehouse before, it sounded like a cool job, except I had to wake-up early for work. While I was at work, I was walking from the truck to somewhere in the warehouse to find boxes of siding, gutters, and downspouts, to put on my shoulder, and then walk back to the truck. Those boxes were filthy, so after doing that all day, those boxes made me filthy. I enjoyed the people I worked with, but my legs were throbbing from being on my feet all day, so I kept looking for work while I was working at the warehouse.

Within a few weeks I had an opportunity to put my degree to good use. Long John Silver's in Battle Creek was looking for an Assistant Manager, and part of the qualifications for the job was a college degree. I had a college degree, but I really didn't want to work at a traditional restaurant franchise, because that was against my vegan principles. I identified with the vegan diet and lifestyle while I was in the military, and I cared a lot about living my vegan principles. I really wanted to go into business for myself, and I thought opening a vegan restaurant would be a good way to share my values, and earn a decent income. But, I didn't know anything about the restaurant business.

I talked myself into applying for the job because it would give me the restaurant experience I needed, and I could work on my business plan for my restaurant in my free-time. Then, I could use my experience and business plan to get financing to open my vegan restaurant, and franchise it. I considered that taking a job at a mainstream restaurant franchise was like me infiltrating the establishment to learn everything about them, and then use it against them. I applied for the Assistant Manager position, interviewed, and I was hired for the job.

I was living at my parents house in Michigan, and commuted to work at Long John Silver's about a half hour away. I liked my lofty goals going into my restaurant career, but I let myself quickly lose sight of my goals. Just like in the Air Force, I became consumed by the daily drudgery, and wasn't reminding myself daily or throughout the day what I was really trying to do. To cope with the misery I unwittingly put myself in; I drank, a lot.

I would get gallon jugs of cranberry juice, and drink just enough cranberry juice out of the jug so I could mix-in a 750mL bottle of vodka. I loved my vodka-cranberry mix, and I kept it on the floor of the passenger side of my car so I could drink it during my drive home after work. I looked forward to drinking it every night after I finished work; it was definitely the highlight of my night.

I worked the closing shift, and was off-work between 10 and 11 p.m. Then, I'd drive away and start drinking my vodka-cranberry mix. I had a good time doing it, and I was pretty drunk by the time I got back to my parent's house. My parents didn't notice, they were always asleep by the time I got home. Some nights I bought gin and tonic water, pulled onto a side street to mix the gin into my tonic just like I did my vodka-cranberry mix, and drank that on my way home. I liked drinking 40s of Camo High Gravity Lager and 30 packs of Miller High Life too, but I waited to drink the beers at home because I thought the beer smell was too obvious, and I knew I wouldn't get away with that if I was pulled-over. I thought drinking my mixed drinks out of the tonic or juice containers was less obvious, and didn't stink-up my car as much as the beer. Although, one evening I didn't have to work, and I broke my "no beer in the car" rule.

My father and I were drinking at the Moose Lodge (now a parking lot) one night; I was drinking mixed drinks, he was drinking cans of beer. After we finished drinking there, I was craving a smoke, so I dropped-off my dad at our house. I only smoked clove cigarettes. The small town I lived-in didn't have a smoke shop, so I had to drive a half-hour to the next closest city that had a smoke shop, Battle Creek. I really didn't know where the smoke shop was in Battle Creek, I just knew how to get to get to the city. Before I left town on my road-trip, I stopped at a quick service grocery store, and picked-up a couple each of FOSTER'S Lager and Ale Oil Cans to drink along the way.

It was a really nice summer evening, perfect weather! I had my music up, and my car windows down as I drank a can of lager, and then a can of ale along the winding road. I kept the full cans of beer and my empties in the brown paper sack behind my passenger seat. I stopped drinking once I was within city limits again.

There wasn't much traffic on the four-lane road in Battle Creek that evening, and I wasn't having much luck finding any open stores at-all. As I was driving, I saw a gas station that was open. I really didn't think the gas station would have my cloves, but I was desperate. The gas station was on my right side, and I was cruising in the passing lane two-lanes away. I didn't want to pass the gas station and have to turn around, so I turned quickly from the passing lane, and tried to pull-into the parking lot. Before I even made it into the driveway of the parking lot, I hit the car that was driving in my blind spot. The good thing was, I achieved my goal, and I did end-up in the gas station parking lot before passing it. The bad thing was, I dented both of our cars in the process.

The accident wasn't that big of a deal, nobody was injured, but the lady driving the car was hysterical because she said she just got her car out of the shop from the same thing happening to her a couple weeks earlier. As the sun was setting, some guy walking-by saw me drive into her car, and told the lady he called the police. I was pretty drunk, so I knew this wasn't going to be good for me.

I walked into the gas station convenience store looking for some emergency provisions. I bought some Little Trees Royal Pine Car Fresheners, spearmint gum, and a pack of Newport 100s in a box. No, they didn't have the clove cigarettes I was looking for, and that didn't bother me too much because I had much bigger problems on my mind. I quickly hung an air freshener on my rear-view window, and I put the other two air fresheners on the shirt hooks in my back seat, only after rubbing one of the air fresheners on my forearms and legs so I wouldn't reek soo bad of booze.

I knew I had to get rid of my empty cans of beer; and anybody who saw me throw anything into the garbage would have immediately checked the trash can, so that wasn't a good idea. I was in-luck. I had a bi-fold back seat; so I quickly and discretely pulled the right-half of the back seatback down while simultaneously grabbing my sack of empty and full beers, shoving it into my trunk, and closing the seatback again. Then I got out of my car, stood in front of the gas station, and started chain-smoking.

I smoked three or four of those Newports within a few minutes. I don't know if it was the nicotine, or my extreme nervousness, but all-of-a-sudden I had an almost uncontrollable urge to defecate. I walked back into the convenience store, and asked the gas station clerk for the bathroom key. He handed me a foot-long wooden-dowel with the key hanging from the stick by a formerly white, but now grey, piece of string. I grabbed the key with my thumb and index-finger, walked outside and around to the side of the building, and opened the door to the restroom.

It really wasn't in that bad of condition. Gang insignias and obscenities were carved into the mirror in typical public restroom fashion, and there were a couple crumpled paper towels on the grey-painted concrete floor, but it was generally well-kept. I lined the toilet seat with a few layers of toilet paper as I normally do, had a seat, and proceeded to have the biggest bowel movement of my life. I wasn't in there too long, but I was expecting to see the police officer already talking to the lady by the time I got out of there, and I was thinking that was going to make me look bad.

When I walked out of the restroom and into the parking lot, I was pleasantly surprised to see the police had not yet arrived, and I started to feel like I was winning. As I was returning the bathroom key to the gas station attendant, I looked over at the lady whose car I hit, and she was nervously sitting in her car. She hadn't left her car since we pulled into that gas station parking lot; so I walked over, and began talking to her.

She told me the guy who said he had called the police really didn't call the police. Seeing this as something in my favor, I tried to negotiate a deal with the lady. I told her I would make monthly payments to her so she could fix her car. Somehow she did not believe me that I would follow-through, and she wanted the police report for her insurance. So she called the police, and within a few minutes, a police officer arrived.

I was still standing in the parking lot, but by this time, I was chewing gum. The police officer spoke with the frantic lady first. When he was finished listening to her side of the story, he walked-over to me.

He was a tall-slender-man, about my age. He took my driver's license, and told me his understanding of what happened. I agreed with him, and repeated to him what he told me. I think he appreciated that I was calm. He confiscated my driver's license, wrote me a ticket, and that was it. No breathalyzer, no long-drawn-out affair, just a ticket, and I was on my way. I asked him what I should do if I get pulled-over on my way home; he said all I needed to do was show the officer my citation, and I'd be good. I thanked him, got in my car, buckled up, and drove away.

I waited a few blocks before I breathed a sigh of relief. I knew I was still drunk, so I took the side streets through the city until I made my way to the highway to get back to my parent's house. I thought about cracking open another one of those beers while I was driving the side-streets to celebrate not getting caught; but I quickly talked myself out of that, thinking I pushed my luck enough for one evening. I made it home safely, and my parents were already asleep.

The next morning my father asked me about the dent in my car; I told him some lady was driving in my blind-spot, and I hit her car when I changed lanes because I didn't check my blind spot. He made a disgusted sound as he turned his back to me, and walked away. I had to get my driver's license back, so I drove back to Battle Creek.

I parked on some side-street, and walked the block or so to the police station. I gave my citation to the young man in the police uniform standing behind a short counter. This guy was not as nice as the guy that helped me the night before.

While he was reading my citation, he turned away from me, and walked a few steps to the see-through letter holder in the wall behind him. He reached into the letter holder, and pulled-out my South Dakota driver's license. He slowly turned, and started to walk back toward me as he was looking down and comparing my driver's license to the citation. The officer looked confused about the situation; so I told him I just needed to pay my fine to get my license back, but he didn't even lift his head or acknowledge me as I spoke to him. Instead, he walked behind a wall at the side of the room, and asked one of his colleagues about it. I heard them briefly murmur to each other; then he returned, still looking down at my driver's license and the citation. He let me pay my fine there, and he gave me my driver's license back.

After he handed-me my license, I quickly, but nonchalantly, left the police station before he had time to change his mind. I walked down the street outside of the police station with a feeling of great relief, and a little more appreciation for South Dakota. The accident, and the whole ordeal, kinda scared-me-straight.

A few days later, I actually went to an automobile insurance office to buy insurance for my car. The receptionist greeted me, told me all of the agents were busy, and I agreed to wait. I anxiously sat in the waiting room for a few minutes; but I didn't want to spend the last few dollars I had that bad, so I just left.

A couple months later, I was at Long John Silver's working a closing shift. It was a nice quiet evening, everything was going smooth, and we were cleaning-up, getting ready to close the restaurant for the night. One of my rabblerousing employees that was under the legal drinking age had a bottle of gin, and a bottle of tonic, in his trunk. He was new to drinking gin and tonics, and didn't know how to mix them, so he asked me for help.

We went out to the parking lot with a cup of ice, and he opened his trunk. He poured a little gin over the ice in the cup filling it about 20%, and then filled the rest of the cup with the tonic. He tasted it, and wasn't sure if he poured it right, so he asked me to try it. I thought to myself: "this is a really bad idea;" but, I took a sip anyway. It was perfect! He did a great job pouring the drink; and I knew I had already screwed-up, so I kept it. I finished drinking it while I was supervising my closing-shift employees, and doing my closing paperwork. Nothing went awry, we closed the store on time, and we all went home for the evening.

A few weeks later, the general manager was checking our stock, and was wondering why we kept coming-up short on the frozen single serving deserts. I didn't realize it was a problem, but I told him I would pay a little closer attention to our staff. A week later, I was working another closing shift with my rabblerousing underage gin-and-tonic guy, and it was another nice night with everything going smooth. I was doing my night-count, and needed to go into the walk-in cooler to double check something. I opened the cooler door, and the rabble-rouser was standing in the middle of the cooler, facing me. He had a white plastic fork in his right hand, the little single serving pie-wedge-box in his left hand, and the box and fork were raised to his face. I caught him just as he finished putting a fork-full of desert into his mouth; and with a full-mouth he said: "you got me." I told him: "yeah, but I can't do anything, because you've got me in your hip pocket."

Had I told our general manager I found who was stealing all of the frozen single serving deserts, my rabble-rouser employee would have told the general manager I was drinking on the job, and we both could have lost our jobs. I double-checked the count in the cooler as I originally intended, and finished my nightly duties. I felt really bad about the situation, but there wasn't anything I could do about it, and all I could think about was how to prevent myself from doing something like that again.

My buddy Quilian called me from Gainesville, Florida New Years Day 2002. He was studying architecture at the University of Florida (UF), and asked me if I wanted to come down and go to school there too. His offer was an answer to an unspoken prayer for me. I had a degree, but I had already moved-on from the idea of using it in an administrative capacity, considering my failed attempts of applying for jobs while I was in the military. Also, I didn't think I'd be a strong enough candidate to compete for any Avionics Technician job.

I considered Quilian's offer as an opportunity for me to get a fresh start since I screwed-up so bad in Michigan. Even though we had just come out of the .com bust, I thought by studying Information Technology and website development, I would be able to work from anywhere worldwide. So I gave written notice to the managers at Long John Silver's, and a couple months later, I was packing my car with my stuff to move to Florida to start working on an Associate Degree in Information Technology.

I wasn't happy working at the restaurant because I chose not to be happy. I should have been happy with my job at the restaurant because the job was easy, I was earning a living wage, I had a sweet car, I was living at my parent's house rent-free, and I had a little independence. Instead, I chose to make the good situation I was in a bad situation, by choosing to be a sad sap again. I was stuck thinking about my short term situation that I was broke, and I was working someplace where I really didn't want to work. I should have been grateful that I had a decent-enough job, and that I was living rent-free. I also should have been thinking about ways to be less broke, and should have kept reminding myself of the long-term goal I was trying to achieve: my vegan restaurant coup. With no perceived better option, I left Michigan, but I was excited about my potential in Florida.

6

Gainesville

Song Suggestions:
Ministry of Sound—The Annual 2002, Disk 1
Carl Cox—Mixed Live: Crobar Night Club, Chicago

On the way down to Gainesville, I stopped in Ft. Walton Beach to see my friend Fred from Ellsworth AFB. He was happy to see me, so we went out for drinks! There were a lot of people out at the bars that night, because people were visiting the area for spring break.

Fred and I chose to go to a tiki bar. While we were sitting at the bar, I noticed a cute girl working the guys sitting at the bar. She was just making her way around the bar, asking guys to buy her drinks as she went. By the time she got to Fred and I, she was wasted. She stood in-between our barstools, looked at Fred, and then looked at me. With a sexy little smile on her face, and an upbeat tone of voice, she asked me if I wanted to buy her a drink. I couldn't buy her a drink. Not because I was morally opposed to buying a drink for a drunk girl, but because I didn't have any money. I shook my head side-to-side, and followed-that up with: "uhhh, yeah, I'm broke!" Then I pointed at Fred, and said: "Fred's buying us drinks!" She turned toward Fred, and then I watched her go through the same routine I saw her repeat six times before. A sucker for a pretty girl, Fred muttered: "oh alright," reached for his wallet, and bought her a drink. She drunkily stood and smiled while exchanging glances with Fred and I as she waited for the bartender to bring her a drink. After the bartender gave her-her drink, she kissed Fred on the cheek, then kissed me on the cheek, smiled and walked away. We finished our drinks, and then Fred drove us to a nightclub.

We saw some cute girls in the parking lot outside of the nightclub, so Fred rolled down his window, and started yelling at them to get their attention. When he got their attention, he stopped the car, started laughing, and told them I was the drummer for Creed. As I was listening to him keep trying to sell the idea, the young ladies were skeptical, but they wanted to believe him at the same time. I was just embarrassed, playing it off, and shook my head side-to-side as I sunk down into my seat trying to go unnoticed. My hair was shaggy at the time, I was wearing a jean outfit, it was dark, and everything I was doing just made Fred's story sound even more believable. The girls walked over to my side of the car, and I didn't even want to roll down my window, but they persisted, so I did.

It was a group of three girls; a tall slim blonde girl in the middle, with slightly shorter brunettes on each side of her. They stood shoulder-to-shoulder outside of my window, and the blonde girl asked me if I was the drummer for Creed. I told her no, but she and her friends didn't believe me. Then the tall blonde girl demanded an autograph from me. Again, I tried to weasel out of it by telling her I didn't have a pen or paper. Fred replied quick and said: "I have a pen!" He reached into his center console, grabbed a pen, and handed it to me. Then I humbly said: "Yeah, but I don't have any paper." The blonde girl made a made a fist with her right hand as she straightened and twisted her arm, showing me the inside of her forearm. She told me: "You can sign here." I thought about how I should sign her arm; if maybe I should make something up, but my signature is illegible anyway. So, I just signed my normal signature, large on the inside of her forearm. Satisfied, they thanked me in unison, and walked away.

When I rolled-up the window, Fred burst out-loud with laughter, and kept laughing as we drove through the parking lot to find a place to park. I was still really embarrassed about it all; couldn't believe he did that, and was surprised the girls went along with it. I didn't even know what the drummer of Creed looked like. When we went inside the club, I was expecting more fanfare, but I walked-in unrecognized. It was early in the evening, and not much was going on in the nightclub, so we didn't stay long.

The next day Fred asked me if I wanted to go down to Panama

City with him. I told him I couldn't afford it, and Fred again said he would buy us drinks. I felt really bad about it, didn't want to take advantage of him, and told him I really just needed to get down to Gainesville and start looking for work. We had lunch at a restaurant on the water, I thanked him for his hospitality, and I left after that.

When I arrived in Gainesville, I really didn't know where I was at, or where I needed to go. I saw a building painted purple called the Mellow Mushroom; I didn't know what it was, but it looked like a friendly place. I found-out Mellow Mushroom was a pizzeria that served pitchers of beer. So; I ordered a veggie pizza with no cheese, and a pitcher of Natural Light. While I was in Michigan I set myself up with a cell-phone, so I gave Quilian a call, and he knew right where I was at. When he arrived, my pizza had just arrived, and I was already half-way through the pitcher. Quilian was not interested to drink my beer or eat my pizza, but he was somewhat happy to see me.

Quilian invited me to live with him in his studio apartment. Quilian slept on a futon mattress elevated by pallets in one corner of the room. Accustomed to sleeping on the floor, I slept in my sleeping bag diagonally from him in the opposite corner of the room. The next night, we went to the Publix grocery store.

All I was interested in buying was beer. I found a case of that delicious Natural Light, and proudly carried it through the store. I saw Quilian before I checked-out, boasted about the case of Natural Light I found, and asked him if he minded if I drank beer in the apartment. He said he didn't have a problem with me buying beer to drink in the apartment, so I bought the case of beer.

When we got back to the apartment, I started cracking-open the beers. Just after I cracked-open my third beer, Quilian made a comment to me that he was a little uncomfortable with my drinking. I rebuked him saying: "I thought you didn't mind if I drank!," and he told me: "You're just doing it to get drunk!" Yep, that was the idea, but I didn't like making my friend uncomfortable, so I stopped drinking in the apartment. We were still cool after that, but Quilian saw I needed something else to do with my time other than spending my nights getting drunk in our studio apartment. So, he took me to another studio, the architecture studio at UF.

At the architecture studio, Quilian and his classmates worked on their models for their program. One evening, Quilian introduced me to one of his classmates, Chris. Chris was also a recently honorably discharged veteran. We chit-chatted a little bit about our military experiences, and got along really well. I went to the studio almost every night, so Quilian and his classmates setup a place for me in the studio where I could work on my vegan restaurant business plan.

One night I was taking a break from my business plan, and was riding my skateboard on campus at UF. The roads were really smooth on campus, so I could get a lot of speed when I pedaled hard. I was enjoying a warm summer evening pedaling hard on campus, until I lost my balance, and fell back on my elbow. My wound didn't look bad, but it hurt too much for me to ride my skateboard, so I just walked back to the architecture studio carrying my skateboard in my good arm. When I told the guys about it at the studio, Quilian suggested that I get it checked-out.

I told him I was broke, and couldn't afford to go to the emergency room. Quilian told me, since we were veterans, we could go to the Veterans Administration (VA) medical center. At the VA medical center, service charges are income based, so poor people pay less. I didn't expect to use any of my veteran benefits when I got out of the military, especially my VA medical benefits. But I was poor, so I went to the VA medical center to get my elbow checked-out.

Since it was late in the evening, I was in-and-out of the VA clinic quick! A few minutes after registering at the front desk, a lady came to get me. She walked me down to the x-ray room, x-rayed my elbow, said I had a hairline fracture, put my arm in a sling, gave me some Motrin, and I was on my way. Because I was soo poor, the trip to the VA only cost me $7.

I didn't sleep well that night at the apartment because of the pain from my elbow. I didn't realize that it was possible to lose sleep because of pain. It was my first broken bone, so it was an all-new experience for me. Other than my broken elbow, hanging-out at UF was a good time. But I was running out of cash, and my credit card was maxed-out, so I needed to find a job.

My hair was a little shaggy at the time, and I didn't think my shaggy hair looked professional, but I couldn't afford a haircut. I explained my problem to Chris. He said he had a pair of clippers, and that he'd bring his clippers into the studio the next night. A man of his word, Chris brought-in his clippers the following night. I was hoping he could just give me a little trim with the guards, but he didn't have that kind of expertise, so he just shaved my head for me outside of the studio. With my new haircut, I was ready to look for work. My friends at the studio were sad to see me leave, but I desperately needed some money.

I really didn't want to go down in income that I was used to earning as an assistant manager at Long John Silver's. As luck would have it, David's Real Pit BBQ was looking for an assistant manager. I drove out to the business park where David's Real Pit BBQ was located. David's place was a stand-alone brick building close to a busy street. I could smell the smoke from the real pit in his restaurant right away. I walked-in, found, and interviewed with David.

David was an authentic, hard-working, small-business-owner. At the end of our tour of his restaurant, we were standing outside in the front parking lot. He asked me why my head was shaved; I told him I was vegan, and Florida was a fresh start for me. He paused a few seconds, and sipped the air with a little hesitation before he said he would hire me to join his crew as an assistant manager. I was happy about that, and looked forward to learning how he ran his restaurant.

David did a lot of business, and he had a lot of fun products that I liked trying. He had a wall of novelty hot sauces that I loved exploring, and I enjoyed eating his seasoned steak fries with Vegenaise and ketchup. His homemade barbecue sauce was also good, but he had a couple things I didn't try, like all of the animal products we slow cooked in the real pit. I still hacked-up the hams and ribs with our meat cleavers, and served it to our patrons, but I was just doing my job.

Nights after cleaning the restaurant, I went back to Quilian's studio apartment with my shirt, pants, and sneakers covered in vegetable grease, animal fat, and the smell of smoke from the wood in the pit. Sometimes Chris was at the apartment hanging out with Quilian when I finished my closing shifts. When I walked into the apartment, those guys immediately burst-out into laughter as they ridiculed my stench while trying to hold their noses and waft away my smells. While I was showering-off the smells from the restaurant, I could still hear their mockery and laughter. Their jokes didn't bother me much, it was funny because it was true.

One busy day, David just finished paying for a load of wood

behind the restaurant, and he asked me why I didn't write down much overtime. The other assistant managers sat around and watched television while the closing crew cleaned the restaurant, and those television watching managers were charging David overtime. I felt really uncomfortable with the idea of doing that. I just liked to do my job; write down the scheduled hours I worked, and leave. So when David asked me why I wasn't putting-in much overtime, I considered telling him about his lazy managers, but instead I told him I didn't realize working overtime was an expectation.

I think he knew something wasn't quite right with his management staff. David encouraged me to talk to him about anything I thought needed addressed in his restaurant; I told him I would, but I knew I wasn't going to be there much longer. It was a toxic environment, but I didn't want to be the whistleblower to help fix it.

I started looking for work again; I liked the money I was earning at the restaurant, I just didn't like the work environment. I interviewed to be a front desk clerk at the Villager Lodge on SW 13th Street. Mr. Patel had a very high opinion of his motel, and he had high standards for his employees. However, his compensation structure was not commensurate with his expectations. Mr. Patel paid minimum wage, and at that time it was $5.15/hr. The crazy thing was, he had us college students competing for an opportunity to work for him. I went through a few rounds of interviews with Mr. Patel before he finally agreed to hire me.

When I started working there, I saw that Mr. Patel was thrifty, and his motel wasn't in that great of a neighborhood. He advertised a continental breakfast, but his continental breakfast consisted of coffee, and individually wrapped Little Debbie snack cakes that he was really stingy with. Also, I saw prostitutes making their rounds up and down the street as early as mid-morning. We had most of our activity around the first of the month when our guests would get their government checks.

One morning, I rented a room to a guy to stay there a few days. But I didn't see that someone else already had a reservation for his room midway through his stay, so I needed to move him to a different room. When Mr. Patel went to his room to get him out, he was already asleep, and Mr. Patel had to wake him up. Mr. Patel escorted him to the lobby to make arrangements with me, but the guy was being very unreasonable, and started getting really upset with me. Mr. Patel saw the situation escalating, and started to escort him out the front door.

As Mr. Patel was turning him toward the door, the gnarly man extended his long scraggly arm toward me, and raspily yelled at me slowly and dramatically: "I will kill you!" I pressed my back against the wall behind the front desk, trying to create as much distance from me and him as I could, but I was only able to step up on my toes and put my heels on the wall because the front desk was soo close to the wall. Mr. Patel ushered him out, and calm was restored to my lobby, but I started to wonder if the guy really would come back to try to kill me. I didn't worry about it too much, but that idea was persistent in the back of my mind. Overall it was a clean job, I was happy to be there, and Mr. Patel was willing to work with my class schedule whenever I figured that out.

My next step was to get enrolled in school. Since I was going to school mostly on a whim, I missed all of the application deadlines for the University of Florida. My only other option was Santa Fe Community College. I found the veteran's office on campus, and waited around for the veteran's representative (vet-rep) to show-up.

I didn't have to wait long, and when he arrived, he helped me get setup to use my GI Bill benefits. I was going to get close to a-grand a month for full-time enrollment! That should have been enough to pay for my classes, but because I was maxed-out on my credit cards, and I was driving a car I really couldn't afford, I needed to use all of that money for my living expenses. When I finished registering to receive my GI Bill benefits, my friendly vet-rep pointed me in the direction of the registrar's office to sign-up for classes.

On the way to the registrar's office, I called my buddy Chris, and he told me to sign-up for my FAFSA. I thought it was a Florida thing, but when I went to the library on-campus and went online, I found out it was a federal thing. I filled-out my FAFSA in the library, and then walked toward the registrar's office. I really liked the look of the white façade of the buildings as I strolled through campus.

When I got to the registrar's office, it was dimly lit and vacant, like a bar in the early afternoon. The registrar lady came up-front from some other room at the back of the office to meet me, and helped me sign-up for classes. I felt clueless about the entire process. I was signing-up for classes, I really didn't know what I was doing, but it felt like something that I needed to do. She told me what it was going to cost me, and told me Nelnet was going to be my student loan servicer. That is where my student loan debt started, with Nelnet, in the fall of 2002.

Quilian's lease on the studio apartment was ending, and he found someplace less expensive to live. The place he was moving-to had some special requirements applicants needed to meet in order to qualify for the reduced rent; really, he was only sharing something like a dormitory room with someone. Quilian told me I could take-over the studio apartment we were living-in. I liked the idea, but I couldn't afford the place on my own. Chris's lease was ending too; I told him about Quilian moving-out, and Chris suggested we check-out the luxury townhomes at Oxford Manor.

Oxford Manor was a gated community; we toured the place, and it was awesome! They had a tanning bed, two designer pools, a recreation room, fitness facility, and they had a roommate match program so we could share a three-bed, three-bath townhome with another student. They were even going to furnish the place for us with new furniture! Descending in price-per-month, the townhome had two upstairs bedrooms. The large room with a private balcony overlooking a swamp was the most expensive. The second medium-sized bedroom upstairs overlooking the parking lot was mid-range, and the smallest bedroom by the front door was least expensive.

Since I was going to be getting money for school from my GI Bill, I felt like I would have no problem affording the nicest and most expensive room in the house, so we agreed to sign one-year leases. Chris just flipped the pages quickly initialing and signing wherever he needed-to as I started to read the entire 20-page lease agreement. When Chris finished signing and initialing he just looked at me and said: "Dude, you want the apartment, right?" I densely replied: "yeah." Then he said: "It doesn't even matter what it says, you want the apartment, so just sign it." I signed, and it was done.

We had a few days before we could move into Oxford Manor. Quilian was at the studio; I hadn't started school yet, and I didn't have to work that night. I was just standing on the balcony-walkway outside of Quilian's studio apartment in the early evening, looking across at the swimming pool. Nobody was at the pool, it was just calming to look at. As I was standing there, Chris gave me a call. We talked for a couple minutes, both didn't have anything going on, so he thought it would be fun to go to '80s New Wave night at Full Circle.

Full Circle was a local nightclub in downtown Gainesville. We lived near the UF campus. The downtown area was a couple miles away, so we had to drive to get there. Accustomed to driving drunk, I drove us to the nightclub.

We were there early, around 8 p.m. Only a dozen-or-so people were there, scattered throughout the nightclub. I had a little anxiety; I wasn't comfortable being there, and I wasn't really sure why.

As Chris and I had a couple drinks at the bar, my anxiety quickly melted away, and I was starting to have a good time. Before we knew it, the club was busy. Chris and I saw a booth full of girls, so we squeezed into the booth with them, and began talking to them.

We had a couple more drinks, and then Chris disappeared. Alone with the four girls, I was not able to keep the conversation going, and our good times quickly became awkward times. Really uncomfortable now, I left the booth, and looked for Chris.

I walked around the night club doing quick scans of the dance floor, bar, and bathroom. I couldn't find him, so I figured he did the quick-bone-stalone, and just ditched me. It wasn't a big deal, I've done it before. Drunk and broke, I left too.

I walked outside to the parking lot; the sun had set, and the street lights were on. I saw my car in the lot where I left it, but there was a group of people standing in front of my car on the sidewalk, talking amongst themselves. I wondered if they were going to try to mess with me; so I kept my head down, and minded my own business as I walked to my car. When I got to my car, they didn't even acknowledge me. I didn't want to push my luck, so I locked my doors as soon as I got into my car, and prepared to leave.

I put my headlights on, but I didn't want to blind the people in front of me, so I switched-down my lights to only have my parking lights on. I kept my headlights off as I backed up; and as I drove forward, there was a big dip to get out of the parking lot. I really didn't want to scrape the bottom of my car as I was turning onto the side street, so I had to carefully maneuver my car across the dip. Slowly I made it out of the parking lot, and onto the side street, without damaging my car. I looked at my instrument panel again, saw it was lit-up like my lights were on, and thought I was good.

As I was driving through the city, I didn't have any problem seeing where I was going because the street lights were on. I had my music turned-up, and I was singing along to a song trying to have a good time, but people kept flashing me as I was driving. That confused me; each time I looked down I saw my instrument-panel lights on, so I figured my headlights were on too, and those people were just being stupid.

A minute later, I saw a police car driving past me in the oncoming traffic. I checked my rearview mirror, and couldn't see where he went, but it was time for me to turn anyway. I pulled into the alley to get to my apartment complex, and I felt like I was ducking behind the building hiding from the police. I looked in my rearview mirror, and again, I didn't see the police behind me so I thought I was in the clear.

I was soo happy to find a parking spot right in front of my apartment. I stopped my car to start backing into the parking space. As I shifted into reverse, I imagined myself quickly parking my car, and strolling toward my apartment as the police drove-by. But before I could even start moving, a car was already behind me, blocking my way to my parking spot.

I was pretty sure it was the police officer I saw a few minutes earlier; but he didn't have his red and blue lights on, so I didn't know what was going on. I thought about driving around to the parking garage at the back of the building, but I was almost certain he was going to follow me, so I just waited for someone to approach my car. I think the nervousness was starting to get to me; because all-of-a-sudden, I had this uncontrollable urge to vomit.

Before I could even think to do anything else, I threw-up on myself. I blocked my vomit from going anyplace else in my car, but it was all down the front of my shirt, and pooled in my lap. Then, I felt like I had to throw-up some more. I wanted to open my car door and throw-up outside of my car, but I was nervous to open my car door because I thought they might shoot me. I still hadn't seen anyone, so I took a chance, and opened my car door to throw-up outside, but I was already done. Still not seeing anyone or hearing anything from anyone, I thought I was cool, so I got out of my car to shake the vomit off of my shirt.

While I was shaking the vomit off of my shirt, I saw the police officers walking toward me. One of the guys asked me: "what's on the front of your shirt?" I was calm, and did my best to maintain my composure on the off-chance they might not suspect that I was drunk, but my responses to their questions didn't help. I replied to him: "I threw-up on myself." They asked me to walk-over to the front of one of the police cars with them. I agreed, and slowly walked with them, still trying to get the vomit off of my shirt.

As I stood in front of his car, he asked me what time I thought it was. In my happy-go-lucky way, I cleverly responded to him: "midnight-30." Most people would have appreciated my fun way of saying 12:30 a.m., but he wasn't amused by my response. After a brief discussion with his partner, they decided to call for an ambulance, just to make sure I was well-enough to go to jail.

I really didn't want to go to the hospital, because I knew that was going to cost me a lot of money I didn't have, so I told the officer: "I don't want to go to the hospital." He told me: "You can choose to go, or I can make you go." I didn't like the way that sounded; and thought it would look better in court if I made the decision for myself, so I decided to go.

At the hospital, they had me handcuffed to the bed, and the nurse prepared to give me an intravenous (IV) saline solution. Happy to be in a bed, I took a little nap. When I woke-up, I looked around the room, and through my doorway. I was alone in the room, and couldn't see anyone outside of my room. Then I looked down at the IV in my hand. Either I was moving in my sleep, or the nurse wasn't gentle with me, but her IV needle created a wound on my hand. I wondered if I could sue. While I was considering that, the officers came back to take me to jail.

As I was going through booking process in jail, I was uncomfortable that they scanned my iris. I figured the option of becoming a career criminal was over for me at that point. After the iris scanner in the narrow booking hallway, was a large circular administrative area surrounded by jail cells.

They didn't even have me handcuffed at this point; while the police officers were looking for a cell for me, I was just milling around wherever I wanted to go. I felt a little panicky, and nervously looked for a payphone so I could call Chris to come and get me, but I couldn't remember his phone number. I felt like throwing-up again, and grabbed a trash can behind the desk. The police officer said I would have to clean it if I made a mess, and the urge suddenly left me.

The cell they found for me was a room with eight bunk beds cantilevered from the walls. On each of the metal bed frames was a thin green vinyl-wrapped foam mattress that had the pillow permanently attached. The room was already half-full when I arrived.

I wanted to sleep at the back of the room away from the door, but it was dark in the room, so I just threw myself down onto the only mattress I could see that didn't have anyone sleeping on it. That bunk was closest to the door on the left as you walked into the room. The sheriffs were considerate enough to leave the lights off for us, but that door opened all-night-long, casting a thick beam of light onto my face until our room was finally filled.

In the morning, the officers made us line-up in a single file line, and they escorted us to a stadium seating room for our remote courtroom first appearance. I looked at the guy sitting next to me in the courtroom. He was a tall, shaggy-haired, unkempt guy, wearing canvas shorts, a short sleeve button-down shirt, and sandals. The man's toenails were caked with dirt. I looked at him, and thought I had sunk pretty low to be in the position I was, sitting next to this dirty guy. I thought to myself: "I'm better than this, I shouldn't be here." I watched as the bailiff turned the television on.

The judge had already been hearing cases in his local courtroom before he started seeing us in our remote courtroom. I watched one-by-one as the defendants were called by name, and listened to what was said, so I would have a general idea of what to do when I was called-up to speak with the judge. When he called my name, he quickly reviewed my file, and released me on my own recognizance. I had no idea that was possible, so I was surprised and happy he let me go.

My car was in the impound lot. Somehow I had just enough money to pay to have my car released to me. Another surprise, I left my cell-phone in the center council, and my battery wasn't dead.

I saw I had seven missed calls from Chris, and a couple voicemails. I drove away from the impound lot, and listened to my messages. It was Chris in my messages. He was talking to me in a calm tone of voice in his messages, but he was telling me he was mad and frustrated that I left him at the bar.

Still driving to the apartment, I called him back to let him know what happened. He said he was hoping something bad happened to me for ditching him. But when he learned I was arrested, he said he didn't want anything that bad to happen to me, and his anger turned to sympathy. The whole ordeal was a traumatic for me, so I quit drinking. The next day I checked the mail, and I was already receiving letters from attorneys that wanted to represent me in court.

The first office I went to was a team of three young attorneys. Their office was next to a busy street, and they were really excited to represent me. I sat in the basic hard plastic classroom chair in front of their wooden desk. Two of the attorneys sat on the desk, while the third was pacing back and forth in the entryway. They discussed my driving under the influence (DUI) charge with me, and their fee would cover me all the way through trial if we had to go there. I didn't know what the heck I was doing, so I sheepishly told them I needed to think about it. They were giving me the hard sell, and wanted me to decide now so they could have more time to prepare for my case. They were a little too eager for me, so I told them no, and walked toward the door. As I was leaving, I could hear them utter sounds of disbelief, and they were a little frantic that I turned down their offer. I was soo confused about my situation, and they did not do a good job of putting me at ease, so leaving felt like the right thing to do.

The next day I met with another attorney. He was a middle-aged-man, in a small office, on a sleepy street. He used to fly helicopters in the military, and had awards with helicopters on them behind him. I liked that he was a veteran, he was calm, and he was nice. In our conversation about my case, he told me his fee would cover me up-to trial. It wasn't as good of a deal as the three young attorneys, but I wasn't expecting to go to trial. I had soo much stress about my ordeal; but my calm veteran was reassuring to me, so I told him I wanted him to represent me.

I really didn't want to tell my parents that I was arrested for drunk driving; but I desperately wanted to get out of the mess I was in, and I thought the middle-aged attorney could help me. I called my parents, and spoke with my father first. He told me he too had been in a similar situation. Hearing him say that made me feel a little less bad. I asked him if he could help me, and he said I would have to ask my mother.

That was the conversation I didn't want to have the most because my mother is very emotional. As I was telling her what happened, I could hear her crying, and trying to hold back tears at the same time. I told her I met with an attorney who was a veteran, and I thought he could help me get out of trouble. My mother's tears of disappointment turned into tears of anger as she chastised me for doing something so dishonorable. For a little more than five minutes, she spoke to me through her disappointed and angry tears, condemning my behavior.

After all of that, she still didn't tell me she would give me money to pay for the attorney. I didn't want to be rude and interrupt her; so when she ran out of things to say to me, I asked her if she would give me money. Still crying and trying to hold back her tears, she told me she would send me money to pay for the attorney, and told me to never do this again. I agreed to what she said, and I was soo relieved to hear her say she would send me money.

The time couldn't pass fast enough as I waited for her check to arrive. But when it did, I was soo excited. I called my middle-aged attorney right away, and made an appointment to meet with him.

I thought it would look really bad to drive my car to his office, so I called Chris to ask for a ride. Chris was busy, but he said he had a 20" bicycle he would let me use whenever I wanted. Chris lived nearby so I walked to his place, picked-up his bicycle, and rode it to meet with the middle-aged man at his office.

The guy's office was really just a one-story single-family home in a residential neighborhood, converted into a little office. I paid his retainer, and immediately felt relieved that my problem was taken care of. I walked down his front steps to where I left Chris's bicycle, and I rode his bicycle home smiling with ease about my situation.

I met with my attorney once more before my court hearing so he could show me the dashboard-camera video of my arrest. The video was of me opening my car door when I threw-up on myself, and a segment of me standing in front of the officer's car. I stood perfectly straight for a few minutes, and then I started wavering a little. My attorney said I looked good in the video, and suggested a jury might side with me if we went to trial. Of course he needed additional funds to go to trial; and, it was completely out of the question for me to ask my parents for more money. I rejected his jury idea, and was starting to regret my decision to not work with the three young attorneys.

When my court date arrived, I met my attorney at the courthouse. As we walked through the courthouse, he saw another attorney he knew, and smugly greeted him. When the judge called for me in the courtroom, my attorney stood-up, and spoke to the judge for me. Then, the judge sentenced me.

The judge ordered me to pay a fine, pay my court fees, pay for an alcohol evaluation, and I had to pay for supervised probation for a year. On top of all that, my license was revoked, but I was eligible to apply for another driver's license after six months. My comfortable middle aged attorney didn't get me any better of a deal than I would have on my own, and wasn't worth any of the money we paid to him. I didn't get a break on anything. I actually think I received a more punitive sentence than if I had just represented myself. I was really upset and disappointed by all of that, but I started doing what the judge ordered me to do.

The additional bills I had to pay for my court fees and supervised probation tightened my economic noose, and made things a lot more uncomfortable for me. With my GI Bill, I was earning close to $1,000 per month, and with my front desk clerk job I was earning around $600 per month. Had I chose to live modestly, I would have been very comfortable with those incomes I was earning. But because I wanted to live-in, drive, and wear the best of everything, I was always broke. And because I continued to make poor life choices by ignoring the laws, I had even more bills to pay.

I kept checking the local newspaper for other jobs I could do that paid more money. I saw an advertisement to earn up to $1,300 per month working in a call-center setting-up appointments to sell water purification systems. The phone interview and the in-person interview went well, but I lost my birth certificate, my driver's license was revoked, and my passport was expired, so I didn't have any documentation proving that I was legally authorized to live and work in the United States of America. Consequently, the water purification company couldn't hire me even though they wanted to.

I saw another advertisement by a real estate broker stating I could earn $2,000 to $3,000 a month selling real estate. I didn't even know what real estate was, but I was fairly certain I could do it. I called the broker, and he told me I needed a license to sell real estate. He told me taking the course to get my license would cost around $1,600, and I should call him back when I got my license so I could work for him selling houses. I wasn't even close to being in a position to pay $1,600 to take a course to get my real estate license, but it sounded like something that might be worth getting-into.

Even though my driver's license was revoked, not driving was not an option for me. I lived on the Southwest side, worked on the Southside of the city, went to school in the Northwest corner of the city, went grocery shopping on the North side, and had to see my case manager on the East side of the city. In court, they mentioned I could apply for a business-purpose-only (BPO) driving permit, but I couldn't be bothered with the rigmarole to try and get that. And, that too was going to cost me more money. Gainesville was a large enough city that I didn't think I needed to worry about getting caught driving on a suspended license. I'm a good driver! I generally don't break traffic laws, so I'm not going to get pulled over for something stupid. Besides, it wasn't like I was cruising the city for the fun of it. I was just driving to the places I needed to go as if they had given me a BPO permit. One rainy rush-hour afternoon, I just finished filling-up my car with gas, and I was about to turn onto a busy five-lane roadway.

I saw a police car driving past me, headed in the opposite direction, but I didn't think much of it. That night, my housemates and I decided to go-out to Cold Stone Creamery for some ice cream. Chris and I hopped into our housemate Issam's van, and Issam drove us to the ice-cream parlor. As we were driving out of our gated community, we saw a police officer driving in. None of us liked seeing that, and Chris joked that he was probably looking for me. We went out to the parlor, had some ice-cream, chatted on our phones to other friends, and went back to our townhome. An hour or so after we got back, a police officer knocked on our front door.

Issam had the little room next to the front door, so he answered the door. The same police officer that arrested me said he saw me driving my car, recognized my car, and knew I was driving on a suspended license. I'm not sure, but I don't think the Mardi Gras party beads hanging from my rearview mirror helped me stay inconspicuous. Trying not to get involved, Issam covered for me, and told the officer I wasn't home. It didn't matter, the officer had a warrant for my arrest for violating my probation by driving with a revoked driver's license. He gave the citation to Issam, and drove away.

Issam yelled up to me in my room, and I came downstairs to talk with him about what happened. We couldn't believe what just happened, and really didn't think it was legal. Since there was a warrant for my arrest, we decided it would be in my best interest for me to turn myself in. So that is what we did. I got into Issam's van again, and he drove me to the county jail, so I could turn myself in.

It was Friday night; I timidly approached the front desk of the county jail, not knowing how long I was going to have to stay there. I told the officers at the front desk why I was there, and they weren't surprised at all to see me. They in-processed me with the leisure of a department store cashier, and led me into the county jail dayroom.

It was a two-story room. To my left, in-between the main floor and mezzanine areas, there was a 20" tube television bracket-mounted to the cinder block wall. Across the room from where I entered, steel double doors led into the two-story walled courtyard that was fenced at the top so nobody could throw anything into or out-of the courtyard. On the right-side wall near the courtyard doors was the stainless steel meal serving window that was closed, and next to that window was a small wooden two-shelf game cabinet with no doors. The main floor of the room was filled with cafeteria style folding tables, and the second-story mezzanine area was filled with bunk-beds.

I arrived relatively early in the evening, so when I walked up the stairs to the bunk-beds, I quickly found an empty bed. I climbed-up to the top bunk, and tried to get comfortable. Within a couple hours, all the bunks were full. But that didn't stop the Sheriffs from bringing-in more inmates.

Guys were carrying-up thin vinyl-covered mattresses, and were starting to line the baseboard of the mezzanine. I watched as the guys lined the border of the wall head-to-toe, and wondered how many more guys they were going to bring-in. I remembered the news stories I heard about jail overcrowding, and was now seeing it first-hand. I had a bed, but I was still a little concerned about the overcrowding. I got a little sleep that night, and in the morning, I was happy to hear they were calling guys to be released.

I listened carefully to every name they called, hoping my name would be next, but they didn't call my name. I spent most of my time, in-between the times the sheriff was calling inmates to be released, daydreaming on my bed. I was very reluctant to leave my bed. I didn't want to do anything I wasn't supposed to do, so I stayed on my bed, and watched how people interacted with each other in the dayroom.

A group of guys were watching television, some guys were sitting at the tables talking, and some guys were playing board games. Out in the courtyard, it was more of the same. Some guys were playing basketball, some guys were talking to each other, and some guys were just standing or sitting around. I looked over at the guy sleeping in the top bunk next to me. I was envious of him that he could sleep-away his time. I thought to ask him and the other guys I saw what they were there for, but I was fairly certain that question was going to either give me answers that were going to make me really uncomfortable, or make them want to fight me. So, I chose not to talk to anyone.

I usually only ventured off my bunk for the meals, even though there wasn't much for me to eat. I basically just ate the piece of fruit on my tray, and gave the rest of my food to the few guys sitting around me that wanted extra food. After a while they were getting used to it, but occasionally a new guy sat in my area, and was surprised that I didn't want most of my food. I thought of it as a strategic moment. If I could make everyone around me a little happier, then things might go a little easier for me while I was in-there.

One afternoon, I mustered-up the courage to venture off of my bed. I saw a couple guys playing checkers at the end of one of the cafeteria tables. I knew how to play checkers. When one of the guys lost and got-up to leave, I sat down to play. We lined up the checkers pieces, and when this guy jumped my pieces during play, he would slam his checker piece onto the board in an uncomfortably intimidating way. It kinda made me mad after a while. I looked down the table at the other guys sitting at the table, to see their reactions to the way he was playing checkers, but the guys weren't interested in what we were doing, and were just laughing and smiling amongst themselves. The more we played, the more I got mad, so I said: "you win," got-up, and went to the courtyard.

In the courtyard too the guys played basketball really rough. I wasn't interested in getting into a fight; so I went to a little open space out in the yard, and did sit-ups and push-ups. After a little fresh air and exercise, I went back into the dayroom. Nobody was watching TV, so I grabbed the remote, and started flipping through the channels. Nothing on TV was interesting to me, so I went back to my bed to daydream.

At night, some guys would sneak off of their beds, and shoot dice for their commissary snacks. It looked like fun, but I didn't have any money for commissary. I didn't want to risk getting caught either; it wasn't worth it to me.

Monday morning my name was finally called, and it was my turn to be released. They gave me a court date and time, and all I needed to do was show-up to not screw it up. Issam picked me up from jail, and took me back to our townhome.

Having finally learned my lesson, Chris and Issam drove my car to the motel I worked-at, and parked it in front next to the busy four-lane street. I removed the Mardi Gras beads, and hung a For Sale sign from my rearview mirror. I couldn't afford to buy a bicycle or use public transportation, but Chris bought a beach cruiser he never rode, and he let me ride it. I rode his beach cruiser everyday to go to work, school, and to Sam's Club for my groceries.

I liked Sam's Club because I could buy my food in bulk at a good price. I always tried to get the most amount of food I could for the least amount of money. I normally bought five-pound bags of in-shell peanuts, large bunches of bananas, ten-pound bags of pinto beans, three-liter jugs of olive oil, and five-pound bags of carrots.

I shredded the carrots on a cheese grater into a large Rubbermaid food storage container, poured store-brand apple cider vinegar over the carrots from my plastic one-gallon jug, and sprinkled some sea salt over the carrots to make enough carrot salad to last me a week. I had a 10-cup electric cooker to cook my rice, and I usually cooked my beans in a pot on the stove because the rice and beans had different cook times.

Sometimes Chris would come home from the studio, and find me asleep on the couch with my beans cooking on the stove. That freaked-out Chris a lot. He was very concerned that I was going to burn-down our townhouse. Fortunately I never did, but there was definitely the potential. Somehow, I almost always perfectly cooked my beans. I mixed the cooked rice and beans together, and seasoned them with olive oil and salt.

We had a few sandwich size storage containers in the townhouse, so I put my rice and beans in the bottom half of the container, and covered the rice and beans with my carrot salad. I packed three of the sandwich sized storage containers like this, and carried them in my olive drab JanSport backpack to work with me in the morning for breakfast, a mid morning meal, and lunch. When I came back from work I had about an hour before I had to leave for class.

It was going to be several hours before I would have time to eat again, so this was my only opportunity to eat. Chris and Issam were at UF when I came home, so I would watch cable TV on my computer in my room and eat my peanuts. My computer chair was a collapsible lawn chair, and I propped-up my feet on my computer tower. I stood-up my five-pound bag of peanuts, and leaned it against the leg of my chair on the floor so I could easily reach into the bag and grab another in-shell peanut to split-open. Chris had a large Asian rice bowl that I placed in my lap when I ate my peanuts. As I split-open a peanut shell, I would throw the peanuts into my mouth, and drop the shells into the Asian soup bowl. I contentedly sat there watching TV and eating peanuts like this until the bowl was three-quarters-full of empty shells. I never went out to eat, and never ate fast food, because I could always buy and cook my own food for less money than it would cost me at even the cheapest fast food restaurant. I got soo much more food for my money by buying, cooking, and preparing my food myself.

In an effort to save even more money, I lived on fried onions for a while. I bought a 25-pound bag of onions, sliced them, fried them in olive oil, and seasoned them with paprika and salt. I liked the money I was saving by eating my fried onions, but my housemates Chris and Issam really didn't like that I made the whole townhouse reek of onions, for days. They had a little intervention with me, and that was the last time I fried onions in our townhouse.

I always carried my backpack with me, and was really good at packing it with all of the groceries I bought. The only time I rode the bus was when I bought the 50-pound bag of rice; it was such a good price on the rice, I couldn't pass it up. It was difficult for me to ride the beach cruiser with the bag of rice on my handlebars, and I thought about walking home while pushing the beach cruiser with the rice on the handle bars, but it was starting to rain. So I put Chris's beach cruiser in the bike rack on the front of a bus, and I carried my bag of rice onto the bus. I happily paid the bus driver the one-dollar fare. Riding the bus really helped me out that day because the light rain turned into a heavy down-pour. I'm sure I could have coordinated something with Issam or Chris to pick me up or go grocery shopping with me when I bought bulk items like this, but I really didn't like bothering other people with my problems, unless I had no other option.

I started having fun riding Chris's bicycle all-over-town, and I was getting into really good shape. I always wore my headphones with my compact disk (CD) player, and usually played some electronic music that kept me pumped-up on my rides. The only thing I had to worry about was the rain; I needed to be able to get to school or work in the rain, and still be dry enough to sit in-class or stand behind the front-desk at work.

I went to the Army/Navy store, and bought a thick yellow PVC rain-suit. I put my backpack in a white plastic garbage bag with drawstring closure, and wore my backpack on my front. I tucked my backpack into the front part of my rain-bibs, and then I wore my raincoat over my bibs so my CD player and my books wouldn't get wet. I was really upset with myself for not thinking to ride the beach cruiser sooner. I used to ride my mountain bike to work when I was in the Air Force, and it wasn't a big deal. I don't know why I was so obstinate, and didn't start riding a bicycle right away.

When my court date arrived, I rode Chris's beach cruiser downtown to the courthouse. In court, I filled-out the income and expense form to show the court I was too poor to hire an attorney. I was earning just enough money to survive, so I didn't have any extra money, and I wasn't about to ask my parents for any more money to hire another attorney that wasn't going to do anything for me. I thankfully met the eligibility requirements to be represented by a public defender, so they assigned a public defender to me, and gave me another court date. With more time to kill before my next court appointment, I continued my work and school routine.

I was at work in the motel, and within a week of putting my car up-for-sale, I had a guy interested in buying my car. Unfortunately though, he was broke like me, but I was desperate to get-out from under that payment. He said he would pay me the money to make the monthly payments, so I wrote-up a contract, and let him have and use my car. A few weeks went by, and when it was time to make a payment, I still hadn't received any money from him.

He wasn't answering or returning any of my calls, and I was getting really anxious. He lived a couple hours away, but I started making plans to get to the city where he lived. I still had the spare key, so I just needed to find my car, and drive it back to Gainesville.

The next day I went to work, my car was out-front, and the key was under the floor mat. I couldn't believe it! I was soo surprised, soo relieved, and soo thankful! There was a little sand on the floorboard of the car around the floor mats, so I knew he took it to the beach, but having a little sand in the car was a very small price to pay compared to having no car at all.

Considering the awful ordeal I just went through, my co-worker had sympathy for me, and also offered to make payments for me if he could keep and use the car. My co-worker was a little bit older, and a lot more responsible. I knew where he worked, and he worked there a few years before me, so I didn't think I was taking that big of a risk again. As before, I wrote-up a contract that we both signed, and gave him the key to the car. The only other difference between this deal and the other deal was that my co-worker actually followed-through, and made the payments to me. With my car situation in order, it was time to get my legal situation in order.

Like I did with the attorney I hired, I met with my public defender only once to strategize before we went to court. However, my public defender tried to get me the best deal she could. In court, the state's attorney wanted to give me 20 concurrent days in jail for violating my probation, but my public defender relentlessly negotiated for me. She kept arguing my case for me, going back and forth with the state's attorney until they finally settled on four weekends in jail, with credit for the one weekend I already served when I turned myself in. She was enervated after fighting for me, but I was very happy with my sentence, and humbly thanked my attorney for everything she did for me. She worked much harder for me than the attorney my parents gave me money for. Again it was up to me to fulfill my side of the deal, and do what was adjudicated in court, so I made arrangements with Issam.

Like any good friend would, Issam faithfully drove me to jail every Friday night, and picked me up every Sunday evening. During our van rides to jail, we usually talked about how surreal of an experience it was, that I could be doing soo much better, and that neither of us ever expected to make weekend trips to jail. On our van-rides home, I talked about what I saw in jail, and what I did to pass the time.

Every week my time in jail was getting easier, and the sheriffs started calling my name to do work in the jail. I really didn't want to work, but I liked that I got to see a few different areas of the jail. And, getting out of the dayroom helped me pass the time a little quicker. One afternoon, I was outside with a few other guys picking weeds out of the rocks in a decorative courtyard area that was river-rocked. Trying to kill as much time as possible, I moped around, stooped, and pulled-out the weeds like I was told. But a couple of the guys I was with didn't even do that. They just stood in the shade, talked, and laughed to each other.

I was mad at those guys because I was working and they weren't, but I kept my comments to myself, and continued working. Ten minutes later, the sheriff came back, and angrily called for those guys. Apparently he also noticed those guys weren't working. I'm not sure what happened to them, but I don't think it worked-out in their favor.

Another day I was working in the kitchen. I had fun working in the kitchen. The guys I worked-with in the kitchen were cool, actually worked, and were all in good moods. They even invited me to come back. I thanked them for the offer, but my time was already up. With Issam's help, I successfully served all of my jail sentence.

Finally doing the right thing by following my court orders, things were starting to go okay for me. I called an office in New Jersey, told them I needed a copy of my birth certificate, and after doing what they told me, they sent me an official copy of my birth certificate. With my birth certificate and disposition papers, I was able to get a Florida driver's license. I still didn't have a car, but now I had enough documentation to get a new job and travel. I was in a good routine riding the beach cruiser to work, school, and Sam's Club, and I even found time to lie by the pool and get some sun after work. But I had enough of Florida, and it was time for me to go.

I always liked Davenport University, often played with the idea of enrolling there, and now was my chance. I got a little smarter too; instead of starting another Associate degree, I decided to transfer my credits toward a Bachelor degree. I applied and was accepted to study marketing in the fall. To prepare myself for my move to Michigan, I started selling things I didn't need like my computer, portable stereo, collapsible lawn chair, and my vintage record collection that I bought at a yard sale. I put all of the clothes I had in a large box, and shipped them to my parent's house in Michigan.

Gabe was out of the military too, and moved back to Pennsylvania to be close to his family. I called him-up one day, told him that I was going to fly to South Dakota to hang out with Mat over the summer, and then I was going to move back to Michigan in the fall. Gabe liked that idea, and suggested I fly to Philadelphia so we could do a road-trip out to South Dakota. Always up for an adventure, I bought a plane ticket to Philadelphia. As time was getting close for me to fly-out to Philadelphia, something changed, and Gabe wasn't able to do the road trip with me anymore. That was a little frustrating, but I had just enough money left-over from selling all of my stuff to buy another plane ticket from Gainesville to Rapid City. Before I left, I went to a café with Chris and Quilian.

It was a nice evening, so we sat outside of the café. We were reminiscing about all the mischief I got into, and talked about having an Irish Car Bomb. I never had one of those drinks before, and I love new experiences! I felt like I learned a lot, and that drinking wouldn't be a problem for me anymore, so we drank an Irish Car Bomb. It was delicious, and a lot of fun! Having that fun drink ended nine-months of sobriety for me, and the next day, I was on the plane to Rapid City.

7

Rapid City

Song Suggestions:
D.B. Boulevard—Point of View
BT—R&R Rare & Remixed (CD 2)

I was warmly greeted by Mat and his parents when I flew-into Rapid City. They were setup nice; and they set me up nice. They had a spare bedroom that I could sleep-in, and they had a spare car I could use when I needed to. Mat's sister Melanie was also flying into Rapid City, and she was in a similar situation as me. We were both broke, and we needed to work, so we started job hunting together.

We read through the classified ads in the local newspaper and saw advertisements for a job we could do. Tourism is one of the drivers of the local economy, so a few hotels were hiring. We found one hotel in Keystone, South Dakota that paid a little more than the local hotels were paying, which was only a few cents more than minimum wage, but we both got really excited about it! Keystone is 20 miles away, and we would spend the difference in hourly earnings on gas, but we were carpooling, so it seemed like we would come out ahead.

Melanie and I drove-out to Keystone, and completed our applications in the office. The hiring manager met with us right away, and she hired us on the spot! The only problem was, all of my clothes were in Michigan, and I didn't have any money to buy clothes to wear to work. But, I had a Herberger's department store charge card that I was making payments on, so I had a few hundred dollars credit available on the card. With money to burn, Melanie and I went to Herberger's to buy some clothes for me.

I picked-out a few pair of black pants, and a few white dress shirts. The pants were like $65 a pair, and the shirts around $40 each. I kinda knew I was spending a lot of money for my clothes, but it didn't seem like I had any other options. And, I figured I'd pay it back eventually, so I didn't think it was that big of a deal.

I still had to pay for my court fees and supervised probation in Florida, and I had a few months left of the 1-year lease that I was paying at Oxford Manor in Gainesville. My room at our townhouse did not go unused. Quilian needed a new place to live-in when I left, and I was happy to let him stay in my Oxford Manor room. There was a month or two I couldn't pay him any rent when we lived together in his studio apartment, so this was my way of paying him back.

I worked dayshift at the hotel in Keystone, and was home around 4 p.m. The only extra money I had after paying all of my bills was about $20. That was just enough money to buy a 1.75 liter bottle of Captain Morgan Spiced Rum from Sam's Club. Not having any extra money to spend on food was a great way to help me stay slim.

I was in great shape from riding Chris's bicycle 19 miles a day in Gainesville, and I wanted to stay in-shape. To help me do that, the first things I did when I got home was 35 pushups and 70 sit-ups. After that, I didn't have anything else better to do, so I drank. I didn't feel guilty about all the calories I was drinking because I wasn't eating, and I always did my exercises before I drank.

I love music, but I couldn't afford to buy all the music I wanted to hear. My solution was to illegally download all of my music and save it on my external hard drive. I didn't feel too bad about stealing my music like that, because most of the music I was listening to was from obscure electronic music artists. I guess some of the music I stole wasn't obscure; I loved listening-to and singing along with Yo La Tengo while drinking double-shots of the Captain. I listened to my music from my external hard drive when I plugged it into Mat's parent's computer that was setup in the laundry room.

Mat's parents lived in California most of the time, and Mat was still in the military, working the night shift, so he was asleep while I was home. But the laundry room was in the basement at one end of the house, and Mat's bedroom was upstairs at the other end of the house, so my boisterousness didn't wake him up. When I was tired of all the drinking and singing, I went to sleep, and did it all over again the next day.

Melanie lived with her fiancé in another house. On the weekends, we all got together at Mat's parent's house. Melanie would give me $10 to buy some snacks for us, and I went to Walmart to buy four bags of store brand potato chips. Melanie would eat one or two chips, and then I ate chips the rest of the weekend. Again, I didn't feel bad about eating all of the potato chips, because I wasn't eating the rest of the week.

Mat's mom, Pam, was in-town one weekend, and decided Mat needed a house. She found a house for him in an established neighborhood in the city, and scheduled a showing. Pam also invited me to come with them to check-out the house.

It was a nice house built in the mid 1950s, owned by an older couple, and it was well-maintained. The showing went well; and after a brief discussion, Mat decided to put-in an offer on the house. Mat's mom was going to help Mat with the closing costs on the house, and I was going to rent a room in the house from Mat.

That process helped me foster the idea I had in Florida, to get my real estate license, and I was starting to understand what real estate was. Pam suggested I contact Mat's real estate agent from the showing to learn more about getting a license to sell real estate. That made sense, so I called Mat's real estate agent, Gale, and setup a meeting with him.

Gale and I had lunch, talked about the process of starting a career in real estate, and how much it would cost me. At the time, I couldn't afford the $1,000 for the real estate class, or the $1,500 for the real estate association fees. But I was about to start school again, and receive a stipend from school for my living expenses. I thought about following through with my plan to move back to Michigan and going to school there, but I really liked the opportunity I had in South Dakota to learn to sell real estate. So, I decided to go to Michigan.

While I was at my parent's house in Michigan, I discussed my real estate plan with them. They were supportive, as long as I kept going to school. So that is what I did, I packed a few things to bring back with me to South Dakota, and headed-back to Rapid City. As we discussed, I moved into a bedroom at the house Mat just bought, and paid him rent for the room. I enrolled in online courses at Davenport University to study marketing, received my stipend, and registered for the real estate course that Gale suggested.

Mat's sister Melanie also liked the real estate idea, and she decided to go to real estate school too. The following month, Melanie and I worked at the hotel in Keystone during the week, and attended Real Estate school on the weekends. When I wasn't working at the hotel, or studying real estate, I participated in my marketing classes online.

By December, we graduated real estate school, the hotel had shutdown for the year, and Melanie and I were getting ready to take the state real estate exam so we could get our real estate licenses. Taking the exam cost a little over $100, so it was really important to me to study and pass it the first time I took it. Fortunately for me, my studying paid-off, and I passed the test on my first try.

My real estate license application to the state needed an official copy of my exam results, and also asked for disclosure about my criminal background. I was nervous about that, because the law refers to convictions as moral turpitude. That's kind-of a vague concept, subject to interpretation, and a lot of minor things could easily be considered deprave. Hoping for the best, I submitted my completed real estate license application to the state.

January 2004 I was elated when I checked the mail, saw a letter from the state, and read that my real estate license application was approved! I already met with the broker at Coldwell Banker, and they allowed me to hang my license there whenever it was granted by the state. I also made an arrangement with Gale to be my mentor, and agreed to pay him a 20% commission from my real estate sales. As I was learning real estate, I was still taking my online courses at Davenport University.

I really needed that stipend money from school, and my GI Bill, to help me pay for my living expenses while I was getting my start in real estate. But, it still wasn't enough for me to get by. I had to start working my front desk clerk job again. I found a job at a hotel in Rapid City, because the hotel in Keystone was closed for the winter. I worked nights at the hotel so I could do my real estate prospecting and training during the day. I didn't know how long it was going to take for me to get a real estate commission check, but everyone I talked to told me it was going to take a while since I was just starting-out.

It ended-up taking me four months to get my first real estate closing, and it was actually a referral from one of my classmates in real estate school. My real estate school classmate was in a different market than the buyer, and the buyers were in the military. Since I was a veteran, my real estate school classmate thought it would be in the buyer's best interest to work with me. Of course, I paid a referral fee to my real estate school classmate.

When I got that first check, it was pretty good, but I had to pay a lot of people. I had to give part of my commission to Coldwell Banker, my mentor, and my real estate school classmate for the referral. After all of that, I still walked away with $2,400, and I was really happy! To show my appreciation for all of the help along the way, I gave each of the office staff a Godiva chocolate bar I bought from Herberger's. And since I had a little money to spend, Mat and I started planning a trip to Philadelphia to visit Gabe.

That summer, we flew to Philadelphia, and Gabe picked us up at the airport. Gabe didn't live in the city, he lived about an hour out of the city in a nice suburban town of Lower Bucks County called Langhorne. Gabe was living with his girlfriend, Heather, in a mansion that the owners converted into apartments. The owners of the mansion did a great job preserving the historic charm of the property, and only had like two units per floor, so there was plenty of space for Mat to sleep on the floor in the middle of the living room, and for me to sleep on an air mattress behind the couch. While we were there we went to the Amish Village, tailgated at a Phillies game, and I met Gabe's childhood friend Robbie, who became my friend too. After a great trip visiting our friends, Mat and I went back to South Dakota, and got back to work.

As the year passed, I was getting better at real estate, and averaged one sale a month. Unfortunately, my first sale was a great sale, and all of the other houses I was selling netted me only around a $1,200 each. Regardless, any sale that generates income is better than no sale.

With the few sales I was doing, I was getting to know my colleagues at the office, and their licensed assistants. One of the licensed assistants was a cute girl, and she wasn't involved with anyone. She gave me her phone number, and one night I decided to call her, even though I was really reluctant to go out with her. In High School, one of my classmates told me to not pee in my own pool. It made sense to me, there are too many people to date outside of work or school pools, making it completely unnecessary to pollute my own pool like that. Following that rule always served me well, until I broke the rule for her.

She used to manage a few gentleman's night clubs; and for the fun of it, we decided to visit them all. At these clubs they served beer and mixed drinks. I was drinking gin and tonic because I liked the way they tasted, and I liked their cool blue glow under the black lights. I had a lot of fun meeting all of the cute licensed assistant's old friends, and the dancers at the clubs treated me very well. At the last club we went to, I was lying down on stage, and the dancer climbed on top of me.

She was kneeling over my face, bent down over my body, and ripped my button-down shirt off of me. As I was lying there, I could hear the buttons shoot off of my shirt like BBs out of a BB-gun. I wasn't wearing an undershirt, so I was half-naked on stage with a half-naked dancer. I really liked the shirt she ripped all the buttons off of, but it was worth it for the experience. After her dance, I had one more drink, and then it was time for us to go because we had to work in the morning.

We walked out to my car, hopped-in, and drove-off. I was driving down the highway no problem, but I was looking for some music to play, so I was veering out of my lane a little. After a few seconds of that, I saw the red and blue lights in my rearview mirror, and I got to spend the night in jail, again. Adding insult to injury, the cute licensed assistant actually saw the police officer sitting in his car across the street from the strip club. She didn't say anything to me because she didn't think I was drunk. In the morning, I called Melanie, and she came to pick me up from jail in Sturgis with her husband Mike.

One good thing about the cute licensed assistant was that she knew a good attorney. She explained to me how he represented someone in her family very well, and how impressed she was with the results he was able to achieve. She called him for me, talked to him a couple minutes to introduce me, and then she handed the phone to me.

I was especially nervous because this was my second offence, so I asked a lot of questions. After answering several of my questions, he recommended we meet at his office. I really didn't want to go to his office; but I desperately needed help, so I reluctantly agreed to meet with him at his office.

The attorney was formerly an attorney for the state of South Dakota. When I walked into his office, I liked to see that his office was clean, well-organized, and uncluttered. I was wearing a suit and tie, but I timidly approached his desk. He had nice brown leather office chairs at his stately wooden desk. His office was carpeted, which I generally don't prefer, but I liked that the carpet helped to keep the noise down in the room as we spoke.

We talked for a few minutes; he explained the worst case scenario, the best case scenario, and his past experiences with people who had similar problems as me. He was expensive to work with, but I really needed help, and he seemed like he was worth taking a chance with. Even with my stipend, I didn't have enough money to pay his fee, but he still agreed to work with me. I gave him the half of his retainer that I had, and told him I would pay the other half after my next closing at the end of the following month.

As I made my payment to his secretary, I didn't have the sense of relief I had with the first attorney I hired. My former state's attorney explained to me he was going to need some assistance from me in the process; to help build a case to the judge that he shouldn't revoke my driver's license. He also told me to not tell anyone about my DUI charge. He said telling people wasn't going to help me, so I didn't tell anyone. I didn't need to go to most of the hearings, but I did produce a letter from my office stating the necessity of keeping my driver's license as a tool for me to do my job, and to be a productive member of the community. At the last court hearing, the judge wanted to see me in court.

My former state's attorney strategically arranged for us to meet with the judge last; because we were asking for a favor from the judge. I think my former state's attorney could sense my trepidation while we waited at the back of the court room. We watched the judge hear the cases in front of us; and my attorney leaned into me and told me the judge was just a man, doing a job.

What he said to me put me at ease immediately, and up-until it was our turn to stand in front of the judge. We were asking the judge for a suspended imposition of sentence; meaning, I was to be sentenced, but I didn't have to serve any of the time in the sentence. The judge asked me if I intended to be a permanent resident of South

Dakota, and I told him I did. The judge pursed his lips, hesitated, granted my suspended imposition of sentence, and we were done. I left the courtroom, and walked down the front stairs of the courthouse as if nothing happened.

As negotiated, I had another closing the following month, and I paid the other half of my attorney's retainer. That was my first year in real estate. My second year in real estate was much better. I didn't stop drinking and driving, I just didn't get caught.

I'm a social person. One night after work, a few of my colleagues wanted to get together for a drink downtown, so we went to a local restaurant/bar that brewed their own beer. We had a couple beers, and a couple girls sat at the table next to ours. The girls were cute, so I sat down with them, and started talking to them.

They were telling me the county fair was in town, and they were going to go check it out. They invited me along, so I met them there. We danced a little at one of the tents, and of course, we did more drinking. We were having a great time until one of the girls was getting jealous of the other girl. It was pretty good timing, because I had to leave anyway.

I was working nights at the hotel in Keystone part-time. Like I said, I was selling houses, but I wasn't making a lot of money selling houses. I left the tent at the county fair and then Jason called me. I spoke with him as I staggered-out to the parking lot to try to find my car. I was glad he called; my conversation with him got me excited, and helped revive me. While I was talking to him, I was walking back and forth in the dusty field looking for my car in the light of the headlights of the cars that were driving by. My car was difficult to find in the night because it was an old Toyota Corolla that didn't have a key fob to flash the car lights. Miraculously I found my car, Jason hung-up the phone with me, and I started to drive to the hotel to work my night shift.

There isn't much in-between Rapid City and Keystone, just some rolling hills, rocks, and trees. It's soo remote, there aren't even any street lights. It's only a 20 minute drive, but I got bored, and fell asleep while I was driving.

I woke up to the sight of sparks outside of my driver-side window, and realized my car was driving along the guardrail on the highway. I jerked the wheel off of the guardrail, skidding a little onto the highway, and kept driving to work. I noticed my car was making a grinding sound now, but I made it to work, and looked at my car in the hotel parking lot.

The driver side fender was smashed causing the wheel-well to rub against the tire, and a line of paint was scraped off of the car all along the driver-side. That woke me up enough to work my shift. I walked into the hotel lobby, got caught-up on the shift-notes from the afternoon shift, and worked the rest of the night.

The following morning, I was still a little shook-up about my accident. I drove my car to a body shop to get a quote to fix it, but the damages were more than the car was worth. Then I started thinking, I might have been soo drunk that I hit some other car on the highway, ran them off the road, and didn't even realize it. I was soo scared about that idea. I called the police department from a payphone to ask them if there were any accidents reported on that highway the night before. I was relieved to hear the officer tell me the only accident reported was someone hitting a deer.

I called Pam, and told her what I did, sans the drinking part. She totaled the Toyota for insurance, and did a little car swap in the family. After the car swap, I ended-up with another gently used old car, a Mitsubishi Galant. A lady at my office was looking for a car for her teenage daughter, and figured the beat-up Corolla would be perfect for her beginner driver, so we sold it to her for a few hundred dollars.

In the midst of all of my partying, I failed a couple of my marketing classes at Davenport University. The online environment made it too easy for me to not do my work, so I wanted to transfer my credits to a local university. I was nervous my failed classes would be reason-enough for a university to reject me, but National American University (NAU) had open enrollment, so they didn't hold that against me. I was really grateful for that, and as part of the transfer, I switched my major to business management. The other important difference was that I had physical classes to go to. Seeing my teachers in-class made it easier for me to hold myself accountable, and do my homework as they assigned it.

Spring 2006, Melanie came over to Coldwell Banker from Century 21, and we started a real estate team focused on helping people our age buy real estate. Our first couple years in real estate, almost anyone who wanted a house could get financing to buy a house because of deregulation. Getting a mortgage was relatively easy, so selling homes was relatively easy, even to people our age that had no money. I was comfortable at Coldwell Banker; they treated me well, and I had a good group of friends that I regularly partied-with. After a couple months, Melanie had another idea. She thought we would be better-off moving to The Real Estate Group, which had a much better commission split.

We met with the owner/broker, Keith, and the meeting went well. I convinced myself moving us and our licenses to The Real Estate Group would be good for business. I especially liked that he had a corner office available in the lower level with a nice view of the city. To help us get started on the right foot, Pam bought some beautiful office furniture for us.

Around the same time, Pam bought a remodeled Victorian house downtown on Quincy Street. In addition to moving to a new real estate company, I moved from Mat's house into Pam's house. She didn't live there, she just liked the house, and needed someone to take care of it for her. Pam did this a few times, and ended-up with a bunch of rental properties.

After the moves, Melanie and I began a marketing campaign to let people know where we were at, and what we were trying to do. As a former marketing student, I designed our business cards and advertisements for the local real estate magazines. Melanie and I were broke, but Pam wanted to see us succeed, so she paid all of our marketing expenses.

I had a lot of fun designing our marketing materials, and Pam was really supportive of us. One of the things Pam wanted for us was notepads with our names and phone numbers on it that we could give away to everyone to help keep front of mind awareness. Unfortunately, after a few months of marketing, we weren't meeting very many new people to give our notepads to. I did get a couple deals done with some past clients, but we didn't gain any new business.

What I was afraid of happening actually happened; business dried-up for me, and Melanie wasn't selling anything either. As time passed, our sales did not improve, and I was broke. My stipends from school helped me keep my nose above water, and my coursework made me feel like I was doing something productive, but I was miserable. I started to think I'd be much better-off economically if I was working some hourly wage job. To cope with the stress, I drank.

I drank every night of the week, and always knew which bar had the best party on any given night. I was like Google for the local party scene; people would ask me where to go, and I could tell them the place, time, and what was going on that night. I had to do something; I wasn't selling real estate, so why not enjoy myself with a night on the town every night of the week? When I sobered-up in the morning, my anguish resumed, and I started to strategize my next move.

Robbie and I talked on the phone a few times after Mat and I came back from Philadelphia. Robbie usually pitched the idea of me getting my real estate license in Pennsylvania, and selling real estate out there. I needed a change of scenery, and I had to do something different to start selling real estate again, so I planned a trip to see him. I visited Robbie that summer, and I met with real estate broker Joel at Fairmount Park Real Estate in Germantown while I was there.

Considering my experience at The Real Estate Group, I didn't want to work at another startup, but I really liked the marketing strategies at Fairmount Park Real Estate. They had a great online presence to attract prospects, along with a strong local network that drove business to their firm, and that was exactly what I needed. Although I was optimistic about Fairmount Park Real Estate, I wanted a backup plan, so I met with Gabe's friend Tracy who also sold real estate.

She was working for a national franchise, Avalar, and was selling real estate in the suburbs. We got along well, and I liked the idea of working out there, but I really didn't want to miss-out on my opportunity at Fairmount Park Real Estate. I told Joel I wanted to work with him at his firm, and he told me to call him when I was ready to come to work.

When I got back to South Dakota, I started my Pennsylvania salesperson license application. I worked on my application at the office, because I didn't have anything else better to do. South Dakota had reciprocity with Pennsylvania; so that made the application process a lot easier, and I was able to submit my application to the state pretty quick. While I waited for Pennsylvania to approve my application, I continued to work on our marketing materials in the office.

I wasn't going downtown as much, mostly because I was running out of money, and my credit cards were close to being maxed-out again. I didn't stop drinking, I just bought a bottle of vodka, and kept it, along with a shot glass, hidden on the bottom shelf of Pam's nice wooden hutch in our office. I kept my office door closed, and did shots throughout the day as I designed our marketing materials.

Mat's father, Dennis, worked for Best Buy in loss prevention, and they paid a decent starting wage. I was desperate for money, so I asked Dennis if he could help me get a job there, and he did! Actually earning money again felt great, and it didn't take me long to get comfortable. Best Buy had a really good employee discount; after a few paychecks, I was able to buy all of the electronics I always wanted, but could never afford. I bought a great printer/scanner, computer speakers, an MP3 player, terabyte external hard drive, a Swissgear business case for my laptop and files, and good usb cables.

Working at Best Buy helped me occupy my time, and because of that, I drank less. But, I started binge eating instead. On the way to work, I ate a couple grilled bean burritos, and two large orders of Potato Olés at Taco John's. Then, while I was at work, I drank energy drinks, ate large snack bags of Combos, Cheez-it crackers, and sometimes ate large bags of chewy candy. I was getting unhealthily heavy for my size. In high school I weighed 145, but months of binge eating and drinking pushed me up to 195. I knew I needed to start exercising, and stop eating soo much, but I was still too distraught to do that, until I received a little hope in the mail.

After a few months of treating myself bad, I finally received my real estate salesperson's license from the state of Pennsylvania, and it was time for me to go. I told Keith at The Real Estate Group I was leaving, and not to tell Melanie because I wasn't ready to do that yet. He didn't tell her directly, but when Keith asked Melanie if she planned to keep the office when I left, Melanie kinda figured it out.

Of course, the first call Melanie made was to Pam. Pam called me-up furious, naturally felt betrayed, and there was absolutely nothing I could say to either one of them to make amends. I felt awful; I wasn't trying to be malicious, I was just trying to do what I thought would be best for all of us. Pam was spending a lot of money on our failing real estate team; I felt really guilty about it, and it didn't seem like it was ever going to be worth it. Still, Pam just thought we needed more time, and that our strategy would catch on. I didn't see it that way. In my mind, our business failed, and it was time to move on.

We didn't have the success we wanted in our real estate team, but I was still doing good in school. I completed my Bachelor of Science in Applied Management at NAU, and because I couldn't afford to start paying-back my student loans, I enrolled in their Master of Business Administration (MBA) program right away. As I was completing my financial aid paperwork, the registrar lady's eyes bulged out of her head when she asked me: "You know you're going to owe $100,000 when you complete this program, right?"

I naively nodded my head in agreement, and eagerly signed the paperwork before they changed their mind about loaning the money to me. It could have been a million dollars I was borrowing, I had no concept of the money, and I couldn't pay it back anyway. I just needed to buy myself more time until I could make it in real estate. So my educational journey continued, and I was doing it all online, again.

Even though I wasn't leaving South Dakota on the best terms with Pam and Melanie, Pam still let me leave a lot of my stuff at her house on Quincy. I packed what I needed into my car, and started driving to Philadelphia. On my drive out to Philadelphia, I called Joel at Fairmount Park Real Estate to tell him I was on my way, and he assured me he was ready for me.

8
Philadelphia

Song Suggestions:
The Clientele—My Own Face Inside The Trees
Armin van Buuren—A State Of Trance Year Mix 2007

Robbie was living with his parents in Langhorne, so when I drove out to Pennsylvania, I went straight to their house. When I got there, it wasn't that late, but it was dark because it was early November 2006. I parked across the street from their house; Robbie came out to greet me, and helped me bring my things into their house. Robbie's parents had a spare bedroom in their two-story colonial, and were kind enough to let me live there for $300 a month.

The next day, I drove to Germantown, to start work at Fairmount Park Real Estate. I parked on the street, and put a couple dollars of quarters in the parking meter. When I went upstairs to meet with Joel, he was surprised to see me, and wasn't sure what to do with me. He wanted one of his agents to train me, but I didn't need a trainer, I just needed to familiarize myself with their brokerage agreements. He wanted to set me up with a computer, but I already had a computer. Really, all I needed was their lead list, and I wanted to start working their leads.

After a couple hours of that rigmarole, I needed to put more quarters in the parking meter, and that's when they told me they had a private parking lot behind the building. I was happy to hear that, but was very off-put about my experience at Fairmount Park Real Estate already. Once we got through the cumbersome process of getting me setup at the office, I needed to get acclimated to the market.

One of the agents gave me a zip code map, and I started driving around and learning the city from South Philly, through West Philly, up to Norristown, and down through North Philly. Knowing the neighborhoods made things a lot easier for me. With all the leads my broker had, and my strong desire to succeed, it only took me a month and a half to get my first settlement.

Joel did a lot of business, and he always drove his cream colored Rolls Royce to the office. He got his start rehabbing commercial buildings in the city, and his real estate office was another extension of his investments. Joel even referred business to me. I usually couldn't help his referrals, but his leads helped me meet new prospects that I was able to close deals with.

What I loved about working in Philadelphia was the public transportation. There was a SEPTA Regional Rail train station about 10 minutes from Robbie's parent's house, so I could drive to the train station, park my car, and ride the train to get to the city. Once I was in the city, I usually transferred to the Broad Street Subway, and then rode the bus the rest of the way to Fairmount Park Real Estate. There was a train station right behind Joel's parking lot, so any appointments I had in the city I could ride the train to center city, and then transfer to a bus or tram as needed. Some days I drove straight to the office, but driving on Route 1 was a death defying drag race between the traffic lights that I preferred to avoid.

Although I was navigating the city very well, and getting deals done, the average sales price of my closings was $70,000. I was working 12 hours a-day, six days-a-week, and that didn't even include my hour-long commute to and from the office. With a 2.5% commission that I split 50/50 with my broker, I was doing a lot of work, but I wasn't earning a lot of money. I was getting frustrated that I was working soo much, and earning soo little. Joel told me to hang-in there, and that the deals would start getting bigger. I knew Joel wasn't lying to me, but I wanted to earn bigger paychecks now, so I began looking for other options.

I started using my weekends to explore the coffee shops in the city. I took-up one of the rare spots in the little cafés next to an electrical outlet, and usually drank herbal tea while I did my online schoolwork. When I was caught-up with my schoolwork, I looked for some salary paying position where I could use my degree.

I wanted to work for one of the banks. With all of my management experience, and desire to travel up to 100% of the time, I thought my qualities made me a competitive candidate. To keep all of my options open, I had my resume posted on a few different job boards. I didn't have anything else going on, so I worked in the coffee shops as late as I could.

I didn't want to get to the bus stop early and waste time waiting around, so I always left at the last minute, and because of that, I missed the bus to the train station one evening. Missing the bus also made me miss the last regional rail train out of the city. I was frustrated about that, but I thought I might figure something out.

Listlessly I walked around the city, looking at the tall hotel buildings all around me, and dreamt to be able to afford to spend the night in one of those hotels. Also, I thought it would've been fun to explore the city all night, but around 11 p.m., it started to rain. I needed shelter, so I walked down the stairs to the underground Suburban train station.

There was a bar near the entrance of the station; I thought drinking at the bar would be a good way for me to pass the time until the bar closed at two in-the-morning, but I couldn't afford that either. Instead, I just walked around the platform. There were a dozen homeless guys spending the night at Suburban Station with me. A few of the homeless guys were milling around, making sounds to themselves as they staggered on the platform. Other homeless guys slept on the benches as a couple police officers patrolled the station.

All of my work was online, and there was no WiFi, so I couldn't surf the internet or work on anything to help me pass the time. I would've loved to have slept on one of the benches, but I didn't trust that the homeless guys or the police wouldn't mess with me. I thought it would be better to stop walking around because I didn't want to draw attention to myself. Instead, all I did was stand in one little area so I could see where everyone was, and what they were doing. The nonsensical sounds of the homeless guys bothered me the most; I was expecting several interactions between them and the police, but the police mostly left the homeless guys alone. Other than daydreaming, I occupied myself by checking the train schedule, the time, and looking for the earliest train I could get onto.

I explored all of my options trying to figure-out the best way for me to get out of the train station and onto a train as quick as I could. The first train I could catch was a little after 5 a.m., and went to the airport. I figured I would get on that train, ride it to the airport, and then ride it back to and through the train station out to the Langhorne station. I definitely didn't want to make this mistake again.

I eagerly watched the clock as it got close to 5 a.m., and then I finally ventured out from my little area so that I could look down the tracks for the light of the train. Shortly after 5, the first train of the day approached, and I desperately hoped it would stop so I could get onto the train. I was soo relieved when I saw the train slow to a stop at my station, and the doors opened. I looked around, and I was the only passenger boarding the train. I liked that I had the entire car to myself, and that I could sit wherever I wanted.

I chose to sit close to the front, next to the window, and I put my knees on the seat in front of me trying to sleep a little on my hour-long train-ride home. When the train got to the airport it stopped, waited a few minutes for passengers to embark and disembark, and then the train started traveling in the opposite direction. The ticketing agent on the train glared at me with resentment as he passed by me, still huddled at the window. We rode to and through Suburban Station, and finally we were on our way out of the city toward the suburbs. It was still raining from the night before. The steady rain on the train window, and the grey morning light filtered through the thick clouds, were the perfect encore to my dreary evening. When we arrived at my stop, I bounded off the train, and jogged back to my car trying not to get wet. My car started, and I drove home.

I was happy that nobody was awake when I got back to Robbie's parent's house; I didn't want to explain to them where I had been, or what I was doing. I probably could have called Robbie or Gabe to pick-me-up from the train station downtown, but I felt like I was already being a burden enough, and I really didn't want to bother them with my problems. The gloomy weather made it easy to sleep, so I slid myself underneath the heavy blanket of the bed, and quickly fell asleep in their warm comfortable home.

I continued lumbering along with my normal routine, until a recruiter from Enterprise Rent-A-Car saw my resume posted on one of the job boards, and called me. We chatted for a few minutes, discussing the job, and it sounded like a lot of fun. Half of me was ready to start earning a salary, and half of me wasn't ready to give-up on real estate. Since she already had me on the phone, I reluctantly agreed to go through their pre-employment screening process. Everything was going good until we got to the DUI question. My most recent DUI was within their disqualification window by five months, so my pre-employment screener had to end my interview. She did encourage me to apply when the time period passed, but I wasn't sure where I was going to be at that point, and I was a little relieved by my disqualification anyway. I liked the idea of long days running in and out of the leasing office, working with the customers, and earning a steady income. But I also thought I could still make it in real estate.

Shortly thereafter, Gabe's friend Tracy called me to see how things were going for me at Fairmount Park Real Estate. I told her I was exploring my options, and she told me to meet with her broker Bill in Huntingdon Valley to talk about selling with Avalar. The average sales price at the time in that area was $400,000. I did some quick math, and figured for all of the work I was doing in the city, if I only sold one house per quarter, I would come out way-ahead. The Huntingdon Valley suburban market was similar to the market I was used to in South Dakota, so I thought it would be a natural transition for me. I called Bill, he said come on over, and I made up my mind to make the move. Then, my phone rang again.

My buddy Robbie was working as a branch manager at Citizens Bank, and he wanted to help me out too. He made a call to human resources, and set me up with an interview to start-out as an assistant branch manager. It was a slam-dunk, the job was mine if I wanted it, but I told the lady from human resources I wasn't interested in the position. She was surprised by my response, but she was cool with it, and I thanked her for calling me. Sadly, I left the city, but I had high hopes of selling some houses in the suburbs.

I did a few open houses, got a few names and numbers, and did a few showings, but I was having a really hard time putting a deal together. After four months, the only thing I was able to do was help a client secure a lease for an apartment at a vineyard. I needed a home sale, but there was no hope on the horizon for that.

I went from making ends meet in the city, to being flat broke again in the suburbs. I got to the point that I didn't even leave home. I worked-on some mailers I wanted to send out, and when I wasn't doing that, I was doing my schoolwork. When I finished my schoolwork, I sat in the sun on the deck at the pool, and smoked a cigar.

I had very little money, so I didn't drink that often, and I didn't eat much. It wasn't a terrible thing, I was losing weight, and I was looking a lot better. I was starting to think that I could be doing schoolwork, smoking cigars, and sitting in the sun back in Rapid City. So, I called Mat to see what was going on in South Dakota.

Mat had finally honorably separated from the military, and was working at a residential treatment facility called Sky Ranch for Boys. Sky Ranch was in the Northwest corner of South Dakota, and was only a stones-throw away from Montana. It was really remote. The closest town to Sky Ranch, Camp Crook, was seven miles away, and had a population of less than 50. Teenage boys were usually placed at Sky Ranch by court order; either because they screwed-up, or their parents weren't responsible enough to prioritize care for their children over their drug or alcohol abuse. The goals at Sky Ranch were to teach responsibility, self discipline, and basic social skills. I didn't have anything going for me in Pennsylvania anymore, and Mat said he could probably get me a job where he was working, so I loaded-up my car again, and headed back to South Dakota.

9

South Dakota

Song Suggestions:
friskyPodcast138—Miss Disk
When Saints Go Machine—Parix

Social Distortion was playing a show in Sioux Falls, and Mat thought it would be cool if we could meet-up there and catch the show. I agreed, so that is what we did. When we checked-into the hotel, they gave us each two free drink tickets to the hotel bar. We didn't use the tickets, because we had a bunch of drinks in the hotel room, but it was nice to have that option. When we were warmed-up pretty good, we headed into the show.

I'm a center of the action guy, so I went straight to the middle of the crowd, close to the front of the stage. As the band played, the crowed was really amped-up, and guys were shoving each other around a little bit in front of me. It was rough, but it wasn't that bad, until Mike Ness started singing Bad Luck.

Like something out of a movie, I got to experience a little bad luck myself. The guy in front of me was leaning forward; but all-of-a-sudden he was falling backward, and before I could do anything else, my cheekbone broke the fall of his clipper-cut blonde head. That hit gave me an uncomfortable amount of pain, and I decided I had seen enough of the show.

When I left the concert, I went to the hotel bar. At the hotel bar, the bartender gave me some ice to put on my cheekbone, and I got to use our free drink tickets for some martinis. When I finished my martinis, I went back to my hotel room, and went to bed early.

I didn't have any money when I made it back to Rapid City, and my GI Bill money ran-out a couple years earlier. I was pretty tense for about a week; but we were nearing the start of another term, and just in time, NAU sent me another stipend check. That made things a lot easier for me.

Then, Mat set-me-up with an interview for a youth care worker position at Sky Ranch. I met with the charge counselor, Mike, and he pretty much hired me on the spot. I was nervous my criminal convictions might disqualify me again, but Mike wasn't concerned about my little misdemeanors. I started working there the first week of September 2007.

I never thought I would be a good parent. I always imagined myself having a child, and my child basically running the house because I didn't have the skills to discipline my child, or teach self-discipline to my child. But being a disciplinarian was a skill I needed to learn quick at Sky Ranch.

I was a group leader of eight youths. When I didn't have confidence to hold them accountable they would start acting out; just for the fun of it, because they knew I wasn't going to do anything about it. Within a few months, I learned the program, and I was pretty good at my new job. By being consistent with each youth, and enforcing the already established rules, I earned the respect of the youths.

We were actually able to have fun during the process too. As long as our staff-to-resident ratios were right, we could go lift weights in the weight room, play basketball in the gym, play Monopoly or ping pong in the game room, go to the sauna, hike, or run around the ranch. But with all of that good, there was still some bad.

One day we thought it would be a good idea to take the golf clubs out, and hit some golf balls. I took a small group of boys out; two boys were hitting golf balls, one boy was playing in the dirt, and one boy was talking to me. I'm watching everyone, making sure they're being safe, and then one of the boys decided he was tired of hitting the golf balls.

He walked over to me with this contorted look on his face. I was talking at him, trying to find out what was going on, and then he raised the golf club like he was holding a baseball bat. Next thing I knew, he was beating me with the golf club. I was blocking the blows with my forearm, and then the golf club snapped in half. I got on the radio, called for help, and Mike came out to restrain the youth. We ended up calling the police, the youth went to jail, and he was not allowed to come back to our facility. Stuff like that didn't happen too often; most often the boys were just defiant, and not aggressive.

The schedule at the ranch was really good. It was four days on-shift, and three days off-shift. The four days on-shift we lived in the staff house on the ranch. The staff house was a six-bed, six-bath building with a kitchen, dining area, and living room. On our three-days-off we went back to Rapid City. It was a two-and-a-half hour drive to Rapid City if you stuck to the paved roads. But, there was a 48 mile gravel road they called the "cut-across." Taking the cut across shaved a half-hour off the trip.

One night, I was driving home on the paved road. I knew there weren't any police looking for speeders in the middle of the night, so I sped on the highways as much as I felt comfortable with. I got my car up to 131 miles per hour (mph) on the stretch of road from Camp Crook to Buffalo, and I could see the reflection of my headlights in the eyes of the deer that were standing on the sides of the road. All the deer made me a little nervous, so I mostly kept my speed around 85 mph. I drove another 50 minutes, and I was right outside of Belle Fourche.

I could see the Belle Fourche city lights in the distance, and I was starting to feel home-free. Then, I could see at the end of the beam of light from my headlights there was a deer standing in the middle of the road. I got some really bad advice from one of my teachers in high school that stuck in my brain. It was in one of my business classes. He said because of liability, most drivers would be better-off hitting an animal, than swerving and hitting something else. So, that is what I did; I didn't slam on the brakes, or try to swerve. I don't even think I let-up off of the gas. I just hit the deer straight-on at 85 mph. I wasn't even wearing a seatbelt. I thought the air-bag was supposed to come out, but it didn't. After I hit the deer, it ran about three steps before collapsing on the side of the road. I was surprised nothing happened to me.

That deer totally could have been the end of me, but, hitting the deer just slowed me down. Literally, it slowed me down. My car couldn't even get-up to 45 mph after that. I drove my car to the St. Onge bar, parked it there, and had a couple beers. After my friendly bartender finished her shift and closed the bar, she gave me a ride home. So, that was the end of the Mitsubishi Galant.

After that, I carpooled to work with one of my coworkers, Rocky Boyd. Rocky was on the same shift as me, and he lived the next block over, so I should have been carpooling with him the whole time. Carpooling with Rocky was great! He listened to good music, I got to relax as a passenger, and I really enjoyed not having the responsibility of a car. But, my car-free life was short-lived. Rocky had carpel tunnel syndrome, and was going to miss work for a while because he was going-in for surgery. I didn't have anyone else to carpool with, so I had to buy a car.

I was in-luck. One of our coworkers, Ross, wanted to get rid of his car so he could buy a newer car from Dan. Dan was in the Air Force, was dating Melanie, and had a Kia. Ross only wanted a few hundred dollars for his Daewoo Nubria, so I bought it off of him. I was still a little uncomfortably tight on cash, so I didn't buy insurance for the car. I could have afforded the automobile insurance, I just didn't want to spend all of my money and be broke again.

So, I drove the Daewoo Nubria back-and-forth to work on the cut-across without insurance. Since my commute was in the middle of nowhere, and there weren't any cops around, I drove that Daewoo Nubria like a rally car on the cut-across. I liked the way the car felt as it raised-up when I drove across the cattle guards, it almost felt like I was getting airborne. Before I got to rally-race my car on my way home, we always had an end-of-shift turnover meeting.

We were about to have one of our turnover meetings, and Rocky, back with us after his surgery, knew I drove faster than I should have on the cut-across. He made a comment before the meeting in a joking-but-warning way, that we haven't had a rollover on the cut-across in a long time. I laughed-it-off, because I really didn't expect that to happen to me. After the meeting, I loaded my car, and thought about slamming a couple beers in the staff house kitchen before my rally-ride home. I decided I would save the beer drinking for home, got in my car, and started driving.

It was a beautiful spring day, bright sun, clear blue sky, and the road was dry and smooth. I was doing my normal 85 mph on the road, still trying to get airborne off the cattle guards. I made it through most of the cut-across, but then I hit a stretch of the road that had thick gravel. My car started drifting from one edge of the road to the other edge of the road, and I wasn't sure what I was supposed to do. I was running out of road, and knew I couldn't just keep drifting.

I thought about what I saw in the movies. They would always slam on the brake, and turn the wheel sharply. So, that is what I did. I imagined myself swinging the rear of the car 180°, and coming to a perfect stop in the middle of the road. I guess that only happens in the movies, because when I slammed on the brake and jerked the steering wheel, my car started rolling.

In the middle of the first roll, I was upside down in my car, and thought to myself: "this isn't right." The car finished that roll, and kept rolling, until it finally stopped upside-down in the ditch on the side of the road. Again, I wasn't wearing my seatbelt, and must have blacked-out after that first roll. When I opened my eyes, I was lying on my back on the roof inside my car.

Glass was everywhere, and the car was off. But somehow, through all of that, the Pioneer MP3 CD deck in my car was still playing some independent rock I was listening to before I rolled the car. I reached up to the ignition to switch it off, and then I thought my car might catch on-fire and explode, just like in the movies!

I flipped myself onto my stomach as quick as I could without cutting myself, and began crawling out of my car where my back window used to be. When I placed my hand in the grass to push myself up, I felt a sharp pain in the palm of my hand. I thought at first it was an injury from the wreck. Then I thought maybe it was some glass. But when I lifted my hand, I was relieved to see that I pressed my palm on a small cactus as I was trying to stand-up. I looked for a safer area to place my hand, and used my nuckles to push myself up. When I finally stood-up, I assessed the situation.

I didn't see any gas leaking out of my car, the car wasn't on-fire, and it wasn't about to explode. I moved my arms, hands, legs, feet, fingers and toes, and everything was working right. After that, I stood there for a minute, and pulled the cactus quills from my hand. As I was doing that, the only thing I could feel that was wrong was that my neck was a little stiff. I didn't have any pain in my neck, it was just a little stiff, so I knew I wasn't hurt that bad. Again, I was close to Belle Fourche, but hadn't made it to Belle Fourche before the accident.

I walked-up to the gravel road, and looked down the road in both directions. The whole area was quiet except for a light breeze and calls from some carnivorous birds as they flew by. I stood there in the road, and checked my cell phone for service. Of course there wasn't any service. I wondered what I was going to do. I remembered Rocky was also going off-shift, and he usually took the cut-across, so I hoped I would see him.

I really couldn't go anywhere or do anything, so I just stood there, looking down the deserted road, just like I was waiting for a bus. Ten minutes later, I saw Rocky casually driving toward me. As he drove toward me, I waved, and he stopped. He made some I-told-you-so comment, and I got into his little Sport Utility Vehicle (SUV).

Rocky knew the guy that owned the tow truck company in Belle Fourche, so he drove me to his garage. As we continued driving down the gravel road to Belle Fourche, I felt pain in my neck with every bump in the road that Rocky hit. It wasn't a lot of pain, but it was uncomfortable. I flipped-down Rocky's sun visor that had a mirror behind it so I could see if I injured my face. All I had was a cut above my eye from some of the glass that broke in my car. When we made it to the tow truck garage, I walked slowly with my back straight, and tried not to move my neck.

The good thing was, Rocky's tow truck friend was available to tow my car. The bad thing was, the tow truck owner was a law abiding citizen, and told me he had to report my accident because there was more than $1,000 of damage. Really, the car was totaled at that point. He called the Belle Fourche police, and Rocky got caught-up with the tow-truck man while we waited for the police officer to show-up. I pensively paced in the garage, wondering how the police officer was going to handle the situation.

When the policeman showed-up, I uncomfortably got back into Rocky's SUV, and we started driving back to my car. The police officer followed us, and the tow truck driver followed him. It only took us 20 minutes, and we were back out at the wreck. While we were driving up to it, I looked at my car upside down on the side of the road, and thought it was kinda amazing that I survived the rollover with next-to-no injuries.

The police officer asked me questions about the accident, like where I was going, and what I was doing. I was really glad that I didn't drink any beers before the drive, because that may have complicated things for me. And fortunately, Rocky was there to vouch for me, because the officer didn't want to believe the answers I was giving him. The policeman still hadn't asked about my insurance, and I thought I was in the clear.

I was thinking he was going to be cool with me, and just write a report with a summary of what happened. And then he asked me for my proof of insurance. I humbly told him I didn't have any insurance. The officer said he would have to write me a ticket for that. I was shocked! I just cheated death, and he wanted to write me a ticket for driving without insurance? Becoming my own defense attorney, I told him I wasn't wearing a seatbelt either, and said if he needed to write a ticket, maybe he could write a ticket for that. He said it was a pretty serious offence, and because of the laws, he had to write the insurance ticket. So, he wrote the insurance ticket, and I had to appear in court in Belle Fourche the following month. I was really disappointed about that.

After we finished all of that rigmarole, Rocky wanted to stop-in at the museum in Belle Fourche. We went to the museum, and Rocky saw another one of his old friends. While he was talking to her, I stood around, and looked into the display cases filled with historical South Dakota pictures and artifacts. I was a little annoyed that Rocky wanted to do a sight-seeing tour, and talk to old friends when I wasn't in the best shape. But, we didn't stay there long, and continued our drive home. Then, Rocky wanted to stop at some road-side monuments, but I told him it would be better if we did that some other day.

We finally made it back to Rapid, my neck was still tight, and I was wondering what I was going to do for transportation. A couple years earlier, Mike bought a pink scooter for Melanie. Melanie drove the scooter once or twice, and the rest of the time it was collecting dust in the garage. I knew she wasn't using it, so I called Mike, told him I destroyed my car, and asked him if I could borrow the scooter for a little while. He was cool with it, so I had Rocky drop me off at Mike's house to pick-up the scooter. The scooter was an electric-start, and kick-start. I couldn't start it with the electric ignition, so I furiously kicked the kick-start to try to get it going. Nothing was working, so I just left it there for Mike to play with.

Melanie called me while I was standing in the garage, and was frantically talking at me, trying to convince me that I needed to go to the hospital to get checked-out. I prefer to stay away from hospitals, but Melanie told me I might have internal bleeding. I didn't know, how would I know? I had medical insurance through Sky Ranch, so I thought it would be a good idea to use my insurance and get looked-at by a doctor, just to be on the safe side.

Somehow, nobody was available to give me a ride to the hospital, so Dennis told me I could take the SAAB 9-3 convertible. Still a beautiful day, I got into the SAAB, and drove it to the hospital. I got checked-out at the hospital, and the doctor told me I had whiplash. He wrote a prescription for me, and I was on my way.

When I went outside, my bright beautiful day had faded into evening, and it was snowing. The snow falling from the sky looked beautiful in the hospital parking lot lights, but the warm pavement was melting the snow into slippery slush. I had no intention to use any of the pills the doctor prescribed to me, but for some reason, I felt compelled to go to the pharmacy to get my prescription filled. So, I started driving to the pharmacy.

Having grown-up in Michigan, I was used to snow, so the drive to the pharmacy didn't seem like a big deal. The roads were a little slick, but I was managing it well, until it was time for me to turn into the pharmacy. I was coming down a small hill, a little too fast, and I was trying to make the turn into the pharmacy driveway. But, the SAAB wasn't turning at all, and just kept sliding diagonally. That made me a little nervous, and I started to think I must not be as good of a driver as I thought I was.

I saw a curb in front of me, and a yellow concrete pole that was holding a stop sign firmly in-place. I wasn't too concerned about the curb, and hoped that it would slow me down so I would stop short of the yellow pole. The car hopped the curb, and kept going until it hit the concrete pole. Now I had to get the car off the curb, back into the driveway, and drive into the parking lot. Even in the snow, somehow I was able to do all of that. When I parked the car, I got out, and looked to see how the car was.

Everything was fine, except the headlight had popped-out of the car. I opened the hood of the car, and looked around in the engine area to see if anything was broken. I didn't see anything broken, so I just pushed the headlight back in, and it snapped right back into place! I couldn't believe it! I was amazed at how well the car was engineered! That saved me a lot of trouble. Elated, I went into the pharmacy, and waited for my prescription.

As I stood there, I was thinking I shouldn't have even gone to the pharmacy. They gave me my pills, and I drove the car back to Quincy, slipping and sliding up the hill this time. The next day, I looked at the SAAB sitting in the parking lot.

I noticed a little yellow line on the bumper underneath the headlight where I hit the pole. I thought about covering it up, but I didn't think anyone would notice. A couple weeks later, Mat was driving the SAAB home from the ranch. Mat likes to drive fast too, and at his high speeds, the wind ripped the headlight out of the car.

A couple weeks later, the broken headlight came-up in conversation. In addition to renting-out her houses, Pam and her family did their own maintenance on the properties. For something for me to do, Mat occasionally asked me if I wanted to help with the maintenance. Some renters moved out, so we were painting one of the rentals.

Mat was standing in the living room near me, and asked himself out-loud in a wondering way, how a little yellow paint mark ended-up on his bumper. I slipped into stupid mode, shrugged my shoulders, and made the "I don't know sound" with my throat. Mat's mother was in the kitchen, and she speculated with Mat about how it happened. Had Mat asked me directly: "Rich, what happened to my car?" I would have been honest, told him what happened, and worked-out a payment plan with him. But since he didn't ask me anything directly, I didn't feel obligated to volunteer any information to him, and I thought there was still a chance there was no correlation between me hitting the pole and the headlight blowing out of the car. I felt a little guilty about it all, but I was in a really bad cash position, and couldn't afford to pay anything to anyone. I probably owe Mat some money for that, but we'll have that conversation when he reads this.

It was time for court, I still didn't have a car, and Belle Fourche is about an hour drive from Rapid City. Pam was still in town, so she offered to drive me to court. She didn't come-in with me, she just stayed in the parking lot, talking on her phone. At my court appearance, the judge and attorney for the state followed the status-quo for sentencing, and made me buy an insurance certification for three years.

So, I had to pay for insurance, even-though I didn't have anything to insure. The cool thing was, Ross and I were on the same shift now. He lived in Rapid City too, so I started carpooling with him to work. When I was in town and needed a car, Mat and Ross both let me use their cars as needed. I was very fortunate I didn't need to own a car those three years I was required to have insurance. If I did own a car, I would have had to pay for the automobile insurance, plus the monthly insurance certification fee. The $75/month insurance certification fee was bad enough for me.

While I was working fulltime at Sky Ranch, I maintained my real estate license by paying my association dues, and staying current on my continuing education. Mat suggested to me that I should get my broker's license. I had enough experience as a broker associate that all I needed to do was take a class, and apply to the state for my broker's license. With Mat's help, I took a few days off-of-work, drove to Sioux Falls, and participated in the broker's class. I successfully completed the class, and my application to the state was approved.

Now I needed help starting a business. I called my old broker Keith, and he gave me the name and number of an attorney that could help me. I called the attorney, and he helped me create a limited liability corporation (LLC) with Mat.

The idea was that Mat and I would manage Pam's rentals. Dennis already had a business account setup with a bank, so Dennis went with us to the bank to help Mat and I open a business checking account. Mat was optimistic for our business, and decided to buy an old burgundy Ford Explorer from one of our co-workers at the Ranch, so we could use it to haul around maintenance equipment that we needed to manage the rentals.

Account maintenance fees for our business account at the bank were $10/month. We didn't have much money in the account, and we weren't managing any rentals, so we didn't have any revenue. After a few months of that, I couldn't afford to keep paying the monthly maintenance fee, so I called Dennis. We went to the bank, closed the business checking account, and I shut down our property management business. Mat was a little frustrated by that, and asked me why I didn't ask him for help to pay the account maintenance fees, but I told him we weren't doing anything with our business, so what was the point of keeping it open? He sighed-a-groan in agreement, and that was the end of our business venture.

I wasn't ready to give up on real estate, so I started another property management company, with me as the sole owner and operator. The main floor of Pam's Victorian home on Quincy Street was setup really nice as an office, but she wasn't using the office space. I asked her about it, and she was good with me running my property management business out of that office area.

As an academic, I called my company Pragmatic Property Management. My real estate colleagues, not academics, were confused by my company name. That didn't bother me too much, because I wasn't that interested to try to earn their business. I knew sales, but I needed to learn property management, so I talked to Keith at The Real Estate Group again. Keith gave me a lot of guidance on developing a lease agreement for tenants. With his guidance, and a little online research, I developed my own lease agreement. Because of the marketing classes and information technology classes I took, I felt knowledgeable enough to build my own website, design my business cards, and start marketing my business.

Dennis gave me my first lead. A military couple bought a house, left the area, and wanted to rent-out the house. They needed someone to attract tenants, collect rents, and take care of any of the maintenance issues that came up. I secured a brokerage agreement with the owners, and had my new tenants sign my lease agreement. Things were going well with me, the owners, and the tenants, so Dennis referred another client to me. I was getting a good start; but because of my student loan debt, I wasn't even close to being able to leave my job at Sky Ranch.

When I finished my MBA, I was $100,000 in debt, and I needed to figure-out something else. I was far away from being in a position to make the minimum payments; but as long as I was going to school I was in deferment, and I didn't have to make any payments on my student loans. I enjoyed school, and being in-school gave me something to do, so I went online to look for a doctoral program.

I would have moved to anywhere in the United States to be in a doctoral program; but I found a university with an online program, Walden University (Walden). I always wanted to study entrepreneurship, but never had the opportunity to major in that. I was really excited when I saw Walden had a Doctor of Business Administration (DBA) Entrepreneurship program. I also liked the values they promoted online, like positive social change. All of that seemed to be an ideal fit for me, so I applied to the University.

As they were reviewing my application, someone from admissions called me, and interviewed me to qualify how strong my intent was to stay in the program. I passed the interview, and the next month, I was in my first doctoral class. Being in the program was a relief for me; but I knew it was only a quick fix, so I started looking for a decent paying job again.

I did the math; to make my minimum payments and live meagerly, I needed to earn close to $65,000 USD/year. I was searching a South Dakota online job-board, and found a job advertising the starting salary I was looking for. It was for a life and health supplemental insurance company. I applied to them, interviewed with them, and they agreed to hire me provided that I obtain my insurance license. I bought an exam study guide, studied for my life and health insurance exam, took and passed my test! I applied to the state, and the state awarded me my life and health (L&H) insurance licenses.

What excited me about the L&H company was that they told me they had a lot of leads, and they said they didn't have enough people to work the leads. My problem in real estate was a lack of leads. I was great working with people who wanted to buy; I was a customer service award winner at Coldwell Banker, I just needed a little help getting introduced to those people.

So I was optimistic about working for the L&H company; but before I could work any of those leads, they had a script they needed me to learn. They gave me a 10-page script of the entire sales presentation they wanted me to learn; I wanted the business, so I learned the script. As I was learning the script, a sales group from the L&H company was going to North Dakota for a week. I was trying keep my job at Sky Ranch while I was learning how to sell insurance, but this was a fantastic opportunity for me to see a lot of sales presentations in only a week, so I called Mat.

Mat had been promoted to a charge counselor role at the ranch. I told him what was going on, and he understood exactly what I needed to do. Like any good friend, he covered for me, and let everyone know I was leaving the ranch.

To sell insurance products in North Dakota, you have to be licensed to sell insurance in that state. North Dakota has life and health insurance reciprocity with South Dakota, so I applied for my North Dakota licenses, and received my licenses right on time. I went to North Dakota with the L&H sales team, we stayed at a cheap motel, and I got to sit-in on a few sales presentations for a week which helped me learn the script. Any downtime I had in-between appointments I was always studying my script; and the guy I rode-up with worked on the script with me on the way up-there, and all the way back.

I wasn't comfortable enough with the script to do any of my own presentations until we got back to South Dakota. After working their leads for a month or so, I was finally able to do a few sales presentations, but I wasn't able to sell any insurance. They weren't the warm leads I thought they were going to give me.

I was working really hard just to get the appointment because nobody wanted to buy any insurance; and, I'm not a salesperson. A salesperson can get someone to buy even when they don't want to buy, I'm not that guy. I found myself in the same position I was in when I was trying to sell real estate. So after only two months; I told the L&H company I wasn't going to try to sell insurance anymore, and I was going to continue to work toward my doctorate.

The insurance experience really messed with my head. I felt like I was doing everything to find something that was going to help me pay-off my student loans, and nothing was working for me. There was nothing left for me to do except focus on school. They were giving me a $7,000 stipend while I was in school, so I really didn't even have to work. I decided to make the most of it; so I called my mother, and asked her if she wanted to go to Macedonia.

My mother and I hadn't been to Macedonia to see our family there in 20 years. My mother had recently retired, and I wasn't doing anything, so it was a good time for us to go. Prior to leaving on our Macedonia trip, I had to do a residency for my doctoral program in Washington D.C. So I did that for a few days in March, and then I flew to my parent's house in Michigan. My mother and I weren't going to Macedonia until April, so to bide my time, I hung out in a coffee shop from open to close doing my doctoral study coursework.

At the coffee shop, I met one of my classmates from High School, and I was about to break my pool rule again. For some reason, I need to repeat my mistakes before I learn from them. Anyway, she was fit, I was fit, and we started talking. We had fun comparing each other's diet and exercise Excel spreadsheets, and while we were talking, I learned she was divorced, had a daughter, and her family was learning the hard way the importance of a living will, power of attorney, and medical power of attorney. She explained to me what those legal documents were for, and introduced the idea that I should have those documents.

She had a great career, and I wasn't doing anything. We hung-out together a little outside the coffee shop, mostly doing yard work at her place at first, then exploring fun places in Michigan. It kinda turned into a relationship; my mother too saw it becoming a relationship, but she didn't like the girl at all. My loving mother did everything she could to put an end to that relationship, mostly by arguing with me about her. I traveled over the spring and summer, but I kept in touch with my classmate while I traveled. In-between trips, we got together, and enabled each other to fall off of the diet and exercise wagon. Even though she really wasn't right for me, I was enjoying my relationship with my classmate, and didn't care that it made my mother mad. At the time, being with her was the best thing I had going for me.

When my mother and I went to Macedonia, we stayed at my uncle's house in Prilep. My grandfather built the house; and my mother and her five siblings helped make the bricks for the walls of the house as he was building it. My mother helped form the bricks, then they hired a contractor that fired the bricks. When the house was built, my mother, her parents, and her siblings, all lived in the house.

I had a good routine while we were in Macedonia. I woke-up at 5:30 a.m., did 50 pushups, 100 sit-ups, and then I went for a five mile run. While I was doing my exercises, I heard the Muslim call to prayer from the loudspeaker in the city. Macedonia is mostly Macedonian Orthodox, but one-third of the population is Muslim. After my exercises I washed my face, brushed my teeth, changed my clothes, and walked to the library.

At the library I did my doctoral research, worked on my proposal, and did my coursework. When the library closed, I went home, ate a big salad, and went to sleep. Occasionally my mother and I had dinner at one of my Aunt's houses; but because I couldn't speak Macedonian, I usually just sat in the corner of the couch working on my doctoral study proposal.

One evening, we came home late from visiting one of my aunts, it was like a little after 11 p.m. My mother and I stayed in the same room at my uncle's house; I slept on the futon, and my mother slept on the couch. My mother was trying to sleep, but she couldn't fall asleep because she had heartburn, and a lot of gas in her stomach. She had soo much discomfort from her indigestion she woke me up, and told me what was going on. I told her to drink some mineral water to help her burp.

She drank a couple gulps of mineral water from her cup, and then she went outside because she felt nauseous. I went outside with her, and just as we made it outside, she threw-up on the front stoop. After she threw-up, my mother said she was feeling a little better, so I went inside to find something to clean-up the vomit. As I was looking around in the house, I heard her cup hit the stone walkway in the front yard. I rushed outside to see what happened, and found my mother lying on her back, stiff as a board. Although I had been through several CPR classes, I had no idea what to do, so I ran back inside the house. My cousin Robert came to visit us for a day, and was sleeping on a couch in the room next to ours.

My cousin Robert doesn't speak English, but I frantically woke him up, and urgently ushered him to come outside with me. I could see he was alarmed, so I knew that he knew something bad happened. He rushed outside with me, saw my mother on the ground, and called an ambulance. He must have called our aunts too, because my English speaking cousin Branko got to our house before the ambulance.

I explained to my cousin Branko what happened, and we waited around for several minutes before the medics finally came. When the medics arrived, they put my mother on a gurney, and loaded her into the ambulance. I got into my cousin Branko's car, and we followed the ambulance to the local hospital.

It was soo weird, the ambulance driver did not have any sense of urgency. There was nobody else on the road, but he was driving much slower than I thought he should, and he stopped at the traffic lights! It took us like 10 minutes to get to the hospital, it was really frustrating for me.

When we arrived at the hospital, the doctor and nurse were already there, waiting for us. When we went into the hospital, there weren't any lights on in any of the halls, except for the security lights. And, nobody else was there. We took the elevator up to the second story, they turned the lights on in one room, and put my mother on a hospital bed. As they were getting set-up in the room, I was pacing in the hallway, and heard the elevator. I walked down to the elevator, and was soo relieved to see my Aunt Elena. She spoke English, so I told her what happened as we walked to my mother's room.

When we got to my mother's room, the doctor was talking to my family. He was trying to figure-out what could be wrong with my mother, and my Aunt Elena translated to the doctor what I told her. The doctor didn't do anything to- or for-her, but somehow my mother opened her eyes, and started weakly mumbling some words.

I was happy to see her moving her head and making sounds, but I was starting to think she had brain damage, because she didn't look or sound normal. I began wondering how I was going to care for my mother who could no longer take care of herself. As I was fearfully contemplating that scenario, my aunt told me the doctor thinks she probably has an issue with her heart. He also said he couldn't do anything for her, and he referred us to the next largest hospital, located in Skopje, a couple hours away. Before we left, we had to pay cash for the ambulance ride, and for the doctor and nurse to be there.

My Aunt Elena rode in the ambulance with my mother to Skopje, and my cousin Branko and I followed them in his car. We have cousins in Skopje, so we stayed with them while my mother was in the hospital. A much larger hospital in Skopje, there was a specialist that determined my mother needed a stent in her heart. They were able to get my mother into an operating room, and perform the operation the same day.

The day after my mother's operation, my Aunt Elena and I went to see my mother. I was very trepidatious as we walked, still thinking my mother might have brain damage because she was unconscious for soo long. We were walking in front of an apartment complex; my aunt stopped, and picked a red tulip from their yard to give to my mother. When we got to the hospital, my aunt put the flower in a clear plastic cup of water, and put it at my mother's bedside. My mother really appreciated the tulip, it made her soo happy. She smiled, and talked to my aunt. I listed closely as they spoke, trying to hear if my mother sounded normal, and then she said a few words to me too. I was soo relieved to hear my mother talking normally, acting normally, and that she didn't have brain damage. For observation, my mother stayed a few more days in the hospital.

Knowing that my mother was okay, I called my father to tell him what happened. I waited to call him because I wanted to be sure one way or the other about my mother's condition. If I would have told my father any sooner, I would have had to tell him speculations, and that would just make him worry. When I told him what happened, he didn't say much; he was in shock like me, and asked me if he should fly out. I told him no, there wasn't much he could do, and there was plenty of family around already to help. He said okay, and told me to keep him updated. I told him I would, and we hung-up the phone.

Just as in Prilep, we had to pay cash for my mother's hospital bill before they would release her, and her medical records. Amongst all of us in Skopje, we pooled our money, and were able to gather the money we needed to pay the bill. With all of our pooled money, my Aunt Elena, Aunt Vesela, and I, went to the billing office in the hospital to pay the bill.

I don't know how she thought she would get away with it, but the lady in the billing office was trying to overcharge us. It was a private room at the end of a short hallway in the hospital. In the room, we put the cash on the table for the bill, and the billing lady counted it. After she counted it, she said she needed more money. Because I don't know how to say the numbers in Macedonian, I told her to write the total of the bill, and she wrote it on a ripped piece of an envelope. I looked at the number she wrote, recounted the money, and the numbers matched. I told my Aunt Elena the money was right, but the billing lady still insisted she needed more money. My aunt was willing to pay whatever the billing lady wanted, but I was determined not to let the lady get away with it. We had a few more back-and-forths like this; the accountant finally accepted our money, and released my mother's medical records. After all of that, we went back to Prilep to spend the last few days of our trip with our family there. Our family was very happy to see we returned safe and well; and after a few days of rest, we packed our bags to head back to the United States.

The experience we had with my mother's heart attack scared us, and helped me quickly realize we were not prepared for anyone getting ill or dying in our family. I started having conversations with my parents about what we were going to do when someone gets sick or dies, and what we were going to do with all of the stuff that is left behind. I remembered the conversations that I had with my

123

classmate about a living will and powers of attorney, and knew we needed some legal help.

I called the attorney that I worked with to create my limited liability property management company, and he recommended to me that I use LegalZoom. I was surprised that he recommended I use LegalZoom, but he said it was a reputable company. With his vote of confidence, I went online to start the process to create a power of attorney, medical power of attorney, and last will and testament for each of my parents.

The power of attorney names who is authorized to make financial decisions for you when you can't make them for yourself. That's important to have so the people you want can access your accounts to pay the bills. The medical power of attorney names who is authorized to make medical decisions for you when you are unable to make decisions for yourself. And the last will and testament names who is responsible to distribute the assets that are left behind. You can also specify who you want to have certain items to help prevent some disputes.

We discussed to what extent my parents wanted life support if they were in the hospital, and if they wanted to be buried or cremated. My parents only wanted medication to prevent pain, and did not want to be artificially kept alive with life support. And, even though we have burial plots in Paterson, both of my parents wanted to be cremated. My mother wanted her ashes spread in one of the flower beds in the back yard that have Peonies in it, because the Peonies can live for 100 years. My father wanted his ashes spread over Lake Michigan. I suggested that it would be one last helicopter ride, and he said: "yeah, sure." My father previously rode in a helicopter when he fought in the Vietnam War, but it wasn't anything he liked to talk about.

Completing the documents was important because we were able to put in-writing what we already discussed. Having it all in-writing helped prevent confusion about who said what. And, we had the documents notarized, making them legally binding. My parents named me as a beneficiary on all of their accounts; so with an original copy of their death certificate, I could do whatever I needed to with their accounts. Having a dozen original copies of death certificates is important because some companies or offices require an original version, and will not accept a copy of an original. Once we took care of all of that, it was time for another trip for me.

I had a lot of room on my credit card, so I bought a ticket to California to hang out with Pam for a few days. While I was waiting for my bag at the luggage carousel at Los Angeles International Airport (LAX), Melanie called me, and asked me to change the name of my company from Pragmatic Property Management LLC to Prestige Properties. She was considering hanging her license at my firm, and helping me grow my business, but thought my business name was too confusing.

I appreciated that she was interested in working with me, but I wasn't excited about changing my business name. I discussed it with Pam, and thought about it while I swam in the Pacific Ocean, ran on the strand, and ran in the high desert. Hanging out with Pam, and going to the wineries in Temecula helped me relax a little. It was a great trip, Pam was an excellent host, but it was time for my return flight.

Back in Michigan, I pitched an idea to my father. My Great-Great Aunt, his Great-Aunt, was turning 100 years old in Connecticut. A lot of our east coast family had been going to Connecticut to celebrate her birthday with her for years. This year was the same; even my cousins and niece from Colorado and family from Florida were going to see her, so I talked my father into taking the trip with me. We flew to New Jersey, stayed at my sister Kathy's house for a couple days, and then drove up to Connecticut with my Aunt Theresa to see our Great Aunt Wally.

Our Great Aunt Wally Feld was born and raised in Germany and could still see, hear, had all of her teeth, and walked around with a walker. She looked great for being 100 years old, and she still liked to eat sweets! I was soo surprised when she ate one of the fresh chocolate dipped Macrons I brought-up from New Jersey. When my Aunt Theresa was young, she used to play her accordion at shows, and our Aunt Wally made dresses for my Aunt Theresa to wear while my aunt was performing. Our Great Aunt Wally loved nature too; she had a squirrel feeder on her back porch, and she kept it filled with in-shell peanuts. I felt very fortunate to meet her; I never got to meet my Great Grand Father Richard, but at least I got to meet his sister.

We had a couple days left before we were going back to Michigan, so when we got back to New Jersey, I took the Amtrak to

Philadelphia to hang out with my friends there for an evening. Robbie and I went to a house party and saw Gabe there. As we did at the off-base house in the military, Gabe asked me about my debt. As time passed, my economic position hadn't improved. I was still living on my credit cards, and my student loan debt continued to grow because I relied on it to float me. Since I was enrolled in the doctoral program, I wasn't really sure how much debt I was going to be-in when I completed my degree. It was a four-year program, so I speculated that I would be $225,000 in debt by the time I completed the program. After I threw that number out at Gabe, Gabe exclaimed with a shocked-gasp, and an un-envying look of horror. The numbers didn't have the effect on me that they should have; I had no way of paying-off any of that debt, yet I still somehow thought I was going to find that great paying white-collar job to easily pay-off my debts.

After the house party, Robbie and I had a few beers at the Hulmeville Inn, and then took a couple growlers back to his parents house. We alternated between drinking and swimming in his pool, and drinking and sitting in his Jacuzzi. My sister Kathy called me while I was sitting in the Jacuzzi, and told me she took our father to the hospital. She said he was coughing a lot, and his chest was tight, so she wanted to make sure he was going to be okay. I asked her if I should go back now; she said no, he's doing alright.

I went back to New Jersey the next day, and saw my father lying in a hospital bed in the hallway. The night before he was sleeping in Kathy's basement, and thought it might have been the humidity of the basement that was making it difficult for him to breathe. He recently stopped smoking after smoking for more than 30 years; which was great, but it didn't take much for him to lose his breath. He was doing fine in the hospital, they were preparing to discharge him, but I was starting to feel really bad about all of this. First I take a trip with my mother, and she ends up in the hospital. Then I take a trip with my father, and he ends up in the hospital too. We went back to Kathy's house, and he slept alright that night.

In the morning, we hired a chauffeur to take us to the Airport. Because I hate being early to just sit around and wait, I am either right on time, or late for almost everything. I underestimated how long it would take us to get through security at Newark, and we ended-up missing our flight back to Michigan. It turned out to be a good thing. While my father and I were standing in the terminal, we discussed what my plans were.

I told him I wasn't ready to give up on real estate, and thought I could grow my property management business into something. That's also where I decided to change my business name. After that conversation, we had more time to kill, so we had a couple beers at a bar in the Airport. All of my life my father was a father to me, was strict with me, and wanted me to do my best. It was really nice to just sit and relax with him for a couple hours. When we got back to Michigan, my parents were both doing good, so I prepared myself to get back to South Dakota to grow my business.

When I got back to South Dakota, I was still pursuing a relationship with my classmate that my mother said I shouldn't be dating. During one of my conversations with my classmate, I told her I noticed I was not as fit as I was before we started dating, and that we got sloppy. It deeply offended her that I didn't overlook our physical health, because of our emotional connection. And I was frustrated that she got mad, and wasn't honest with herself. Eventually our relationship ended, and I was grateful for that. I did a reality check, didn't like what I saw in myself, saw where I wanted to be, and was working to change it.

I followed-through with my business name-change plans, and registered Prestige Properties as the name my company was operating under. I marketed my business as PrestigeProper because there is a glut of Prestige Properties on the internet. I continued to base my real estate office out of Pam's home on Quincy, and I began running along the bike path first thing in the morning, 13.4 miles, three times a week. Melanie also followed-through, hung her license at my firm, and started recruiting for me. I ordered new distinguished yard signs, created a new website, and designed new business cards. I also joined the chamber of commerce, my church choir, and the board of directors at my local natural foods cooperative. I even volunteered on local political campaigns.

The first political campaign I had the privilege to participate in was Mat's run for District 32 House; but, he ran as an Independent. At first, we thought running as an Independent was a great idea, and that Mat would appeal to Democratic and Republican voters. But on election night, we saw we were wrong. I saw first-hand that an Independent candidate does pull votes from both sides, but it is soo marginal, that an Independent candidate doesn't have a realistic chance at winning. More often than not, Independent candidates only unfavorably upset close elections.

I learned a lot from Mat's campaign; people got to know me, and I had the opportunity to join another campaign, Ritchie Nordstrom's run for city council. Unlike the House seat, the city council seat was non-partisan. We were competing against the incumbent who held the seat for the majority of a decade. To gain a competitive advantage, we met with local leaders of religious, fraternal, and athletic organizations. Ritchie went door-to-door talking to voters, and routinely held his yard sign while waving at passing motorists. To keep front of mind awareness, and inform voters, we regularly sent mailers.

The election had four candidates running for the seat, and the results were too close to call, so we had a runoff election. We sent-out another mailer to remind people to vote, and in the runoff election, we beat the incumbent! Ritchie kept that seat for a few terms after that too!

My diet and exercise routine, refreshed marketing campaign, and local networking was working. In less than a year, I grew my business from managing three units, to managing 13 units. Four of those units were from a federal client, Fannie Mae.

All of that growth came at a price. In the process of growing my business, I maxed-out all of my credit cards, and spent all of my stipend money from my student loans. I was earning money, but I wasn't earning enough money from my property management business to cover my minimum monthly expenses, so I needed to get a job again.

I started working at a local residential treatment facility, Wellspring. I couldn't work with any of the youths until my background check cleared, so they had me painting doors a few hours a day. I was so happy to do whatever they needed, because they were paying me for every hour that I was there, unlike all of the work I did while I was trying to grow my business. When my background check cleared, I was able to start working with the youths. Working with the youths is a tough job mentally, and sometimes physically, and the pay wasn't great. With prior experience, I earned $9.63/hour. People with less experience were earning less, so it was easy for people to call-in when they didn't feel like working, or had absolutely anything else better to do. I was soo pitifully broke, and soo happy to actually be earning money for my time, that I worked every extra shift that came up. Some weeks I worked a little over a 100 hours.

While I was working with the youths, my father went to his dentist for a routine dental exam. My father's dentist thought my father might have oral cancer, so he referred him to a specialist. After a couple more tests and exams, they confirmed it was oral cancer, and recommended surgery.

My father went-in for a day, that turned into a week, that turned into months of intensive care. He was at University of Michigan Ann Arbor, and that was a three-hour drive from our house, so my mother only visited him once a week. While she was there, she put the phone to his ear so I could talk to him. It was me talking to him, because they cut his tongue out. There wasn't much I could do for him, so I just kept working. Finally, after five months of he's improving-he's declining-cycles, I flew to Michigan to see what was going on.

When I walked into my father's room, he was soo happy to see me! He sat up in his bed, pulled his top sheet down, and energetically mouthed the words: "let's go!" I really wanted to walk out of that room with him. I imagined us standing in his room at our house, talking like we used to. But they had soo many tubes coming-in and going-out of him, that I knew he wasn't physically capable of leaving that hospital. I solemnly shook my side-to-side as I told him: "no dad, we really can't do that, that's not going to work." He just shrugged his shoulders, pulled the sheet back on him as he lye back down in his bed, and resigningly closed his eyes.

I watched as the nurses did some maintenance on him, and I pulled my mother out of the room with me to discuss with the doctor what was going on. They were giving him blood every week because his body wasn't making blood. His pancreas was failing, and he had MRSA. I told my mother: "he's in really bad shape, this isn't what he wanted, we need to stop!" When she finally understood the severity of my father's condition, she agreed with me, and we asked the doctor to remove all of the devices that were keeping my father alive, except the pain medication. There was soo much more space in his room, and it was a lot more peaceful.

We decided to leave him for the night. Before I left, I shook my dad's hand, and he mouthed to me: "take care of your mother." Still holding his hand, I assured him I would. A couple days later my mother was boiling some noodles in the kitchen, and I was listening to: Why?—Good Friday, on my computer in my room.

A nurse called us from the hospital, said my father wasn't doing that great, and said we should probably come to the hospital. We stopped what we were doing, quickly put some decent clothes on, and drove to the hospital. As we were getting closer to the hospital, I started craving chocolate chip cookies. My mother and I worked well together making baked goods, so I told her we should bake some cookies sometime.

When we got to the hospital, my mother was nervous, and tears were rolling down the sides of her face. I tried to give her encouragement as we walked through the hospital to his room, and it seemed to help assuage her fears. We made it up to his level, and started walking toward his hall. I looked around the corner at his hall, and could see the lights were out in his room. Just as we turned the corner, we saw the nurse, and asked her about my father. She said he was deceased; and we hadn't missed him by much, maybe 15 minutes. I asked her if he went peacefully, and she reacted with a body response like it was a strange question. But then she thought about it, and said in a way that surprised herself: "yeah, he was a little restless in his bed, and then he died."

My mother and I sat in his room with him. The nurse asked us if we wanted a priest. My mother, not knowing what else to do, agreed it was a good idea. But it was Friday night, and my father wasn't religious, so it didn't make sense to me. I made some derisive comment that he was probably just finishing his scotch and the nurse started to chuckle, but abruptly stifled her chuckle. I appreciated that she understood my humor. With a little more persuasion, I convinced my mother that we did not need a priest to come and say some prayer for us. Instead, we just sat with him. I called the mortician, and let him know my father was dead. One of the nurses at the hospital told us they would keep my father until the mortician came and got him to be cremated. I stood by my father's bedside, touched his arm with the back of my fingers, and he was already starting to feel cold to the touch. He had only been dead for like 45 minutes. My mother touched him too, and was also surprised that his body was turning cold so soon. We stayed there for a few more minutes, and when we ran out of things to say, we left his room. My mother was soo sad, she was crying soo much, but I was determined to not make his death the death of me or her.

While I was at my parent's house, reflecting about my father's life and death, I was standing in my father's room. My mother and father slept in separate rooms across the hall from each other. My mother slept with an electric blanket, and my father liked the room cool. Also, my father woke up for work an hour earlier than my mother so the two-room thing worked best for them. Anyway, I was looking around his room, and saw a cookie jar. I didn't expect to find anything in his cookie jar, but when I opened the lid, I saw a handful of chocolate chip cookies in the bottom of the jar. I figured the cookies would be hard or stale; but when I bit into a cookie, it was soo soft and delicious, it was wonderful! I couldn't believe it, it made me soo happy!

I sat on my father's bed; hugging the cooking jar in my lap with my left hand, and eating the cookies out of the jar with my right hand. As I sat on his bed, I dangled my legs back-and-forth like a child. I remembered the craving I had on the way to the hospital, and figured the cookies were my father's metaphysical gift to me.

I told my mother about the cookies I found in my father's room, and reminded her about the cookie craving I had on the way to the hospital. She said she had a feeling that my father had already died before I even said that. She told me she didn't say anything at the time because she didn't want to upset me while I was driving, thinking I might cause us to wreck. I don't think I would have caused us to wreck; but, you know how I drive.

When we finally got the call from the mortician, my mother and I drove to the funeral parlor to get him. My father's ashes were in a clear plastic bag, inside a black square plastic box. When the mortician handed us the box, my mother and I were both surprised at how heavy his ashes were. We paid the man, and drove back to the house.

When we got to the house, I called EasyRotor Helicopter. I asked the pilot if he was okay with me spreading my father's ashes while he hovered over the lake. He said he didn't have a problem with that, so I scheduled a half-hour ride with him to fly over Lake Michigan.

A few days later, it was time for our helicopter ride. As my mother and I drove to the airport, I realized we were driving the same route my father drove to work every day for 20 years. I mentioned that to my mother; she shrugged her shoulders with ambivalence, and we didn't say much to each other after that. When we got to the private airport, our helicopter arrived, and the pilot pulled-off the side door to make it easier for me to spread my father's ashes. The pilot told us a few dos and don'ts, and then we took off. I really liked the change in my field of vision as we ascended into the air, flew over the city, and flew to the lake. It only took a few minutes, and we were already flying over the beach. The beach was busy with people as we flew over, but after a few more minutes, our pilot found an area where there wasn't anyone on the lake or the beach. There, he hovered the helicopter about 100' above the water.

Before I spread my father's ashes over the water, my mother wanted to feel what my father's ashes felt like. She dipped her thumb, index, and middle finger-tips into his ashes, and rolled his ashes between her fingertips. I thought that was a little weird, but my mother encouraged me to do the same. I knew I wouldn't have another opportunity to do that, and really didn't want to miss-out on that experience, so I did it too. They weren't soft and light like wood ash, his ashes were dense and a little gritty. After a minute of that, we dusted our finger tips into his bag, and I started emptying his ashes from the bag over the water.

It wasn't as clean of an experience as I thought it would be. I got ash all over the landing skid of our pilot's helicopter. I was thinking, if anyone saw us from the beach, they might think something was wrong with our helicopter, and call emergency services because they were seeing a grey cloud behind us. Fortunately, nobody called emergency services, I safely emptied my father's ash bag, and we flew back to the airport. I apologized to the pilot that I got ash all-over his helicopter, but he wasn't bothered by it.

It would be nice to say emptying my father's ashes over the water gave us the closure we needed to move on, but there were a lot of things we needed to take care of first. With an original copy of my father's death certificate, we went to our local social security office to let them know he was dead. We also learned how much money my mother would receive from my father's social security as his surviving spouse, and told them where to deposit the money. My father always paid all of the bills. As a result, my mother didn't know how to pay the bills or balance the checking account, so I taught her how to do those things. My mother didn't know how to use the lawn mower either. I was going to pay a landscaping company to cut the grass for her; but she didn't want to spend $65 per week to have the grass cut, so I taught my 69 year old mother how to mow the grass with the riding lawn mower. My father had a life insurance policy, so I helped her claim his death benefit. With that money, we were able to take care of some maintenance things at the house that we deferred.

The shingles on the roof of the house were worn, and the roof was sagging, so we fixed the sagging, and put a metal roof on the house. A few windows in the house were old and inefficient, so we replaced those windows. The water softener was outdated and inefficient, so we replaced the water softener, and I taught my mother how and when to put salt in the water softener. As my dying father instructed me, I took care of my mother. I stayed at the house with her to teach her, or help her do whatever she needed, and considered moving-in with her permanently. We continued like this for most of the summer of 2012, until Mat sent me a text message.

He was asking me if I was interested to go to school in North Dakota, to study petroleum production, and try to get a job in the oil field. Mat, like me, sometimes has crazy ideas that are not well thought-out. I knew I needed to do something different, but I really wasn't sold on the idea of going to school in North Dakota. My options were to move-in with my mother and try to find some managerial job in Michigan, or go to school in North Dakota. Either way, I had to go back to South Dakota to shut down my business, pack my stuff, and move out of the house. So, I bought a plane ticket for a flight back to South Dakota.

I was off to a good start already. The girl sitting on the plane next to me liked to drink, so we drank a couple beers on the plane during our flight from Grand Rapids to Minneapolis. Then we had time between our flights, so we drank another beer at the Rock Bottom bar in the airport. We finished our drinks, and went our separate ways to our gates. On my way to my gate, I met another girl, and we also had a beer at Rock Bottom. The same server served me both times at Rock Bottom (no longer open at the airport), and she gave me this look of: "I recognize you, what are you doing?" I gave her a look of: "Please don't say anything." My server was cool with me, and didn't say anything, so I gave her a decent tip.

By the time I got back to Rapid City, I already had a good buzz. As usual, Melanie and our friends warmly greeted me. The night I arrived it was Summer Nights on 7th Street in Rapid City. That's an event where they shut down a couple city streets for a live concert, there are vendors in the streets, and some people drink. A couple friends of ours were bar tenders, so they escorted us to the bars, and took care of us with a beautiful array of mixed drinks all night. It was a very good welcome back celebration that evening.

The next day I didn't have anything I needed to do except shut-down my business, pack, and figure-out where I was going to move-to. Until I could figure that out, I started working at Wellspring. As before, I worked whenever they needed me, and I was grateful to be earning money again.

Just as I was getting back to work at Wellspring, Dan was getting out of the Air Force. He had a realistic chance to get a job with Boeing, but he was also considering the oil opportunity in North Dakota. Dan loved researching everything to do with investing or spending his money. When he told me he was considering rejecting a stable and comfortable opportunity with Boeing, for a not-so-safe bet in North Dakota, he got my attention.

I started imagining myself in Michigan, working as an assistant manager at a gas station, and calling Mat and Dan in North Dakota. I imagined them gleefully smiling, telling me how great of jobs they had, making me resent my choice as I stood in the middle of the convenience store with my mobile phone to my ear, wearing my assistant manager uniform, and re-stocking the candy bars. There was no way I was going to miss-out on this; if there was any chance we were going to make it in North Dakota, I wanted to take that chance. Mat was already enrolled at the school; but Dan and I missed the deadline for the fall semester, so we had some time to kill until the winter semester started in January.

Dan wanted a transition job, so I introduced him to the hiring managers at Wellspring. We were leaving in a few months, but most residential treatment facilities have staffing challenges, so even part-time temporary work is very helpful. I was good at my job; me giving Dan the face-to-face introductions helped speed-up the hiring process for him, a lot. They gave him a tour of the facility, and then they started filling-out new hire paperwork.

One night, Dan and I had the night off. Dan needed new tires, and I didn't have anything else to do, so I went with him. There was a bar across the street, and we both like to drink, so we went to the bar to help pass the time while we waited.

I was in the mood for vintage port, but all they had was 10, 20, and 40 year old port, and not vintage port. I tried each of those ports, and they were expensive, but I was disappointed with each of the ports I tried. Dan, not knowing anything about port, thought the wines tasted good. I assured him the wines paled in comparison to vintage port. When they finished with his tires, Dan drove me to the liquor store.

Vintage ports are hard to find. When we went to the specialty liquor store, and there were 28 bottles in the cooler, I bought all 28 bottles. Some of the ports didn't have prices, so the cashier had to call the owner to find out how much to charge me. And because I bought soo much, they gave me a 10% discount. I was a little nervous about the total as he was ringing-up the ports, but I had just received my doctoral stipend. Actually, it was my last doctoral study stipend because they just cut me off from borrowing anymore money. In any case, I had $7,000 to spend. I happily paid a little over $2,600 for my ports that ranged in vintage from 1963 to 2007, and I was excited to get a good start on my vintage port collection. That night, Dan and I drank a 2007 Niepoort Vintage Port. It was young, and could have stood several more years maturing, but we still really enjoyed that vintage port, much more than all of the decades-old ports we drank in the restaurant.

As I was shutting down my business, I got a call from a guy who was interested in me managing a half-dozen units for him. I've seen this a few times in real estate; where there is no activity for a long time, and then the last few days of a listing all-of-a-sudden there is significant interest. I already made-up my mind I was shutting down my business, so I reluctantly rejected his offer.

Packing-up my home office, I exasperatedly put my license in an envelope, and sent it back to the real estate commission to deactivate my brokerage license. I did everything I could to try to make it in real estate, and had no intention of doing again anything in real estate in any capacity. I told all my clients to find another broker, and helped them through the transition process.

Dan and I had already applied, and were accepted into the petroleum production program at Williston State College in North Dakota. We had rooms reserved for us in the 21 years old and over dorms on campus, so everything was setup nicely for us. Dan and I also told the managers at Wellspring we were moving to North Dakota. All I had to do now was get my vintage port collection to my mother's cellar in Michigan.

It was a few days before Christmas 2012. Getting my wine, and a truck full of miscellaneous stuff to Michigan, was one of the last things I needed to do before my move to North Dakota. I still didn't own a car, so Mat let me borrow his truck, an F150 with a lift-kit. Dan had never been to Michigan, so he decided to go on the road-trip with me. Dennis warned us that a winter storm was approaching, but I wasn't concerned about the inclement weather, because we had unseasonably warm weather up until that point, and I'm a good driver in winter anyway.

Dan and I left in the morning, and as we drove to Minnesota, it was getting colder and colder. By the time we made it to Minnesota, it started snowing hard, and getting really windy. The more we drove into Minnesota, the worse the weather was becoming. When I saw trucks in the ditches west-bound on the interstate, I thought it was strange the ice was only on their side of the road. Even if the cars were in the ditch on my side of the interstate, I still wouldn't have been concerned. I've driven past people like that too many times before, and never ended-up in the ditch, so I kept driving at 65 miles per hour until I drove under an overpass.

As I passed an overpass, a heavy gust of wind hit the truck, and I started to spinout toward the shoulder. I jerked the wheel hard trying to get back onto the interstate, but that just made the truck start to roll. Of course I wasn't wearing a seatbelt, so when the driver side window broke as the truck was rolling, I was ejected from the truck. Dan, who was wisely wearing his seatbelt, safely stayed inside the truck during and after the truck rolls.

After he freed himself from the truck, he called for me. I heard him, and really didn't want to respond, but I knew I had to respond so he knew I was still alive. I groaned a response to him like I groaned to my mother when she yelled at me to get out of bed and go to school. The sound of my groan implied: "I hear you, I understand you, I know I need to move, but I'm not moving right now."

I landed on my back in a snow drift, and really didn't want to get up, but with Dan's help and encouragement, I got up out of the snow drift. I didn't want to go back to the truck either. I wanted to pretend the whole incident didn't even happen. But he walked me over to the truck, sat me down on the tailgate, and put his beanie on my head to help keep me warm. As I sat there, Dan went up to the interstate to flag-down some help. I was happy to be sitting there; and that my only responsibility at the time was to sit there and wait while Dan looked for help.

A kid stopped his car on the interstate shoulder, and said we were so far down the embankment, he didn't even see the truck as he was driving past. I must have had a pretty good rush of adrenaline, because I hopped down from the truck, and staggered up the hill to sit in the kid's car as we waited for the ambulance to arrive. I was really excited talking to the kid in the car, explaining to him what happened.

Then the ambulance arrived, so I walked over, and started talking to the paramedic in the back of the ambulance. I really didn't want to go to the hospital. But when he asked me what year it was, I told him 2013. When I saw him angle his head at me with unpleasant surprise, I realized I told him the wrong year, and we all decided it was in my best interest to go to the hospital.

They drove me to the Mayo Clinic near Rochester, Minnesota, took me to the CT scan room right away, and cut-off all of my clothes. Dan was in the room too, watching the process, and I looked across the room at him with a look of: "Dude, a little privacy please!" He looked away quickly, and stepped out of the room while they slid me into the scanner.

After all of the scans, they put me in my own intensive care room. They wanted to give me a lot of drugs, but I was refusing all of the drugs they wanted to give me because I don't do drugs. I was having trouble sleeping, and I heard them say to Dan that I wasn't doing too good, but I didn't want to believe them. Dan walked over to me, and told me that if I didn't take the drugs, I could die.

I reluctantly took all of the medications they wanted to give me. I even agreed to take an IV of some trial drug serum that was supposed to help with the healing process. With all of that, I actually slept through most of the rest of the night. In the morning they were saying my vital signs were looking a lot better.

I was ready to go, but I knew I couldn't go anywhere by myself, and I had to wait for Dan. Dan spent the night in a nearby hotel. When he came back to my room late-morning I was very relieved, because I was starting to feel trapped in my intensive care room, and I knew it was very expensive to stay there.

I felt good, and wanted to be discharged, so the specialists began visiting me one at a time. I told them I was planning on flying home; and they told me not to do that, because I would die if I did. I had eight broken ribs, a cracked vertebrae, and a bruised shoulder. They said the pressure on the plane would push my broken ribs against my lungs, puncture my lungs, and I would not be able to survive the flight. I really didn't like that scenario, so I decided renting a car was the best option. Before I left the hospital I had to get some clothes, because all I was wearing was my hospital gown.

The nurse who was staying with me in my room was very cool, and robbed the hospital for me. She picked out a pair of socks, shorts, fleece pants, and a fleece top for me. The off-brand clothes weren't anything I would normally buy, but it was a lot better than what I had, which was nothing. Besides, I wanted a pair of fleece pants for years, so it was really nice that she gave them to me.

I didn't have any shoes either. I took my shoes off while I was driving the truck, so when the truck rolled, I lost my shoes. The guy who was working with my nurse thought he might have a pair of shoes for me. He went to his locker, and came back with an old pair of Asics that actually fit me! The people in-charge of taking care of me in my intensive care room went far above what was expected of them, I really appreciated that.

I passed all of my specialists' medical checks, and had clothes and shoes to wear, so I was ready to go. Before I left, they offered me a prescription for pain killers. Considering my last prescription experience, I respectfully declined their offer. I asked them about drinking alcohol, and they said I should avoid alcohol because it wasn't going to help my healing process. Everything else was as good as it was going to be, so I started walking, very slowly, because it hurt to move any faster than baby steps.

We took a taxi to the nearest car rental place. Unfortunately for me, it was Hertz. I wanted something with 4-wheel drive, just in case the weather turned bad again, so I rented a little sport utility vehicle.

Before we began our journey, we stopped at a gas station to fill-up, bought some snacks and a drink for Dan, and Ibuprofen and Motrin for me. My discharging doctor told me I should alternate between the two every three hours to help keep my inflammation down, so that is what I did. Because we were going through the automobile insurance company to pay for all of our expenses, including the medical expenses, Dan was saving all of our receipts.

As we drove back to South Dakota it was a sunny, but cold day, and the roads were mostly clear. Occasionally there was a little snow drift in the cruising lane, and that made me a little nervous, but Dan managed it well. I was doing good alternating my medicines, and with Dan's good driving, we made it back to Rapid City safely. We turned-in my Hertz rental at the airport, and Dan added the paperwork to our receipt stack. Dan and I waited at the airport for a few minutes, and Pam and Dennis came to pick us up.

The first night back we had dinner at Pam's house. Everybody made jokes about me and my driving, and that made me laugh, but laughing, sneezing, and coughing were painful. After dinner, I prepared myself to try to sleep.

Pam had a really comfortable couch in her living room that I could sink into. I thought that would be a good place for me to cushion my broken bones and sleep, but I forgot that I don't just sleep in one spot, I naturally reposition myself throughout the night. In the middle of the night I was trying to reposition myself on that couch, but it sucked me in, making it really difficult for me to move at all without feeling pain. Fortunately for me, the vintage couch was low to the floor.

Over the course of an hour I was able to turn my body perpendicular to the couch, slide off of the couch, and sit on the floor with my back against the couch. But now I was pinned between the couch and the coffee table, and there was no way to pick myself up without injuring myself more, so I just sat there until someone finally woke up. Pam was the first to find me, and Dan came over for breakfast, so one on each side of me they gingerly helped me up off of the floor.

Learning my lesson from the couch experience, I tied a dog leash to the end of my bed so I could use it to pull myself up from the bed, and gently lie myself down. Because of the natural need to reposition myself throughout the night, and not being able to sleep on my front or either of my sides, I alternated between sleeping on my bed and sleeping on the couch. I would sleep a couple hours on my back in my bed, use the dog leash to help myself pick myself up and out of bed, walk downstairs, and sleep sitting-up on the couch for a couple hours. On the couch I had a large pillow behind my back so it would be easier to sit-down and stand-up from the couch. I did this every night, and during the day, I tried to rest more and eat clean.

I knew I needed some exercise, and that it would help my recovery, so I tried to take the dog for a walk. The dog, a corgi and blue healer mix, loves walks, so it was going to be a great thing for both of us. I put the leash on her, and we attempted to go for one of our usual walks, but I was still walking baby steps. We made it outside, and as we walked, she was soo excited she kept jerking her leash, trying to move at a quicker pace. The dog jerking the leash was pulling my arm and uncomfortably twisting my rib cage. After a block of that, I had to stop, and turn around. She looked up at me with disappointment, and I could tell by her slow walk that she knew we were going home. When we got home, I unleashed the dog in the house. Trying to walk the dog (now deceased) was far too painful for me, but I still wanted to try walking by myself.

I decided to go to the grocery store to get some healthy food to eat, so I slowly walked just under a mile to get there. I got to the grocery store okay, so I started shopping. At my infantile pace, I picked-up a few things, and put them in my grocery basket. But after walking around the store and buying my groceries, I was too exhausted to walk home, so I called a taxi. Getting in and out of the car was a challenge, but it wasn't nearly as bad as trying to walk that mile again.

I hadn't packed any of my stuff remaining in the house yet. I wasn't really in good enough health to do most of the packing myself, so Pam came over one day to help me. She packed all of my belongings into big grey tote bins (totes) for me, and I hung out with her while she was doing that. With all my stuff packed into totes, I rented a UHAUL.

Mat and Dan kindly loaded my stuff into the UHAUL for me. Dan had a few things he was moving to North Dakota too, and I was happy to share my UHAUL with him. With everything packed and loaded, we hit the road again. But this time, I was driving by myself.

10

Williston

Song Suggestions:
Estiva feat. Josie—Better Days
KAASI & TÁCHES—Heartbeats

Mat was leading the way to North Dakota, driving the new truck he bought since I totaled his old truck. Dan was driving his car, and I was following them with my 17' UHAUL. The six hour drive to Williston was a lot for me. During our drive-up it was a windy day, so I was wrestling the steering wheel to keep the truck on the road, and at times I was afraid a gust of wind was going to knock the truck over onto its side. When we made it to Williston, and the streets were covered in snowpack. I backed-up the UHAUL to the front door of the dorm building, and Mat and Dan unloaded the UHAUL, putting my stuff into my dorm room.

Part of my packed stuff was a case of Guinness beer. I was buying several cases of Guinness beer at a time at Sam's Club, because they only did seasonal bulk-buys, and they would usually sell-out before I finished drinking one case. I had a case left, and I knew I wasn't supposed to drink, but I wanted to thank Mat and Dan for their help. Also, I wanted to celebrate making it safely to North Dakota, so we started cracking-open the Guinness beers in Dan's room. That night I got to meet one of our classmates, Ed, and he enjoyed drinking the Guinness beers too. A little later that night we met another one of our classmates, Matt (spelled with two-ts), but he was drinking mixed drinks. Mat and Matt shared a bathroom the next set of rooms over from Dan and I.

The dorms were setup so that two rooms, one on each side, shared a bathroom. Each dorm room had a desk, and a steel frame bunk bed so the college could put two people in a room if they needed to. There wasn't a flood of enrollment at the college, so there wasn't a threat of sharing the room with someone. Because of that, most guys just gave the top bunks to the dorm manager to put into storage.

The steel frame bunk bed worked great for me. I stored my grey totes on the top bunk, and at the middle of the bottom of the bedframe of the top bunk there was a bar that bowed down so I could easily grab onto it, to help pull myself up from the bed. That bowed bar worked a lot better than the dog leash I was using. I still had too much pain to sleep through the night, so I used the time I couldn't sleep to unpack my totes, and organize my room. I usually live-streamed National Public Radio (NPR) from either Boston, Vermont, New York, or Colorado while I was unpacking to keep-up with the news and also for a little entertainment.

Our dorm building had been around since the early 1970s, and had not been updated at all. So all of the carpets, furniture, and appliances were worn, and near the end of their useful lives. But we really didn't care about the condition of the building.

We were paying $180 a month in rent because we were enrolled at the college. If we weren't living in the dorms we'd have to pay $1,000 to rent a room in somebody's house, or even more to live in one of the few available apartments. Because of the limited housing and the high rents, people drove their motor homes to North Dakota, or they brought their camper-trailers in-tow. And because of the limited places to rent a recreational vehicle (RV) lot, some of the people coming to the area lived in their RV in the Walmart parking lot.

There were soo many people coming to the area because they just finished drilling the exploratory wells in an oilfield called the Bakken. They determined the boundaries of the oil play, and also developed systems to cost effectively drill and hydraulically fracture the oil wells horizontally. Oil was around $100 per barrel, so organizational leaders were trying to move fast to produce as much oil as they could in the highly profitable market. Consequently, there was a lot of work for everyone in and around the oil field. Most of the oil companies were looking for people with experience. We didn't have any experience, which is why we were studying petroleum production at Williston State College.

Williston is at the top of the Bakken, Dickinson is at the bottom of the Bakken, and it takes about two-and-a-half hours to get from one city to the other. They aren't large cities, only around 25,000 people in each, but they are the two most populated cities in Western North Dakota, so most of the oil companies doing business in the area are located in those cities. Although we were enrolled in college, we didn't want to be there any longer than we had to. We planned to drop-out as soon as we got hired someplace. We wanted to get internships at one of the exploration and production companies, but it really didn't matter how we found our jobs, as long as we got jobs.

School started a couple days after we got there. We lived in the same hall, and had the same class schedule. Dan and I carpooled with Mat in his new Toyota truck, aptly named Tundra. I rode in the back seat, and actually learned to wear my seatbelt. I also encouraged everyone else to wear their seatbelts too. It wasn't easy for me to get in and out of the truck with my broken bones. Slowly, with Dan as my spotter, I carefully climbed into and out-of Mat's truck. I wasn't able to walk at a normal pace either, so I normally fell behind as we walked to school, through school, and everywhere else. Mat always apologized for walking ahead, and would tell me that he forgot. School was easy, it was only a couple hours three times a week, so we had a lot of time to kill.

Matt and Ed were already working at Walmart, so they helped Mat and Dan get jobs at Walmart. Walmart was paying $17 an hour, couldn't get enough workers, and couldn't keep their shelves stocked. Basically, Walmart was selling a lot of their inventory almost as quick as they could get it on the shelves.

I was still enrolled in my doctoral program, so I occupied my time by doing research, writing, and editing a couple hours a day. The rest of the time I was binge eating, binge drinking, and binge watching shows on HULU and Netflix. I wasn't healthy enough to lift weights or run, so those weren't options for me, but riding a bicycle wasn't too bad.

Matt had a bicycle he didn't ride because he too just bought a truck. Matt let me use his bicycle whenever I wanted, and even gave me the key to his bike lock. Riding his bicycle was one of the activities I looked forward to. I rode his bicycle all-over Williston buying groceries, and lottery.

I was desperate to get out of my student loan debt, so I bought a lot of lottery. I plotted a route so I could buy lottery tickets at every lotto retailer in Williston; at the time, there were 14 locations. The route was pretty much a loop around the city. I went grocery shopping at Walmart and Albertson's, got $60 cash-back from my Discover card at each store, and used that money to play any game that had more than a $10-million payout. I chose games with $10-million payouts and over because I wanted to split the winnings between Mat, Dan and I, and still be millionaires after the cash option deduction and paying taxes on the winnings. I wanted to split the money with Mat and Dan, because without Mat and Dan deciding to move to North Dakota, I wouldn't have moved to North Dakota either. The two weekdays we didn't go to school I was doing my lottery runs to stay ahead of the Tuesday-Wednesday, and Friday-Saturday drawings. And on the weekend, I was doing my grocery shopping-cash runs. I wasn't doing any other exercise, so I think all of the bike riding I was doing was helping me heal.

Occasionally I would walk to the post office when I needed to mail a letter, and I regularly tested my abilities, like trying to walk a little faster. In the dorm, I tried doing sit-ups and push-ups when it didn't hurt so much to get in and out of bed. One day, coming back from a walk to the post office, I started to jog a little. It felt soo good to be able to almost run again. I was soo happy to be able to start to move freely like I used to. I thought about all of the stuff that I lost in the wreck, all of the expensive stuff that I valued soo much, and I didn't even care about all of that anymore. I just wanted to be able to move freely without pain again. The whole experience helped me be a lot less materialistic than I used to be.

I was spending $120 a week on lottery tickets for weeks. I think the most I won on a ticket was $16. Since I was starting to move around more freely without pain, and I really didn't like how fast I was burning through my cash, I applied for a job at Walmart too.

I completed the application, had an interview, and she wanted to hire me, but we had to wait until my background check was completed. A few days later, I received a letter in the mail from Walmart. The letter said Walmart wasn't going to hire me because my character wasn't aligned with Walmart's values, and referenced my public indecency offence from a decade earlier. I was a little surprised by that, but I wasn't too disappointed. Instead, I tried using my degrees again, and applied for administrative jobs at some of the local oil field companies.

While I was completing my applications, I was checking my credit card statement, and noticed I had a $1,758.76 charge from Hertz for an 11 day car rental! I only rented the car for one day, and my charge was only supposed to be $186.57. I turned the car in, they gave me a receipt, and I thought we were done. The numbers were close, so it looked like someone just typed something wrong. I called Hertz to try and resolve the issue.

When I called Hertz and explained the situation, they weren't interested in helping me find a solution to my problem, so I told Discover Card I was disputing the charge. Discover was great; they refunded me the difference between what I was actually charged, and what I should have been charged right away. I made a couple more calls to Hertz, and inadvertently found-out that they didn't close my original rental when I turned the car in. So, in their computer system, it looked like I was still using the car.

But it was too late, Hertz already submitted the balance of the bill to a debt collection company because I disputed the charge. Thankfully, Dan saved all of our receipts from the wreck for the insurance claim. So when I received the collections notice, I followed their dispute instructions, and sent them copies of all of the receipts including the rental agreement Hertz gave me when I rented the car. I sent all of that paperwork to the debt collection company via United States Postal Service (USPS) certified mail, and saved a copy of my certified mail receipt. I asked the collections company to rescind the bill, cease further collection activity, and to reply to me in writing within 14 days.

Fourteen days came-and-went, and I didn't receive anything from the debt collection company. I did receive a signed copy of the receipt from the USPS that the collections company received my dispute paperwork, so I know they received my dispute paperwork, but they didn't reply to me. I'm pretty sure they stopped collections activity, because I didn't see or hear anything from anyone else about it, so I'm calling it a win.

By now it's March 2nd 2013, and it's the one year anniversary of my father's death. At first, I didn't think much of it. It was a Saturday, I didn't have anything else better to do, so I decided to walk to the store to pick-up some snacks. On the way to the store I started thinking more about my father, and remembered stories he told me.

One story was about him and a friend drinking at a bar. My father's friend was a big guy, with a thick beard. In addition to drinking their beers, they wanted to do flaming Sambuca shots. So they ordered shots of Sambuca, lit them on fire, blew out the flames, and drank the shots. Except my father's bearded friend didn't blow-out the fire all the way; the Sambuca spilled onto his beard, and he lit his beard on fire. My father told me he just laughed at him as the guy was trying to put-out the fire in his beard. I would have laughed too.

To commemorate my father's life and death, I decided I needed to go to a bar, and drink some Sambuca shots. So, I skipped the grocery store, and went to the bar. The first bar I went to didn't have liquor, but they had beers on tap. First I drank a dark, thick, delicious beer, and I was already buzzed. They also had an IPA beer that looked good, so I drank a glass of that too. I was definitely legally drunk at this point, because I drank the beers in quick succession, but I really wanted to drink some Sambuca.

I walked to another bar, they served liquor, and I was happy they had Sambuca. But, they didn't have the clear Sambuca that I wanted, they only had Sambuca Black. Still, I was happy I was drinking Sambuca, so I did a couple shots there. After my quick little shots, I decided to leave. I had the equivalent of about 6 drinks in about an hour-and-a-half; I was drunk, and I was hungry.

I walked to the Dominos and ordered a pan pizza, no cheese, extra sauce, peppers and onions. I was sitting on the little bench in front of the cash register, and passed-out while I was waiting for my pizza. When I opened my eyes, the two workers in the pizzeria were giving me strange looks, maybe because it was two-o'clock in the afternoon and I was wasted. In any case, I took my pizza, and started walking back to the dorm.

I walked on the sidewalks in the city, and ate my pizza while I was walking. The sidewalks were mostly cleared of snow, but there were still some icy patches that I tried to walk across. I ended up slipping and falling as I was trying to carry my pizza box, eat pizza, and walk across the ice. After a few falls, I gave up on that, and threw what was left of my pizza into someone's garbage bin at the curb. I kept walking, and then my mother called me.

I could hear the sadness in her voice as she asked me if I knew what day it was. I choked-up right away, and started to cry a little as I told her: "yeah," and then I heard her start to cry. I had just rounded a corner, and I saw a few police cars parked on a side street of the main street. I wasn't sure what was going on, so I stopped walking halfway down the block. Then, I saw one of the police officers walking toward me. Starting to sob, I told my mother I needed to go, and we hung up. My hand was bloody from falling onto the sidewalk after I slipped on the ice.

The police officer asked me what happened. I tried to tell him it was the one year anniversary of my father's death; but I was crying soo much I could barely speak, and I think all he heard was: "my father's dead." He walked with me to his police car, I showed him my driver's license with my dorm address on it, and he drove me back to my dorm that was only about three blocks away. He walked me to my dorm room, and told me to drink some water. I did what he said, and I went to sleep.

When I woke-up the next day, I was grateful he didn't arrest me. He was soo nice, I was expecting him to check-in on me all day, so I didn't drink. I was surprised when he didn't come back to check on me. I guessed maybe it was his day off, but I was still appreciative of what he did for me.

Spring break came, and we had a week off-of-school, so I decided to visit my mother in Michigan. I had a lot of time, but I didn't have a lot of money, so I took the Amtrak from Williston, ND to Chicago, IL. Then when I was in Chicago, I took another Amtrak from Chicago to Battle Creek, MI where my mother could pick me up to take me to her house. It took a little over a day, and I spent most of the time trying to sleep or daydreaming, but I enjoyed seeing some cities that I had not seen before. At my mother's house, I helped her around the yard, worked on my doctoral study proposal a little, and applied for jobs at more oil companies. I discussed job opportunities I saw with my mother, and was starting to get excited about the progress I was making as I passed each stage of the vetting processes, until ultimately my applications were rejected.

When I got back to North Dakota, I actually got an email from Valero. They wanted me to compete for one of their openings at their refinery in Corpus Christi. This was my first opportunity to get a job in the energy industry. I told them I would be there; booked a flight, reserved a hotel room, and rented a car. I only flew down for a day because I didn't have the money to spend any more time down there.

As soon as I flew-in, I found a Mediterranean place to eat at, checked into my hotel, and went to the beach. It was an overcast day, but I still enjoyed the warm weather, seeing the water, and wading into the Gulf of Mexico. When I got back to the hotel, I could see a very inviting hotel bar on the top floor of the hotel from the parking garage. I loved the idea of going up there to get a few drinks, but I was trying to get a job, and I really didn't want to impair my ability to get that job. So I went to sleep without drinking, and made sure I was well rested to wake up early and show-up early for the refinery test.

I was one of the first few people at the testing facility waiting for the door to open. Again, it was an overcast day, but the weather was still better than the snow in North Dakota. The testing center was a large metal building that looked like a barn you would see on a farm.

When the test administrators arrived, I walked-in, she highlighted my name on the roster, and gave me my test booklet. It was a timed exam with a few sections testing different aptitudes, but the biggest section was about process flow. I spent a lot of time looking at the pictures trying to figure-out how fluids would flow in a process. I was studying petroleum production, but we hadn't yet discussed how fluids flow through process equipment. A few people there were just trying to get a better paying job from their already good paying jobs, and were able to quickly finish the test sections. I ran out of time, and wasn't able to finish my exam. I did well for what I did, but it may not have been enough.

After the exam I went to the Mediterranean restaurant I found, talked with the guys working there about my move to North Dakota, and then I drove to the airport to catch my flight back to North Dakota. A few weeks later I received a call from one of the hiring managers that I did well on the exam, but they had other candidates that were better qualified for the job. It wasn't too much of a surprise for me. That's what most of my previous job applications were like.

I was starting to get desperate again. I saw lots of trucks hauling trailers of water for hydraulic fracturing jobs (fracs), and I thought I could get my commercial driver license (CDL) so that I could drive one of those trucks. I studied an online exam-prep for about a week before I took the CDL exam. When I took the exam, I passed the exam on my first try! Right away the driver's license office issued me a CDL learner's permit endorsement for my driver license, so I could drive a truck in CDL school. CDL school was a couple hours away, and was going to cost me $7,000. I didn't have $7,000, but I had a credit card that I could charge the $7,000 to. I enrolled in the class so a seat was reserved for me, and it was nice I didn't have to pay for the class until I got there.

A couple weeks before the class started there was a job fair in Williston. There were around 60 companies represented at the job fair. The first hour of the job fair was reserved for veterans, so veterans got to walk around and talk to the recruiters before everyone else. Mat, Dan, and I went to the job fair during the veteran hour, and I again tried to make one of my degrees work for me. Mat and Dan went to one room, and I went to the other room.

I found a couple tables from company representatives that sounded like something that would suit me well, but nobody was at the tables. I milled around the area a little, and started talking to recruiters at other tables, trying to track down the recruiters I was looking for. Eventually, the recruiters I wanted to talk-to showed-up to work. They seemed soo disinterested to be there, and were similarly uninterested in me. It was soo strange, I was wondering why they were even there. Deflated, I walked to Mat and Dan's room, and found them walking toward me in one of the aisles.

When I stopped to talk to them, Mat's and Dan's eyes were wide-open with excitement. They said they saw one of their co-workers from Walmart, and their co-worker was saying that he talked to a recruiter that was recruiting for jobs that we were going to school for. Mat told me they talked to the recruiter. He said their starting wage was $24/hr., and that I should go talk to the guy. I started to get excited too, but I was also thinking it was a little too good to be true. I went over to the contract company table, introduced myself to the recruiter, and talked to him about the job.

It went well; he was easy to talk to, and he said that all of the applications he gets go straight to his junk e-mail box. He gave me an application, offered me some Wood Group swag that I politely declined, and we shook hands. After that meeting, Mat, Dan, and I began walking to the door, and felt a little more hope than when we first arrived.

As we were leaving, the exclusive veteran hour was nearly over, and we saw a long line of more than 100 people who were waiting to get into the job fair. I was shocked to see soo many people looking for jobs, and felt soo privileged that we were able to get into the job fair first. As soon as we got back to the dorms, we started filling-out our applications.

I still had the printer/scanner I bought when I worked at Best Buy. I told Mat and Dan that I would scan and email our applications to the recruiter. When they finished filling-out their applications, I scanned our applications into .pdf files, and gave each file the same name as their respective email subject lines.

I knew all of the applications went to the recruiter's junk email, so I wanted our applications to stand-out when he browsed his junk email box. I sent all three of our applications to the recruiter, one-at-a-time, each with similar email subjects, and all within a minute of each other. So when the recruiter scanned through his email, he would see a block of similarly titled emails as a way catch his attention like: Daniel's Application, Met you at the Job Fair, Mat's Application, Met you at the Job Fair, Richard's Application, Met you at the Job Fair. My email strategy worked.

About a week later, we were on our way to school, and Dan's phone rang. It was the recruiter calling him, and he was setting up interviews for one of the local petroleum production companies that was looking for contractors to work for them. He setup an appointment with Dan, and then the recruiter asked about Mat. Dan said Mat was right next to him, so Dan handed the phone to Mat. The recruiter setup an interview time for Mat, and as I was listening to their conversation I was hoping the recruiter would ask for me, and he did! I spoke with the recruiter, got an interview time, thanked him, and hung-up the phone. We went to class that day in great moods, then after class, we got to prepare ourselves for our interviews.

11
Dickinson

Song Suggestions:
Jenna G—Rising
Linnea Schössow—Someone Like You

Normally when I prepare myself for an interview, I make sure my appearance is flawless. I always get my hair cut, wear a well put-together outfit, put on nice shoes, and I shave. But all the times I did that in the past, nobody ever hired me. I've always gone out of my way to try to impress my interviewers, and it's never worked-out for me. This time I thought: "f-it; take me as I am, or not at all." I went to the interview with shaggy hair, I had a little scruff on my face, and the cuffs on my pants were ripped at my heels. Regardless, at a quick glance, I still looked somewhat respectable. Mat and Dan on the other hand, did what I normally do, and looked polished.

Mat, Dan, and I all had interviews within 15 minutes of each other, so we carpooled down to Dickinson for our interviews, and walked into the office together. I thought we would just hang out in the reception area as we took turns interviewing, but there wasn't a reception area. When we walked into the building, we were immediately in the workstation area, but nobody was at any of the workstations. We could barely hear people talking behind a closed door at the back of the room, and we were a few minutes early anyway, so we just stood and waited near the entryway. Similar to our college dorm, this office had been around since at least the 1970s, and neither the building nor the furniture had been updated. It actually made the interview process a lot less intimidating for me.

We didn't have to wait long, and got to see our interviewer and the interviewee leave the interview. I listened to their exchange as they opened the office door, and walked-out into our area. It seemed like it went well for the prospective worker. He sounded knowledgeable, and I kinda thought we weren't in a good position to compete with the guy because we didn't have any experience, and we didn't know much about the oil field.

When our interviewer saw us, and heard how the interview was setup, he was unpleasantly surprised. He wasn't quite sure how to handle it. Trying to lighten the mood, I suggested in an upbeat way that we could have a group interview. He wasn't sure the recruiter would approve of a group interview for us, so he gave him a call. After a quick discussion, the recruiter said he was okay with it, so our interviewer went along with it.

Next was the logistics of the interview. Our interviewer thought we'd be alright meeting in his office. He pulled-in a few more chairs, and sat behind his desk. Then one of the interviewer's operators, Mat, Dan, myself, and the Health, Safety, and Environmental guy filed into our interviewer's office, in that order, for our group interview.

Our interview started with each of us answering the same question, then our interviewer had each of us answer separate questions, and after an hour-and-a-half he and the other two company guys took a break. They all came back from their break, and our interviewer asked us if this was going to be our last interview. I didn't really understand what he was asking, but Mat and Dan chuckled and smiled. Mat replied to him: "yes sir," and Dan followed-up with: "I hope so." I just looked around the room at everyone's faces in bewilderment at what was going on. We all shook hands, and Mat, Dan, and I left.

Mat and Dan were convinced our interviewer wanted to hire us, and were in great moods. I wasn't so sure about it, and remained skeptical about the situation. My thinking was, anyone can say anything, and it really doesn't matter until you get something in writing from them. Dan was soo sure we got the jobs he gave notice to his manager at Walmart that he had a new job, and was probably leaving soon. Mat and I just continued our normal routines.

A few days passed, and I got a call from the recruiter talking about the next steps: getting a medical exam, getting drug tested, sending-in a copy of my driver's license, proof of citizenship, and other pre-employment screening paperwork. I started going through the rigmarole, and was still skeptical that they were actually going to hire us. A week after we finished all of our pre-employment screening stuff, the recruiter called us again, and told us to meet him at the office in Montana. It was a step in the right direction, but I was not yet convinced we had jobs.

Williston is close to the Montana border. We only had about an hour drive from our dorm to his office. When we showed up at the office in Sidney, MT they were having a safety meeting, so everyone at the time that was working for the company in the Williston area showed up to the meeting. It was intimidating walking into the safety meeting room.

The safety meeting room was filled with about a hundred oil field guys with oil field experience, and then there was us in our civilian clothes. We had no idea what we were doing, so we just sat, and paid attention to what was going on. Toward the end of the meeting they made us stand-up in the crowd, and introduced us to everyone. We were relieved when the recruiter found us at the end of the meeting, and led us to his office to fill-out paperwork.

It wasn't until we started filling-out our new-hire paperwork that I finally started to think that we had jobs, and that this was our first day of work, April 25, 2013. After we filled-out all of our paperwork, and completed driver's safety training online, the safety guy gave us field safety orientation. Then, we went back to the recruiter's office to get trucks issued to us.

He had a couple sets of keys. We walked out to the parking lot to find the trucks, and get their information to have them assigned to us. The trucks he gave us were only a couple years old, white Ford F250s, with toolboxes mounted on the sides of the bed. After Mat and I got our trucks, it was late-afternoon, and we were done for the day. The recruiter didn't have a truck for Dan, so Dan drove Mat's personal truck back to Williston, while Mat and I drove our work trucks. The recruiter told us gas cards were in the truck, and he gave us pin numbers so we could use the fleet cards to buy gas. I was soo surprised by that; not only did they give us trucks to use, but they also bought the gas for us to use the trucks.

Our second day of work as contractors, we went to Dickinson. Dan got his truck down there, and the safety guy gave us our safety gear. The safety guy gave us clear and tinted safety glasses, hardhats, and five different types of gloves. He gave us cotton gloves, impact gloves, nitrile gloves, cutting gloves, and Mechanix gloves. He also gave each of us 4-gas monitors. The 4-gas monitors had an audible alarm, vibrated, and flashed when oxygen was too low, carbon monoxide was too high, hydrogen sulfide was too high, and when the lower explosive level was too high. The idea of monitoring 4-gases was interesting to me; all I really thought about was oxygen in the air, and didn't even think about other types of gas in the air.

After we were equipped with all of our safety gear, then we had to find guys to start riding around with. I was lucky enough to ride with the specialist. His expertise was way more than I needed at the time, but he still walked me through process piping, and helped give me a good foundation to build on.

A few days after we hired-in, Matt interviewed, and was hired at the same company we were working for. I don't know what changed with him; but he went from the nice guy who let me borrow his bike anytime I needed, to being a mouthy jerk. Some guys have fun talking trash to each other and making fun of each other, but I'm not one of those guys. We were all still living in the dorms, Matt didn't have his truck yet, and didn't know where to go for the weekly safety meeting, so he rode with Mat and I down to Dickinson.

Mat was driving, Matt was sitting in the front passenger seat, and I was sitting in the passenger seat behind Matt. As we were leaving the parking lot at the dorms, Mat wasn't sure where we were going, and I was trying to help him out. Matt chimed-in with one of his irrelevant rude comments, and that set-me-off right away. First thing in the morning this guy is starting-in on me. I had previously told the guy, many times, don't joke with me, I don't like your jokes, and he just cracked one of his jokes. Animalistically, out of complete basic instinct, I precisely threaded my arm between the headrest and the passenger side door, and swatted him across his face as hard as I could.

He puffed-up quick and asked me: "you wanna go?" I didn't want to go anywhere, I just wanted him to stop making rude comments to me. So that was the beginning of our two-and-a-half-hour drive. During the whole ordeal, Mat didn't say or do anything, he just kept driving. The rest of our time in the car was pretty much silence between the three of us. The good thing was, Matt stopped making stupid jokes with me. The bad thing was, I became very guarded with the guy, and really didn't want anything to do with him. Other than the drama with Matt, things were going well for us.

They were pretty much staffed-up in Dickinson, but needed a little help in the central and northern parts of the Bakken. Williston was about a 45 minute drive from our wells. There were places to live in Williston, but our interviewer wanted us to live a little closer to our wells in the central part of Bakken, so he suggested we live in Watford City. As we began apartment hunting, Mat was adamant about none of us giving all of our money to a landlord, so I tried to find the cheapest place for us to live.

12

Watford City

Song Suggestions:
Ry & Frank Wiedemann—Howling (Âme remix)
Nicolas Coronel presents Mestiza Records on FriskyRadio
June-10-2013

The population in Watford City before the boom was less than 2,000. It was one of those small towns with a traffic light, a main street with a few businesses, and that was about it. Watford City is surround by miles of fields with rolling hills, so there is lots of open land, but no place to live. During the boom in 2013, the population surged close to 7,000. People from around the country, and even from overseas, were coming to the area looking for work because doing almost anything in and around petroleum production paid better than most other jobs anyplace else. Hence, there were more people coming to the area than there were places to live.

To capitalize on the burgeoning population, landowners starting building RV parks. People coming to the area that were bringing their own campers to live-in actually had a place to park them other than the Walmart parking lot. Some landowners started mobile home parks, and brought-in manufactured housing such as mobile homes, duplexes, and multiplexes to rent-out. Other investors bought land and campers, put the campers on the land, connected the campers to utilities, and rented-out the campers. Homeowners even let people park their RVs in their yards for a fee.

The place Mat, Dan, and I moved into was homemade. The owner of the field built 26' long, 11' wide, and 8' high stick-built boxes, that he turned into duplexes, so each half was 13'x11'. From a distance they looked like coffins. And just like a cemetery, there wasn't much space between each of the sites. They were insulated, vapor wrapped and sided, and each unit had a window, door, and a built-in combination heater and air conditioning unit. Inside, there was a bunk bed constructed out of 2x4s and plywood, a little sink and mirror, desk that folded down against the wall, chair on castors, refrigerator, 13" flat screen television connected to satellite, kitchen sink, wooden drying rack for dishes, laminated counter top, and a bathroom with a toilet and shower. Each unit had its own water heater, but it was a small water heater, so there was only five minutes of hot water.

The property manager wanted $1,600/month for each half; but, that included the satellite television service and electricity. Each half was only supposed to have two people, but he was sympathetic to veterans, so he let the three of us rent one 13'x11' half. Dan slept on the bottom bunk, I slept on the top bunk, and Mat slept on a futon mattress on the floor. Dan and Mat woke up close to the same time, and got in each other's way as they prepared themselves for work in the morning. I waited until they left before I put myself together for work. Because our living space was soo small, we referred to the place as: "the box."

After a couple weeks, I finally received my first oil field paycheck, $2,183.82. I desperately needed that money because paying the security deposit for the box left me with a little less than $300 in my checking account. While we were doing our on-the-job training, we were getting a lot of overtime, so the checks were a little bigger after that. I did some student loan math when I got my first paycheck. I figured, at the rate I was going, I could comfortably pay-off my debt within nine years. My student loans needed to be paid-back in 10 years; so I'd be paying them off one-year earlier, and I was good with that.

When we hired-in, I didn't know anything about petroleum production, so my focus was just to learn the job. To be able to focus on the job better, I took a leave of absence with school. Taking a leave of absence enabled me to stay enrolled in the program, didn't require me to do any doctoral study work, and I was still able to get in-school deferment on my student loans. After a few weeks of riding around with different guys, learning what we were supposed to do, and learning what we shouldn't do, I was finally beginning to understand what our jobs were.

The job we were doing is sometimes called lease operator; but, most of the people in and around the industry refer to the people that do that job as pumpers. And most pumpers are responsible for several oil wells that are usually grouped into a route. As we were training, we didn't have routes, so we rode around with pumpers who did have routes.

Pumpers' primary responsibilities are to keep the wells producing fluids, look for leaks, and report production. The fluids that are flowing-up the wells that petroleum production companies drill are oil, water, and y-grade gas. As the fluids come to the surface they are all mixed together, so we use surface equipment to separate the gas from the oil and water, and then we separate the oil and water. We sell the gas and oil, and pay to have the water sent to a disposal. They refer to it as water, but it's really a radioactive brine. For the locations that are connected to pipelines, oil and gas go down their respective pipelines to their respective mid-stream facilities for further processing. Pipelined water is sent to a facility to be pumped back underground. Locations that aren't connected to pipelines have their fluids trucked-out.

The good thing about training was that we weren't responsible for the wells on the route; the bad thing was, we didn't have routes. Without routes, we were just extra guys helping out, and they didn't know what to do with us. We were starting to get used to the daily routine, so it was a huge privilege and great relief when our interviewer finally assigned routes to us. My first route partner was a kindly older guy that had a different way of running the route than what I was used to; but it didn't matter, I just wanted to do whatever it took to keep my job.

They were drilling, fracking, and building locations as fast as they could, so there was no shortage of new people, and keeping everyone safe was paramount. Most companies had a safety program where guys filled-out safety cards, and described on the card a safe or unsafe behavior they witnessed at work. Because of the high level of activity, and the strong focus on safety, we had weekly safety meetings.

At one of our safety meetings, I was in Sidney for the meeting. They needed people to read and count the safety cards that workers turned in, so they asked for volunteers at the safety meeting. Normally that was my thing; volunteering, and getting involved with everything. But that was when I was broke. Now that I was actually earning money, it was time for me to start taking care of myself. So when they asked for volunteers, I derisively kept my hand down as I saw other people's hands go up. From all of my past experiences, I knew they were just wasting their time, and that counting those safety cards wasn't going to help them get ahead in their jobs, or in the company. I wasn't looking for something fun to do to waste a lot of time, I just wanted to earn as much money as I could, and I didn't want anything to get in the way of that.

When we started our jobs we had a four-day-on, and three-day-off work schedule. On their days off, Mat and Dan usually drove five hours down to Rapid City. I didn't want to spend the money, and I still had a very negative sentiment toward Rapid City, so I just stayed in the box. The company we worked for had a lot of online training courses we needed to take for professional development and promotion. I really wanted anyone who had any say about my employment to make every excuse possible to keep me around; so on my days off I did their online trainings, even though I wasn't being paid for it. I followed the same routine in the box that I had at Williston State College. I studied in the morning, and in the afternoon I would drink myself silly.

During our time in the box, rents were soo lucrative, investment groups came to the area buying land. On the land they bought, they built apartment developments. I started to see Tyvek wrapped structures, about the size of shipping containers, filling a field that I passed on my way to work. I wasn't sure what they were going to do with the structures until I saw a crane starting to stack the structures to build apartment complexes.

There was only a two-lane road into and out of Watford City, and there was no highway around Watford City. So all of the traffic going to Dickinson or Williston had to go through Watford City. To manage all of the traffic there was one traffic signal, and one red stop light. The road going into and out of the field was also under-developed. It was a hilly two-lane highway, with steep embankments. The speed limit was 65 mph, but trucks usually drove 55 mph at most.

One afternoon, I was headed-in from the field to go back to Watford to complete my production report. Everyone else was finishing their workday too, so there were about nine vehicles caught behind one of those guys going ten below the speed limit, and I was third in the row. After a few miles of bumper to bumper driving, I felt obligated to try to pass the guys in front of me, so I slowly pulled-out into the oncoming lane to start to pass. As I was pulling into the oncoming lane, I noticed a car in my blind spot, and then I saw a cloud of dust as the car started to go off of the road. I pulled back into my lane, and the car continued to pass. I was soo freaked-out about what just happened. As I continued to drive bumper-to-bumper, I imagined an alternate scenario: I could have hit the car, forced them off the road and down the steep embankment, potentially killing a car-full of people. I had just started the job, and I came really close to losing my job, and having a lot more legal and financial problems.

A few more miles down the road, I saw the same car that passed me, but it was pulled-over in a driveway on the side of the highway. The driver was walking around the back of his car as his passenger was getting out of the car. The driver looked like he was expressing shock about our near-wreck as he paused with one hand on his head and one on his hip. I was a little shocked too; I was thinking this is not the job for me, I should not be driving for work. But I was also grateful that nothing happened to either of us. The good thing about the experience is that it made me a little paranoid about moving into the next lane, and I'm a lot better about checking my blind spot to see what's going on around me before I change lanes.

After three months of living in the box, I was happy with the amount of money I was able to save because of my relatively cheap rent, but Mat and Dan were sick of the box. Dan found a two-bed, two-bath apartment in a building North of town that they just finished building. The property manager wanted $2,700 per month, and we had to pay the utilities. Absorbed with the lesson Mat taught me about not paying any more money to a landlord than I had-to, I was surprised Mat was eager to spend soo much more money for rent. I was not at all interested in paying more money for rent than the $533 I was already paying for my share. But around this time, Ed applied to the company we were working for.

Ed was going through the hiring process, and also needed to move to Watford. Mat and Dan pitched to me the idea of Ed moving into that two-bedroom, two-bathroom apartment with us. With Ed moving-in, and splitting the rent and utilities with us, I agreed to move into the apartment and pay $675 for my share of the rent.

Compared to the box, the 1,000 square-foot apartment seemed palatial to me. I couldn't believe how quickly I got used to living in such a small space, and how comfortable I was living with not much stuff. Since it was four of us living in a two-bedroom apartment, two of us slept in one room, and two of us slept in the other room. Mat bought a bunk bed for us, that he split in-two, so he and I could sleep on opposite sides of the room. Ed and Dan had a similar arrangement in their room. Four months into the job, we got a call from our interviewer.

Our contractor jobs were working-out well for us, but our interviewer said there were some company positions open, and that we should apply. We applied, and got hired-on as company men. They ended-up paying us a little more in salary and benefits, so switching from contract designees to company men made it worth it. I had almost no expenses except for rent, food, booze, and my phone. Also, I worked as much as possible, and did not take any vacation. By keeping my expenses low, and working overtime most days, I was able to save most of my money. After five months of work, I had $20,000 in my checking account. Having all of that cash gave me options; I liked having options, but I wasn't used to having money.

I was walking through the Walmart parking lot, and someone was trying to sell a Hummer H3 for $23,000. I really liked the Hummer H3s, and now I was able to buy one if I wanted to. I wasn't even thinking about how much money the gas was going to cost me, or the registration, or the insurance. All I thought about was that I needed a couple more paychecks, and I could buy that Hummer, and still have a nice cushion in my checking account. So I took a photo of the For Sale sign with the guy's phone number on it, did my shopping in the store, and went back to the apartment.

At the apartment, I told Mat I was thinking about buying a Hummer. I told him how much it was, and he told me it was a lot of money. I thought about it for a few seconds, and realized he was right, that was a lot of money. I had to work months to save-up all of that money, and in a minute, it all could have been spent on a vehicle that was just going to sit unused most of the time. Adding insult to injury, it was also going to lose value over time. I was really glad I told him what I was thinking about doing, and grateful that Mat didn't just go along with me and say: "yeah Rich, you should buy that car, you worked hard for it, you deserve it."

Being broke, I always wanted stuff, but never had enough money to buy anything. So once I started earning money, it was really tempting to start buying all of that stuff I could all-of-a-sudden afford. Mat helped me change my mindset, so I started thinking about it like: "Do I really need that?" or, "How often am I going to use that?" or, "Isn't there a less expensive option?" When I changed how I looked at buying things, a lot of the things I wanted to buy just didn't make sense anymore.

The other weird thing about the money we were earning was the mindsets of the people we worked with. Meeting guys on location doing service work, most people talked about their jobs like prison sentences: "I've got 2 to 3 years and I'm done," or "I'm doing 3 to 5 years and I'm out." There was a couple reasons for that. Most people resented being in North Dakota because they were away from their families. And most of those people only wanted to stay up there long enough to pay their debts off, and then go do something else, anywhere else. I never really looked at my job as a prison sentence. I was grateful to be there, because being there gave me all the money I never had, so I could pay for things like school.

November 2013, my leave of absence with Walden was ending. I was reading my doctoral study proposal, and it inspired me. I really wanted to complete the program. I thought having a doctorate would make it easier for me to work my way into a white collar position, doing something I really wanted to do, higher-up in the company. I was earning enough money, and my expenses were low, so I was easily able to afford the tuition for the term to continue my doctoral program. So, I registered for another term, and paid $7,190 up-front for the term.

Shortly after I re-enrolled in school, they changed our work schedule to 7 days on, and 7 days off. Ed and I ended up on the same schedule; so when we worked, Mat and Dan had days off. Ed enjoyed his oil money by flying to the coasts to see his family on his days off. As usual, Mat and Dan went to Rapid City on their days off. I still didn't go anywhere. I liked being in school again, I was happy I was able to afford school, and I enjoyed doing something productive with my time off. However, the not going anywhere part was about to change.

Even though workers were flooding the area, employers were still having a hard time finding enough people to fill their open positions. To help attract people, some employers were offering to pay people to commute to and from work, give them a place to live while they were at work, pay for their meals during their work week, and give them lots of time off. Our company was one of those companies that decided to offer those incentives, and they referred to people who lived someplace else but worked in North Dakota as rotators. I was content just to have a job. But Mat, looking-out for his friends, said we could live in one of his parent's houses in Rapid City, and carpool back and forth. That way we'd all have a better quality of life not having to live in Watford City, and we'd be making more money.

I did the numbers real quick, and I saw myself coming out ahead economically, so I signed-up for the program. Because I still didn't own a car, I paid for my carpool buddy's gas both ways. I figured they were saving me a lot of money because I didn't have to pay a car payment, insurance, maintenance, or registration fees, so, I expressed my appreciation by filling their tank. Since Ed and I were on the same rotation, he was the lucky carpool buddy to get free gas, and I was lucky that he drove a fuel efficient 1991 Ford Taurus.

13

Quincy

Song Suggestions:
Miike Sno—Burial
Grizzly Bear—Two Weeks

When we were accepted into the rotator program, I rented another UHAUL, and loaded it with my stuff. Pam had a room open at Quincy, so I was moving into Quincy, again. When I loaded the UHAUL to move from South Dakota to North Dakota a year earlier, I was fed-up with South Dakota. For 12 years I did everything I could to earn a living wage in Rapid City, but nothing worked for me, so I was relieved to leave. And now, all-of-a-sudden, I was back in Rapid City. It was bittersweet for me; I was resentful of Rapid City, but I was happy that being there put more money in my pocket, and that I was not in the same pitifully poor economic state I was in when I left. I liked seeing Rapid City with a changed perspective, winning at life.

My old boss from Sky Ranch moved into the room I used to live-in at Quincy, the master suite. He was as surprised to see me as I was to see him. I don't remember what we were talking about, but I concluded the conversation saying I didn't care what people thought of me. I told him the only opinion that matters to me is what my boss thinks of me, because my boss signs my checks, and that's what keeps money going into my checking account. My old boss emphatically agreed with me.

Shortly thereafter, we had a discussion about the internet. Initially, Mat was paying for internet at the house. But Mat, like me, was interested in keeping his expenses low. As much as I needed the internet for school, I really didn't want to pay that bill. Since Mat moved out of his mom's house, he understandably said he wasn't going to pay for the internet anymore. That made sense to me; but I only lived at the house half of the month, so I didn't want to pay for the internet either. I told my old boss that if I needed the internet, I would just walk the six blocks to the public library and use their internet, and I encouraged him to do the same. He was disappointed by my response, and decided to pay for the internet at Quincy. Since I wasn't pitching-in for the internet bill, I walked to the library to use the internet there.

It was nice to get out of the house, and the people at the library were interesting. A quarter of the people there were on Facebook most of the time, another-quarter of the people were doing learning activities, the third-quarter of the library people were just there to socialize, and the last-quarter of the people at the library were homeless. Unfortunately, the homeless people sometimes caused problems.

Because of soo much unwanted activity at the library, the library managers hired a private security company to patrol the library. I wasn't intimidated by any of that, I was just there to do my schoolwork. So that is how I spent my days off of work in South Dakota; at Quincy, or at the library on Quincy doing my schoolwork. When it was time for work, Ed and I carpooled back to North Dakota.

I was really happy with what I was earning with my job in North Dakota. The more time I spent with the company, the more money I was making! After we hired-in as company men, they gave us a pay raise, cost of living adjustment in our favor, a profit sharing bonus, they paid me to keep a healthy weight and not smoke, and we had a deal with Verizon so I got a corporate discount on my personal phone! It was amazing! I couldn't believe how good things were going for me; I wasn't used to having good things happen in my life, and I started to think that I shouldn't have such good fortune.

And then, I backed-into a containment dike with my work truck, and twisted the truck bumper a little. At that point, everything stopped, literally. I called my boss, he picked me up, and we left my truck on location so I could get drug tested. My route buddy had to finish the route for me; my driving privilege was suspended pending asset manager review, and I had to complete a five-hour long defensive driving course from the National Safety Council. They did give me my driving privilege back, and all of that drama helped me learn an important lesson. I learned when good things are coming my way I need to humbly accept them; because they are positive consequences of something good I'm doing, and I just need to keep doing what is working.

On our drives down from North Dakota, there are several small towns along the way, and there are a couple different roads you can take. All of those small towns have bars, and Ed and I like to drink, so we went to a different small town bar every week. We went to Club 85 in Fairfield, ND, Borderline Bar in Reder, ND, the Main Bar and Grill in Scranton, ND, Newell Bar in Newell, SD, and we had a beer at the convenience store in Hoover, SD. I drove most of the time, and I was paranoid about getting another DUI, so I only drank one red beer (beer mixed with tomato juice). I liked the red beers because I thought it helped keep the beer smell off my breath, just in-case I got pulled over. I drove Ed's car soo much he let me keep his spare key, and even let me borrow his car while we were on days off in South Dakota.

Ed's car was hideous, but it reminded me that superficial image stuff is nonsense. Ed's 1991 Ford Taurus was mostly driven in Massachusetts, and was a little rusted-out. To prevent the rust from spreading, Ed covered and filled all the rust spots with Bondo body filler. When stuff broke on his car, he always went to the salvage yard first for parts to fix his car, and he usually fixed the car himself, so Ed was good with his money too.

After a year and two weeks in the oil field, even with paying tuition for my doctoral classes, I was still able to save-up $40,000. I wasn't going anywhere, buying, or doing anything, I just worked and did my schoolwork. I usually worked a few hours overtime per week, and I worked all the extra shifts that came available. I hadn't earned much money at all for soo long, I really didn't want to miss-out on any opportunity to earn money while I could, so I still wasn't taking vacation. Relaxing a little in Rapid City on my days off was enough for me; but I was starting to think I needed to do something with my money, so I asked my mother.

My mother told me I needed to invest my money, so I started looking for investments. I wanted something safe, and paid 8% interest, but I couldn't find anything. One of my days off I was at a coffee shop, and thought to look at my student loans.

I went online, logged-in to my accounts, and checked the balances of my student loans. Great Lakes managed four loans for me; I also owed money to ACS, and NELNET. My debts ranged from $18,000 to $45,000 across all six of the lenders. The numbers weren't that big, so my debts seemed manageable, and I didn't even have to make any payments because of my in-school deferment. I wondered how much interest my loans were, so I looked at my account details, and saw my interest rates varied from 2% to 7.9%. Unfortunately I had only one $20,000 loan that was 2% interest.

When I saw that most of my loans had interest rates between 6.9% and 7.9%, I quickly realized the best investment for me was to start paying-down my highest-interest student loans. So May 28, 2014, right there in the coffee shop, I made a $30,000 payment. I didn't want to spend all of my money, just in case they fired me. I wanted to be sure I had enough money to start all-over-again someplace, pay for some hospital bill if I needed to, or hire an attorney to defend me in court for another criminal offence.

I was kinda excited about the big payment I made, so I kept checking my student loan account until the payment posted. A few days later, the payment finally posted. I really liked to see the balances go down so much. And I was soo surprised at how good I felt after I made the payment, I really didn't expect that. I liked the feeling soo much that I wanted to make more payments! But, I needed to keep my $10,000 just-in-case money.

Another surprise I had when I was checking my student loan balances was that the numbers were going up, daily. I didn't realize that they calculated the interest daily, and added-in the interest to the principal daily. After all of that, I still wasn't really sure how much I owed, so I decided to add-it-all-up.

I wanted to write down my student loan balances because it was a lot to keep track of, I didn't want to get confused, and I didn't want to make a mistake. I grabbed a pen, and one of our old business notepads. I checked my accounts, and wrote-down the balances: $28,788.43, $18,133.53, $45,092.80, $44,256.74, $24,601.30, and $18,505.42. Adding it all up, after my $30,000 payment, I still had

$179,378.22 left to pay. That is when I realized I originally had $209,000 student loan debt, and that the government had cut me off at $200,000. So the $9,000 part of my debt was all interest my loan had accrued.

I wanted to make more payments, but I didn't want to make small regular payments. My loan balances were soo large, and I was paying soo much in interest, that small payments would make almost unrecognizable changes to my account balances. I wanted that feeling again that I got when I made the big payment and saw my balances drop, so I elected to only make big payments.

I thought refinancing my loans wouldn't make sense for me, and I really wasn't going to save that much money, because I was going to pay my student loans ahead of schedule. I also didn't have any economic confidence in myself. It was only a year earlier that I had less than $300 in my checking account; I didn't think there was any way I would qualify for the loan. So, I talked myself out of trying to refinance my loans. Also, I was still enrolled in school, and had in-school deferment, so I had the luxury of not making any payments if I didn't want to.

For the next 10 months, all I did was my oil work and schoolwork. I didn't go anywhere, and I tried not to buy anything. Once every-other-month I would buy an album, and that was a big deal for me. I did have Pandora and DI.FM subscriptions, but I'm passionate about music, and I listened to music on one of those platforms most of the day while I worked. After almost two years in the oil field, and by continuing to live frugally, I saved-up a little better than $48,000. So March 2015, I paid an additional $34,000 to Great Lakes for my student loans.

Around the same time, my friend Jedediah was finishing a backpacking trip in Europe, and needed a place to stay. The basement at Quincy was 1,200 square feet, so I told him he could move in with me down there. I slept at one end of the basement, and he slept at the other end. Jedediah was vegan straight-edge; he didn't eat animals or animal byproducts, and he didn't smoke, drink, or do drugs. I was vegetarian and didn't smoke, and I respected that he liked keeping his head clear, so while he was my basementmate I didn't drink at home, and really didn't drink-out much either.

Jedediah didn't have any money, and was looking for work. He found a job at one of those high-end specialty olive oil shops. It was a nice place, and he wanted to look-the-part, so he went to the thrift store to find some clothes to wear to work. He put together some really nice outfits; I was surprised that he found such nice stuff for so little money. He inspired me to start shopping at the thrift stores too.

We were outside in the parking lot at Quincy one evening, and I don't remember what we were talking about, but he finished our conversation with this hardcore look on his face and excitedly said: "that's punk!" I kinda thought he was just kidding around, and didn't think too much about it, until I started seeing and hearing a trend. I saw a beach cruiser for sale at SAMS Club; and nostalgically, I wanted to buy it. I told him about it, and he said: "that's not punk." I thought about it a minute, and thought about the bicycle I was currently riding, and realized he was right. The bicycle I was riding someone had literally thrown down the street, and left it in the middle of the street. I picked it up, saw it as a good bike, fixed-it-up, and started riding it. A decade later I was still riding it. Then I saw Jedediah making his own flat-breads. He learned to make the flatbreads from a woman in a village in Central America when he was backpacking there. Except in the kitchen at Quincy, he was using an olive oil bottle to roll-out the breads. The olive oil bottle looked like a bottle of wine, and I was finally starting to get it. Punk is doing things yourself; from growing or preparing your own food, to finding new uses for old things, and making the most out of the little that you have.

Jedediah has been through Central America, South America, and most of Europe hiking, hitch-hiking, ridesharing, camping, couch surfing, and farming as he went. On all of his travels he had very little money, like $1,000 or less. His largest expense was air fare, but he always took the greyhound bus to the biggest city where he could get the least expensive flight out of the country.

I really appreciated Jedediah's youthful exuberance. One day we were baking bread by hand, and we were waiting for the dough to rise, so we kicked a soccer ball around the city, in the rain. Another day we rode our bicycles to the bakery, picked up a loaf of sourdough bread, and went to the olive oil shop where he worked.

The shop was closed, and he had a key, so we hung out in the back of the olive oil shop for a while. He had a few sample bottles that were nearly empty, so we turned the bottles upside down for a few minutes, and poured what was left of the olive oils onto a plate, dipping our bread into the olive oils to finish-off the little sample bottles. Full on calorically dense bread and olive oil, we rode down the road to the school of mines.

Somebody left a soccer ball in the open-air stadium; so we kicked the ball back and forth, and then we created our own little soccer game taking turns being goalie. It was soo much fun! Even though we were both in pretty good shape, our quadriceps burned the next day.

At the end of the day Easter Sunday, Jedediah and I were riding our bicycles in an alleyway downtown. All of a sudden, I noticed I was riding by myself, so I stopped and looked back. I saw Jedediah open the lid of dumpster, reach inside to grab something, and then he took a bite out of it and started chewing! I tried not be judgmental; but I thought it was a little weird, we weren't that broke. Then he called me over to see what he was eating. A supportive friend, I walked my bike over to see what was he was soo excited about.

Inside an open garbage bag in the dumpster, behind a bakery, were big full loaves of bread in the shapes of bunny rabbits! There was no dirt on them or anything, they were perfectly clean loaves of bread. It was soo cool! We both had backpacks, so we each put a couple loaves of the bunny rabbit breads in our backpacks, and laughed with elation as we rode away. I was still a little uneasy about eating food out of a dumpster; so I cut the crusts off of the breads, and joked with Jedediah that I skinned the rabbits. The rabbits were delicious dipped in my blend of olive oil, balsamic vinegar, garlic powder, Italian seasoning, and cayenne pepper.

Although I quit drinking at Quincy, Mike still liked to party at Quincy. It made sense, the safest place to party is at home, but it made Jedediah uncomfortable. And because Jedediah was uncomfortable, Mike was uncomfortable, and that put me in an awkward position. Recognizing the contentiousness, Jedediah started calling some of his old friends. After a few calls, he found a guy that had a basement to rent, so he moved into his own basement apartment a short bicycle ride away. Because Mike and I were still cool, I stayed in the basement at Quincy.

Jedediah, like me, is a glutton for punishment. He regularly puts himself in very uncomfortable positions that are physically, mentally, or emotionally challenging. We don't do it intentionally; it just turns out that way, but the struggle is really important. We need the suffering to learn from, and grow from it, like lifting weights in the gym or studying. It's all a lot of suffering, but after it, we're stronger and smarter. Inspired by Jedediah, I re-learned to do things on my own, and that doing things myself was almost always better than buying something prepared or paying someone to do it for me. Jedediah helped me re-develop my self-reliance, and have a lot more fun by cooking my own food, biking around the city, buying used stuff, and not drinking while having fun. I had a lot of great experiences hanging around with Jedediah and not drinking; but when he moved out, I joined a wine club, because I enjoy that too.

With a renewed spirit of empowerment, I finally had the courage to try to refinance my student loans. I received solicitations from a couple banks that offered to refinance my student loans. I applied to both, and both banks rejected me. Frustrated, and now determined, I started looking online. I saw a company that piqued my interest, SoFi. I started to consider SoFi, but felt a little uneasy about it because I didn't know anything about them. The next day I received a letter in the mail from SoFi, and that legitimized them to me, so I applied to the company to refinance my student loans right away. After a few weeks of my loan officers asking for documents, and me sending the documents they wanted, my loan was finally approved. They funded $108,896.81 on 11/23/2015, and all of my Great Lakes loans were paid-off.

I had the option to get a fixed rate loan, or a variable interest rate loan. In my High School business classes I heard horror stories of people who went with variable interest rate loans, so I knew it was a bad idea. At the time though, we were still recovering from the Great Recession. Interest rates were not increasing, and consumer confidence didn't seem that great. So I didn't think it was that risky to get a variable interest rate loan. I wanted to save money, and the variable rate was one-quarter percent lower than the fixed rate, so I thought I was going to come out way ahead by going with the variable rate.

As soon as my loan was funded, my interest rate on my variable rate loan increased. That's when I also learned that my interest rate wasn't calculated based on our domestic Federal Reserve rates, it was calculated based off of the London Inter-Bank Offer Rate (LIBOR).

I became angry about the situation. I was upset that I overlooked that my rate was based off of LIBOR, and that I had chosen the variable rate. But instead of raising hell with the bank or trying to refinance my loan again, I used that negative energy to motivate me.

I still didn't have a good understanding of interest, or how it was calculated, so I started tracking my account balance every day. I just did the simple math of subtracting yesterday's balance from today's balance. I found I was paying $11.03 in interest per day. I became obsessed with reducing how much interest I was paying every day. I had been saving-up my money most of the year, preparing my account for my annual $30,000 student loan payment, but I was soo frustrated about my poor loan choice, I paid $8,897 right away. When I subtracted my daily loan balances again, I was happy to see the daily interest I was paying dropped to $9.52 per day.

After my $8,897 student loan payment, I had about $20,000 left in my checking account. I was starting to think I wanted to make $20,000 my new safe amount for my checking account. Oil prices were falling, my company was getting rid of people left and right, and who knew when I would be the next to go.

I had my mother's house in Michigan as my permanent address, and my billing address, so my mother received letters from my student loan lenders. Because I was in another state, my mother opened the letters, and let me know what the letters were about. Most of my lenders really didn't send anything to my mother's house because I setup all of my accounts so I could do everything online. ACS on the other hand, still sent account balance letters to my mother's house monthly. Even though I was doing good with my student loan payments, the letters made her nervous, and she was tired of seeing the letters.

My mother is a retired woman on social security. She is good at keeping her expenses low, so that she can keep most of the money she earns in retirement. It took her a couple years to save up the money, but she had the money to payoff ACS, and she really wanted to do that for me.

I owed ACS almost $20,000. I had the money to pay it off, and my mother had the money to pay it off, but that is all the cash we had. If I paid it off, I wouldn't have any money left. If my mother paid it off, she was only going to have $4,000 to spare. We didn't want either one of us to get any of our accounts too low, but we decided I would keep the cash I had. So if something happened on my side, I would have the money to pay for it, and if my mother needed money, then I would send her whatever she needed. After we discussed it, my mother mailed me a check. I deposited it to my account, and then I made a $19,895.23 payment to ACS. I was really grateful for that; she helped me speed-up my student loans repayments. So now all I had left to pay was my SoFi account and NELNET. SoFi was a little over $100,000, and NELNET was close to $24,000.

New Years Eve 2015, I was in the library as usual. The computer keyboard of the only available workstation had a broken foot, so I couldn't put the keyboard at a good angle to type. I looked for stuff around me to prop-up the keyboard, but nothing was quite right. I had just used my library card to log-into the computer, so I had my wallet out. I put my wallet under the keyboard, and it was perfect! I briefly thought that I shouldn't use my wallet because I might forget it; but my arrogance won, and I told myself I wouldn't forget it. So, I left it there, and continued my work.

There was a lot of activity around me because it was New Years Eve, and the library was closing early, so the librarians were scurrying around the library trying to get their work done. As it got closer to 4:00 p.m., I watched as the librarians passed by me because I was waiting for someone to tell me to shut down my computer and leave. Finally, I was the last one at the computers, and I couldn't stay any longer. I packed my stuff into my backpack, and drug my feet to the door. As soon as I left, a librarian locked the door behind me.

It was too early to go home, and I didn't know what to do. Before I went anywhere, I called Jedediah. He just finished work with the forest service, and said we should hang out. I told him I'd pick him up because he rode his bicycle to work, and Mat was letting me use his truck again. I loved the olive oil shop experience I had with Jedediah, and told him I would buy some bread and olive oil for us. That was when I realized I left my wallet under the computer keyboard. So I hung-up the phone with Jedediah, and tried to get back into the library.

I stood at the door with my hands around my face to look through the glass door into the building, and there was one guy standing, looking down at something on the desk. I knocked on the glass doors, but the guy couldn't hear me, and just walked away. I walked around to the side of the building, hoping I could catch someone leaving the building. There, I saw a lady standing outside of her minivan with books. I asked her if she worked there, but she said she was just dropping-off books that she borrowed. Then I walked around to the other side of the building looking through the windows as I went, and I couldn't see anyone else in the building.

I kept a few hundred dollars in my wallet, just in case the vehicle I was in broke-down during my commute between the Dakotas, and thought the cleaning crew would probably pick-up my wallet. The library was closed New Years Day too, so I had to wait until the day after that to try and get my wallet back. Frustrated, I got into Mat's truck, went to pick-up Jedediah, and told him what happened. He said he would buy bread and olive oil for us, and while we were driving, some other friends he knew were calling him and asking him what he was doing.

We ended up having a little vegan-straight edge potluck New Years Eve party at Jedediah's apartment, and watched a few independent short films (indie shorts). Around 10 p.m. I started falling asleep watching the videos, so I just went home and went to sleep. I was happy to get out of bed in the morning, sober, and not hungover, but I still had an unproductive day because I was mostly worrying about my wallet.

The following day, I wanted to get to the library before it opened, so I could be the first person in the door. I was 10 minutes early, and there were already a few other people standing outside the door, waiting to get in. I was getting nervous that they were going to get into the library before me. Making the situation even more uncomfortable for me, a couple people were smoking, and the wind was going my direction. I quit smoking when we hired-in as company men, so I hated breathing their smoke, but I had a decent position at the doors. Getting into the library before anyone else was more important to me at the time, so I had to suffer a few minutes. When the library finally opened, I wanted to go to the front desk and have them check their lost and found, but the people that got to the library before me were already going to the front desk. Since that plan was foiled, I thought I would go back to where I was sitting, on the off-chance that a day-and-a half later my wallet would still be there.

As I walked toward the computers, I looked around, and saw the floor still had ripped pieces of paper on it. When I approached my workstation, the keyboard looked the same as I left it, and really stood-out compared to the four other keyboards in my row of computers. I thought someone probably picked-up my wallet, and left something else under the keyboard. But, the table still had eraser rubbings on it. It looked like nobody had been in the place since we left, not even the cleaning crew. When I picked up the keyboard, my wallet was still there! I checked my wallet, and all of my credit cards and cash were there too! I couldn't believe it! Grateful to God, I put my wallet in my pocket, and reflected in astonishment for a few minutes about the whole experience. Then, I reflected about my time in the doctoral study program.

I liked going to school because I always had something to do on my days off. Also, school helped me keep my mind active, in a good way. But after a year and a half, I was in the selfsame spot. My doctoral study proposal was complete, and my committee members had no intention of approving my proposal so I could conduct my research to complete my doctoral study. Considering all of that, January 2016, I dropped-out of the doctoral study program.

The term was about to start, I was downtown at the public library using their internet, and I called my committee chairperson to let him know I was dropping out of the program. He called me back a few minutes later, and told me I had a good book, and that he would like to do a co-authorship with me. Immediately I was flattered by his compliment and suggestion. I thought: "Really? Co-authorship with me? Wow!" And then I remembered that three weeks earlier I submitted my proposal to him, and it wasn't good enough for him. But now, I had a good book, and he wanted to work with me? Nothing changed with my proposal; it didn't make sense, so I did not take him up on his offer. I was making the right decisions, but dropping out of the doctoral program messed with my head a little.

I committed six years of my life to that program, and all of a sudden it was over, it was like a divorce. I felt really bad about it. I looked at myself as the problem, and kept thinking what I could have, or should have done different. Eventually, instead of feeling bad about it all, I just felt bitterness and resentment toward the University, which was actually consoling for me. Also, I needed something to fill my time, so I started looking at everything that was offered in my local community.

Now that I had time to myself during my days off of work, I wanted to enjoy it a little bit. I did yoga at a local studio, and I joined a private club that overlooked the city. I also liked getting dressed-up, walking around downtown, and exploring the local restaurants. After dinner, I went up to my private club, had a few drinks, and looked at the city lights. When I wasn't in the mood to dress-up, I took-out my long board, rode to the closest bar or casino, and went bar hopping and casino-hopping the rest of the night. If I was going to bars on the outskirts of the city, then I'd ride my mountain bike instead.

After having fun on my days off for a few months, it was the first day of the golf season Spring 2016. I went to the golf course with Mat and his girlfriend, and Melanie and her boyfriend. I just bought a cooler full of beer, 18 holes, and rented the golf cart for the day. I was a little uneasy going out there for the day, and my first drive out of the tee box sliced deep into the rough. I drove out to where my ball went off of the course, gave the area a quick glance, and decided not to look for it. I drove up to Mat's cart, told him I needed to leave, and said I was going to look for a job. He said okay, and handed me the keys to his truck.

I called-up Wellspring again. They changed their name to WellFully, but I still left a message to setup an interview. I also went to the library and completed an application for another residential treatment facility, the Black Hills Children's Home. I wasn't sure who was going to hire me, so I kept applying for work. Learning from my shaggy hair appearance and ripped-pants experience at my oil field interview; I reminded myself that they are either going to make an excuse to hire me, or they are going to make an excuse to not hire me.

I found a couple more jobs working for the city at the Civic Center, so when I applied to those, I chose not to take those applications too seriously either. Normally when I filled-out an application, I made sure that every line was filled, every question was answered, and I always double-checked my work. When I did all of that, nobody ever hired me. So instead of filling out the applications completely, I just put-in the bare minimum information, and some of the information was even on the wrong lines.

After making my calls and submitting my applications, I needed to get back to the golf course. On my way back, Mat called me, and asked me to pick-up lunch. I was grateful that he let me use his truck. So, buying lunch for everyone, and delivering it to them on the golf course wasn't a big deal for me. By the time I got there, they were just finishing-up their game, so I hung out for a few minutes, and was happy to be our designated driver home.

Around this same time, Mat asked me if I was interested to move into the basement at Woodridge. Woodridge is a nicer part of town than Quincy. The Woodridge area has great views of the city, is quieter, and the air is cleaner. So when he offered me a place to live in Woodridge, I gladly took it!

14
Woodridge

Song Suggestions:
Jaded—Made in China
Descendents—Catalina

Mat was living upstairs, and Mat likes the convenience of having the internet at home, so Mat paid for internet service. Mat also paid for Netflix and Hulu subscriptions. A good friend, Mat let me use his internet connection and Netflix and HULU accounts, so that was another treat for me. At the time, we were on the same shift, so we could carpool together back and forth to North Dakota. But because we're not boss, and we just do what they tell us, Mat had to switch shifts. Mat's boss had a spot he needed filled on another route on the opposite rotation in Dickinson, so Mat switched shifts, and I was out of people to carpool with.

After eight years of not owning a car, I exhausted all of my options, and needed to buy a car to commute back and forth between the Dakotas. I'm not a craigslist person; but it doesn't hurt to look, so I looked to see what was available on craigslist. I wanted something fuel efficient, that was in decent shape, and cost less than $5,000. I really didn't think they were going to have anything good, or that the seller was even going to be legitimate. I was surprised to see a couple cars from a couple sellers that seemed to meet my needs. One of the cars was a 2001 Mitsubishi Eclipse GT. I missed the Eclipse I had, couldn't afford the GT when I bought my GS, so I thought of it as a great opportunity. Another guy was selling a 2004 Volkswagen (VW) Jetta. The Jetta photos didn't look honest. He didn't have photos of the whole car, and he had Harley Davidson floor mats in the car. I was really skeptical, but I still wanted to see the car. I made appointments to test drive the cars with both of the sellers back-to-back in the same evening. I had my mind set, that one way or another, I was buying a car on that test-drive night.

I asked Ed to drive me down to Dickinson; he hung-out with me for the first test drive, but then he had to go. My first test-drive, the Eclipse, was a disappointment because the car didn't sound or feel right. But, I wasn't too concerned about it, I still had the VW to test drive. Ed dropped me off at the mall, and then he drove back to Watford City. I was a little nervous at that point, because my ride back to Watford City left, and I had to work the next day. I put myself in a bad position; so, I was very motivated to buy a car that night. Worst case scenario I could pay for a taxi back to Watford City, but I really didn't want to go that route, because that wasn't going to solve my commuter car problem.

The VW seller told me right away he didn't know anything about the car. He told me he just bought cars at auctions, did minor repairs, and sold the cars. I appreciated his honesty, and that put me at ease with him. As I was test-driving the car, I liked the way the car sounded and felt, so I negotiated a price with him. He wanted $3,700, and I wanted to pay $3,500, so we settled at $3,600. He told me he didn't have the title yet, and I said I didn't have cash or a money order. We were both a little uneasy about doing business with each other, but I wrote him a personal check, and he handed me the key. I was trusting him that he was going to get the title, and he was trusting me that I had money in my checking account. When I got to Watford City, I noticed I took a huge risk because the license plate didn't even have a registration sticker on it. Thankful I made it home safe without getting pulled over, I kept the car in my garage, and I didn't drive it anymore.

A few days later, my VW seller called me. I was relieved to receive a call from him, and I didn't mention anything about the registration sticker. On the phone, he told me he had the title, and he said he called my credit union to do a verification of funds for my check. Everything was good, so we decided to meet at a gas station halfway between Dickinson and Watford City.

As I was driving the car to the gas station, the car seemed to drive well, but I noticed the check engine light suddenly came on. Nothing changed with the car, it still sounded good and felt good, so I wasn't concerned about it. It's an old car, something is always breaking or wearing-out. Putting any money into it only buys a little time until something else wears out, makes the amber light turn on, and needs more money to fix. I saw a good YouTube video by a mechanic about dashboard warning lights for old cars. He said to treat the warning lights like traffic signals; amber means keep going with caution, red means stop because it's not safe to drive. As long as the thing started, stopped, and ran okay, I didn't care what sensor or cosmetic thing was broken on it. I was not interested in putting any more money into the car than I needed to; I learned that lesson when I had my Tracker.

When we met at the gas station, he handed me the title, and I gave him back his Harley Davidson floor mats. I was disappointed to see he was hiding a hole in the floorboard under the brake pedal, but that didn't bother me much, mostly because the hole didn't go all the way through the car. I didn't say anything about the hole in the floor either, I was just happy to have a halfway decent car at a halfway decent price. I made it back to Watford City without getting pulled-over, again, and registered and insured the car the next day.

I hate paying for insurance, so I shopped around to get the best deal I could for my insurance. I wanted to work with a company that gave me cheap insurance, and was easy to work with. I found a few companies online, but I was having a difficult time getting my car insured. Frustrated, I thought about working with USAA because I'm a veteran. Ed worked with USAA, and loved working with them. Everyone I knew that worked with USAA loved working with them. So, I created an account, and called them.

I really wasn't expecting to get a good deal. After a brief discussion with my USAA insurance agent, he found some cheap insurance for me that I could automatically pay with my credit card. Since I was able to pay my insurance premium in-full, I bought six months of insurance, and received a little discount for paying my insurance in-full. After my discount, I was only paying $24 per month for my automobile insurance.

I felt good that I finally legally possessed the car. As long as the car lasted five months, I would be able to recoup all of the money I spent to buy the car, register, insure, and fuel-it. Really, if the car lasted long enough for me to get my money back that I spent on it, I would have been happy to start the process all over again. And if the car survived beyond that, I considered I was making a profit from driving the car on my commute. Since my company was paying me to drive back and forth from North Dakota to South Dakota, and my car was fuel efficient, I actually did start making money on my commutes.

On one of my commute days that I was driving to South Dakota my bladder was full, and I needed gas, so I stopped at a gas station in Belfield. While the car was filling-up, I went inside to use the restroom. The single occupancy men's room was busy, and the single occupancy women's room was not in-use. There was a hand-written sign on the women's restroom door that said women only. I waited for a few minutes, but the guy wasn't coming out of the men's room. The women's room still wasn't occupied, and I didn't see any women walking toward it, so I decided I was going to use it.

I closed the door, locked it behind me, and before I could even start using it, someone was pounding on the door and yelling at me through the door. I was really confused, and a little scared to leave the room. I didn't hear any other commotion outside the door, so I opened the bathroom door to see what was going on. Immediately, this old man, apparently the owner of the gas station, started yelling at me for trying to use the women's room. He said he just spent thousands of dollars remodeling the bathroom, because guys had ruined it by peeing all over the floor.

I am a very conscientious bathroom user. I always make sure I leave the bathroom clean, because I don't want the person that uses it after me to think it was me that dribbled on the floor or seat. I've often cleaned-up other people's messes, and this guy was yelling at me like he was fighting for women's liberation.

I told him I was a paying customer, but it didn't matter to him. So I left him to keep protecting his women's room, and went across the street to peacefully use the men's room over there. I even bought a bunch of snacks that I wasn't interested in buying at the convenience store across the street, just to spite the old man. I never returned to the old man's gas station, and refuse to return to his gas station. Not because he's using his women's room to advocate for women's rights, but because of the way he treated me.

After that set of days off, I was preparing to drive back to North Dakota, and I had my car parked at the top of the driveway at Woodridge. The Woodridge area is a hilly residential community, so the house sits on-top of a leveled-out part of a hill, and the driveway goes up the hill to a landing at the house. I was loading the car with my stuff, had music playing in the car, and I had the car running so I wouldn't drain my battery. Because my car is a manual transmission, I couldn't leave the car in gear, so I just had the parking brake set.

Dennis came over for something and said: "You're not going to destroy this car too, are you?" I assured him my car destroying days were over; he did what he needed to do, and left. A few minutes later, I had a couple more things to load into the car. I was walking in the basement, about to go outside, and noticed I couldn't hear my music anymore. I figured Dennis turned the volume down on the radio; it's a nice neighborhood, he probably didn't want to upset the neighbors. But as I stepped outside, I didn't even see my car. This time I thought Dennis was messing with me, and drove my car over to his house. But as I looked up the hill to his house, I didn't see my car in his driveway. I turned my head, looked down the driveway, and saw my car sitting on the edge of the hill. The back tires hopped the curb, and the front tires were still in the street. I couldn't believe Dennis was right, I was going to destroy this car too.

I looked down the steep hill behind my car, saw a house, and imagined what would have happened if my car would have kept going down the hill and hit the house. I pictured the rear of my car busted through the side of the house, a hole in the house around my car, and broken boards, glass, and siding around my car. There would have been a lot of damage to the house, and I wasn't sure I had enough insurance to cover all of the damage.

Before Dennis could see my screw-up, I quickly got in the car, and drove it back up the hill to the top of the driveway. This time I set the brake, turned off the car, put it in gear, and finished loading the car. Knowing my car's limitations, I was a little more careful thereafter.

Even with my incomplete, and improperly filled-in applications, I was starting to get call-backs. First WellFully called me, and a week later, the Black Hills Children's Home (Children's Home) called me. I wasn't sure who was actually going to hire me, so I started going through the hiring process at both places. While I was doing that, someone from the city called me to be a banquet server. Again, I wasn't sure which job was going to work-out, so I took that job too. A week later than that, I got another call to be a stage hand. The stage hand job was the one I wanted most because it paid $15/hr; the problem with that job was that they didn't have enough work for every day, it was just a couple times a month, but I still took that job. So I went from one job, to five jobs, in about three weeks.

Now I had the problem of figuring out how I was going to manage all of my schedules. I decided to give priority to WellFully because they were the least flexible in scheduling; they did their scheduling early in the week, and they needed the most help. When they put me into all of the open spots they had, I called the Children's Home, and told them what days or nights I was able to work. And if I still had some openings I would call the Civic Center and see if they had any events I could work. One time I actually worked a shift at each place, and ended-up working 24 hours.

When I worked 24 hours, I worked the night shift at the Children's Home, a morning shift at WellFully, then I worked at the Civic Center frying food all afternoon. It was really tiresome, but I loved it! I loved riding my bicycle back-and-forth between jobs, staying productive, and making progress toward my goals.

The only day I had off was Tuesday, every other week. That was my commute day from Rapid City back to North Dakota. I always looked forward to that day so I could just sit in my car for five hours and do nothing.

It was tough working all of those jobs, but I knew I was doing everything I could to earn as much money as I could. And I hated just sitting around in my basement. If I ever found myself at home, doing nothing, I felt like I wasn't doing my job, which was working to pay my student loans off.

I had a nice little routine that helped keep me going, and gave me something to look forward to. When I finished work for the day, usually around 11 p.m., I stopped at the convenience store on my way home and bought a bag of chips. Then when I got home, I would pop open a bottle of wine, and watch a couple episodes of Broad City and Mr. Pickles before I went to sleep. I was still working my five jobs, I would just drink a bottle of wine on occasion.

One day, I was talking to Melanie about my five jobs. She said I could pay-off my debt a lot sooner if I lived off of my incomes from my part-time jobs, and used all of my North Dakota money to pay toward my student loans. I hadn't really thought about it before she suggested it. I liked the experience of choosing, buying, and drinking a case of red wine blends every month; but I also liked the idea of using all of the income from my highest paying job to pay my debts a little sooner. What she said got burned into my brain, and before I was even consciously considering it, I was already working toward it.

I didn't know how much money my lifestyle was costing me; so I started keeping written logs of how much money I was spending every month, and what I was spending my money on. I grouped my regular expenses into: phone and internet services, booze, food, miscellaneous one-time expenses, and gas for my car. My monthly bills were already low, but when I had an understanding of where my money was going, then I was able to start setting budget goals for myself in each of those expense groups.

My goal was to get all of my living expenses down to $800/month. I planned to pay $350/month for rent and $450/month for other regular expenses. The regular expenses I budgeted for were phone and internet services, $125/month, $50/month for booze, $100/month for food, $25/month for miscellaneous one-time expenses like an oil change, and $150/month for gasoline. By being really strict on myself with all of my expenses, I figured I could use all of my oil field earnings to pay $5,000 per month toward my student loans.

Naturally, as I was tracking my expenses every month, I wanted to try to make the amounts I was spending on my bills even lower. I checked the Verizon website, and tried to find a less expensive plan. I didn't even know it was possible, but by making a quick call to Verizon, I was able to cut my cell-phone bill in half. And thanks to what I learned from Jedediah, I started buying rice, beans, and olive oil in bulk again, and only ate meals that I prepared myself.

Every break I had during my pumper job I pulled-out my monthly expense-log and analyzed it. I was always looking for every opportunity to spend less money on everything. And of course, when I saw an opportunity to spend less, I would set new a new goal for myself.

I reflected on how much money I spent on food, how I felt, and tried spending less money on food. I didn't quit drinking; but I did quit the wine club. Instead of spending $150 per month on wine and snacks, I started buying tall-boys of beer from the gas station when I bought my bag of chips, and began spending less than $40 per month on my snacks and drinks. Thanks to Melanie's advice and my intensity, I was finally able to live off of the little money I was earning from my four part-time jobs. I had all of my monthly expenses down to really low amounts, and used all of my earnings from my North Dakota job to make bi-monthly payments toward my student loans.

It became an obsession for me; constantly trying to spend less money, and earn more money. As I set and met my goals, I used that satisfaction from my achievements to sustain my drive to continue to work toward my goals. I loved the feeling of achieving my earning and paying goals, but I was soo surprised how exhausting it was to spend less money. The deprivation I was putting myself through was tough mentally, because I wouldn't allow myself to buy treats or snacks. The deprivation was also tough physically because I craved those treats and snacks.

Some months were better earning and spending months than others. I usually earned a little more than $1,000 per month from my part-time jobs. Strategically working as much as I could at the highest paying jobs; the most money I earned in a month with my part part-time jobs was a little over $1,250 dollars. My best month where I deprived myself the most I spent a little under $616 on rent and my other regular expenses.

Like me, the company I worked for in North Dakota was also continuously looking for ways to spend less money. So, they decided to get rid of the rotator program that generously paid for my apartment in North Dakota, gave me a stipend for my meals while I worked, and mileage compensation for my travel to work in North Dakota from my basement in South Dakota. My company said I could still keep my job, but I would have to live in North Dakota full-time.

The whole reason I joined the rotator program was for the cash incentives, so when they took the incentives away, I had no reason to continue to drive back and forth to South Dakota. Even though I was in a great routine, and all of my jobs were helping me make amazing progress on paying down my student loan debt, it made the most sense to me to quit all of my part time jobs, and move to North Dakota. As all of that was going on, I got a call from my niece.

15

Vermont

Song Suggestions:
Rationale—Deliverance
Jbre x Dougie Kent—Stimulation feat. SaneBeats &
Margret Kramer

After working almost every day for a year, I was making really good progress paying my student loan debt, and then my niece called me Spring 2017. She told me my sister Sue was dead, and she was going to spread her ashes at Warren Falls, a place my sister loved to spend her time. My sister was in Florida when she died. She had just finished a medical appointment, was crossing a busy road to get to her car, and was hit by someone driving a car.

Ironically, decades earlier, my sister Sue accidentally killed a person with *her* car. The man my sister hit with her car had mental and physical handicaps. As if it were a penitential duty, my sister dedicated the rest of her life to helping people with mental and physical disabilities. To help her do this, she earned a Master degree in specialized education, taught in special education schools, advocated for children and adults with disabilities, and even adopted a boy with autism. But, she liked to party too.

I hadn't seen my sister in a few years. When I saw photos of Sue; she looked rough, and it wasn't because of the accident. She wasn't taking good care of herself, and I could see it in the deep lines in her face. I looked at a photo of myself I had recently taken, saw the lines at the corners of my eyes and thought, "I need to take better care of myself." So, my sister's horrific experiences inspired me to start taking a little better care of myself a little more often, because I don't want to look old, and I don't want to get sick.

I flew to Vermont to reconnect with my sister Sue's common law husband and my niece. I say common law husband because they were committed to each other for decades, and raised two children together, but they never married each other. When I flew-in this time, it was a lot like the first time I flew-in. They knew when I was arriving and leaving, but I wasn't sure anyone was going to greet me at the airport.

As I walked through the airport on my way to baggage claim and ground transportation, I looked for any familiar faces at all. I started walking around a little in the arrivals area, but did not see anyone looking for me there either. I thought maybe they were running late, or trying to surprise me. But after a few minutes of standing and looking around, nobody showed up. I really didn't want to force the issue, so I rented a car.

I looked at the Enterprise counter, and was disappointed to see it was busy. I really didn't feel like waiting at Enterprise so I started to explore my options. Nobody was at Hertz, but I definitely wasn't going to go with Hertz. I looked at the next counter over and saw another brand I had never tried, but always wanted to, so I saw this as a great opportunity to do that. I rented my car from the budget brand, that was comparable to anything I'd get at Enterprise, and I was on my way. One thing that was nagging me, that I wanted to take care of, was getting into Canada.

I kept on hearing that Canada wasn't letting people into their country with DUIs. I have a couple DUIs, and really didn't like the idea that Canada would reject me if at some point I decided I wanted to go back, so I wanted to make amends with Canada. Everything I saw at the Canada Border Services Agency website was vague about what I needed to do clear my name with Canada, and most of the pages online directed me to speak with someone at the border. Watford City is two hours from the border, and I dreaded the idea of a four hour trip just to talk to a border agent for a few minutes, so I never made time for the trip. Here in Vermont, I was only 45 minutes from the border, so I thought this was the perfect opportunity to speak with someone at the border. With that idea in mind, I headed-out on Interstate 89 North.

While I was driving to the border, I was starting to get a little anxiety about what I was trying to do. I didn't know what they were going to say, was thinking the worst, and started to think they might just ban me forever. When I arrived at the border, I told the border agent that I didn't want to go to Canada yet; I just wanted to learn what I needed to do now, to be allowed to go into Canada in the future for short tourist visits. The border agent took my passport, put a form in it, and told me to drive around and park. I stepped inside the dimly lit building; the atrium was cold and uninviting, and the vaulted-ceiling-room almost seemed vacant. In the middle of the large understaffed work area, there were two guys sitting at computers that didn't bother to look away from their terminals as I approached the empty counter. I saw another guy in a dark blue uniform hurriedly walking from one side of the building to the other. Everyone was ignoring me, so I was a little confused about what I was supposed to do, and was getting concerned about where my passport ended-up. I nervously stood behind the line painted on the floor in front of the counter, and tried to wait patiently.

The guy walking around finally stopped, asked me what I wanted, and told me to sit in the area near the door where I walked-in. I went and sat a few seats from the door. As I waited, a few more border agents came in from outside with a tall elderly man in the middle of them. They only walked-in a few feet, stopped, and stood near the door. The border agents seemed frustrated as they each took turns exchanging responses with the old man, and the old man appeared to be confused. The situation didn't look good. I wasn't really sure what was going on because they were talking in some other language. After standing there and talking for a few minutes, they all walked together outside, got into the back of an ambulance, and the driver casually drove away.

The whole situation wasn't helping my anxiety at all. I was really starting to regret my "go to Canada and make amends" idea, and began thinking about just getting up and leaving. But they had my passport, and I really needed that f-ing thing. As I was about to start panicking about my situation, finally, the guy who told me to go sit down called me to the counter.

He leisurely said to me that my record wasn't that bad, but because of my two DUIs, he wouldn't allow me into Canada. He told me since my convictions were soo old, I should just talk to an attorney to get my criminal record expunged. He kept my passport and paperwork, and told me he would give it to me on the other side when I continued to drive around the building to get back into America.

He assured me the paperwork made it look like I didn't even go to Canada. A little relieved, I thanked him, and walked out to my car. As I drove around the building, I looked for the man, and saw him standing on the sidewalk with my passport and paperwork. I rolled-down my window, he handed me my passport and paperwork, and told me to drive around to talk to the American border agents. That was a little more complicated of a scenario than what I was used to from the several other times I had driven back into the United States, but I went along with it.

When I drove to the American side of the building, there were two huge vehicle doors near the building entrance. I didn't want to park in front of the doors in case they were for emergency services vehicles, so I drove past them to the closest non-handicapped parking spots I could find. I parked, and slowly walked to the entrance.

Two American border agents stood at the desk behind one computer as I walked-in. There was only like two feet separating the door and the front desk and two more feet behind the front desk and the back wall. When I walked-in, I handed one of the guys my passport and paperwork. He quickly glanced at my paperwork and exclaimed: "Rejected!?" with a shocked and questioning tone. I was a little surprised by that too, and shrugged my shoulders as I considered how the Canadian border agent deceived me. The guy with my passport did a little data entry on his computer, and the other guy walked over to the only other computer that was at the desk. There was nothing but an empty white wall behind these guys, and a single glass door to their left side. After a couple minutes, the guy with my passport mumbled something to the other guy, and the other guy started approaching the guy with my passport, still muttering exchanges between each other.

The guy with my passport started asking me about my criminal convictions. I was thinking to myself: "oh my f-ing god dude, why does it seem like I'm back in court for this stuff." I told him about all my adult convictions, and when I said that was all, he shook his

189

head sided-to-side and said with a calm, but arrogantly questioning tone: "stealing?" I shook my head side-to-side and responded to his one-word question with a one-word answer: "nope." He didn't seem to approve of my response, and started muttering to the other guy like "this guy just lied to me, what are we going to do with him?" The other guy seemed a little less concerned about the situation.

Defeated, and a little annoyed, the guy with my passport handed it back to me. I reflected about my response to his stealing question, and thought my stealing conviction wasn't anything I needed to mention because I was a juvenile. Apparently everything matters federally, but it was weird that he didn't say anything directly to me about it. As I walked-out, I was confused, but I was happy to have my passport back.

When I drove away, I was thinking about what the Canadian border agent told me. I kinda liked the idea of trying to expunge my record, and considered which attorney I should contact about it. But the more I thought about it, the more I did not like the idea. I kinda wanted to keep my criminal record because I saw it as proof that I existed on this planet at some point in time.

Finally back in Burlington from that tortuous trip to Canada, I needed to find a room for the night. Before I came to Vermont I was hoping I would have the option to stay with family, so I didn't book a hotel room in advance. I was really discouraged about not being able to see people in my family, and not making amends with Canada, so I pulled into the parking lot of the first hotel I saw.

It was some decent national chain down the road from the airport where I knew I would get a standard room at an average price. I walked up to the front desk, rented a room for my stay, and went to my room on the second floor with my bags. I looked out the window, and all I had for a view was part of a roof-top, an empty parking lot, and a little greenspace. Still hung-over from my Canadian anxiety trip, this room and view were not helping to put me at ease at all. It didn't feel like the Vermont I remembered my sister taking me through, and seemed like any other busy city in the United States. Not willing to settle, I went back to the front desk with my bags to check-out of the room. The lady at the front desk assured me everything in the area was full, and I wouldn't have much luck finding anything else. A gambling man, I checked-out of the room anyway, and started looking for something else in their foyer.

After a quick search online, I found some better rates in Stowe than where I was at in Burlington, so I decided to go there. I liked the idea of Stowe much more. Decades earlier, my sister and her common law husband were giving me a tour through the local area. As we were driving through Stowe on our way to Ben & Jerry's, my sister's common law husband told me Stowe was where the rich people live. As a teenager, I felt privileged just driving through the small town. As an adult, I liked having the option to stay there.

When I got to Stowe, it was late. I drove to one of the places I saw with a good rate. When I walked in, it seemed more like an old walk-up apartment building than a hotel, and I couldn't find anyone to talk to about the room. So I drove back down the road to the other place I saw that had a good rate online. I pulled into their pothole filled parking area in front of their motel rooms, and thought I might find a neon-lit front desk sign; but, I was out of luck again. I didn't even get out of the car this time, I just turned around and drove back to the center of town. On the way into Stowe, I saw a well-lit bustling hotel that I thought for sure I would be able to get a room at. I considered driving back to it, but it wasn't in Stowe, and I really wanted to stay in Stowe. As I pulled up to the traffic light, The Green Mountain Inn was pretty-much right in front of me. I kept driving by it, and they seemed to be open, so I decided to check 'em out.

I walked through their foyer to their burgundy carpeted front desk area. I didn't wait long, and a young man greeted me at their vintage wooden front desk. I told him I just wanted something simple. He told me they were remodeling their little single rooms, and most of their other rooms were already reserved, so all that was left was the king Jacuzzi suite with a fireplace. I didn't want to spend that kind of money on a room, but I needed a place to stay. The room was available for all of my stay in Vermont, so I went ahead and reserved the room. Even though I still had $34,612.92 in student loan debt, and shouldn't have been spending my money like that, I was happy I was able to afford my stay in the suite.

There were several buildings with rooms and guest services at the inn. My suite was in the building toward the back of the property. I drove around to the back parking lot, and found an open space close to my building. At the edge of the parking lot, a sidewalk lined with ambiently lit trees and foliage traversed the buildings and facilities on the property. I grabbed my suitcase and backpack from the car, and walked along the sidewalk to my building.

When I stepped-up through the front door and into my building, I was surprised to see a beige-painted lift-rail along the stairs leading to the second story that completely didn't match the style of anything else I had seen at the inn. I gazed at the lift-rail in wonderment as I carried my suitcase up the stairs. At the top of the stairs, I found the door to my room.

My room was as described: gas fireplace at the front wall, a seating area with a little table between the windows that overlooked the post office on the side wall, king-size bed on the back wall, and the Jacuzzi tub on the wall after that. Even though the building itself was old, the bathroom was nicely updated with a glass enclosed shower, tumbled travertine tile flooring, and a simple but elegant vanity. I was spending soo much money on the room, I wanted to get my money's worth, so I had to explore the place. I dropped-off my bags in my room, and went downstairs to check-out the community area.

The community area had a couch, coffee table, and armchairs that did match the property. It was the off season, so nobody else was down there with me, which was actually really nice. I sat in one of the armchairs, and looked around the room for a few minutes. It was quiet and peaceful, I really enjoyed that. I thought about going to the gas station, getting some beers, and going to the pool for a night swim. But, I wasn't there for a leisure trip, I wanted to reconnect with my family. I thought using the fitness area would be a productive use of my time. But somehow I tweaked my shoulder, and was still recovering from that, so that wasn't a good option either.

I went outside and followed the sidewalk. I didn't have to walk too long before I found the arcade. It looked like fun, so I went inside. Again, nobody else was in there. I played one of the arcade games for a few minutes, but it didn't feel right, so I left.

I continued down the path and found the pool. A guy and his girlfriend were sitting around a fire-pit near the pool, so I went and talked to them for a few minutes. I really didn't want to tell them why I was in Vermont, but it came-up in conversation, and that was really unpleasant. I didn't enjoy telling the story, and they were a little sorry they asked, so, that didn't last long either. After our awkward conversation, I decided to go back to my room and go to sleep.

I fell asleep quickly, and was sleeping okay, but it was a windy night. As the wind gusted, I could hear the stop sign by the post office banging against its signpost as if it was missing a bolt. And when that wasn't waking me up, the sound of the wind rattling the vent on the roof did. So, I didn't sleep that-great that-night in my expensive suite.

In the morning, it was a drab overcast day, and it was sprinkling rain. I hadn't heard anything from my niece yet. Prior to me coming out to Vermont, we were talking about getting together for lunch. Over-the-phone, it sounded to me like she was interested to do that, so I kinda just wanted to sit around and wait for her to send me a text or give me a call. The weather too gave me a good excuse to sit in my suite and continue to write this book. After pacing in the room for a few minutes, I went on Facebook.

My niece and I were Facebook friends, so I thought maybe she messaged me on Facebook. I didn't see any messages from her, but I saw that she posted some photos of the falls where she spread her mother's ashes. That motivated me. I decided I needed to at least see the falls where my niece spread my sister's ashes; so, I went out to my rental car.

When I made it out to the parking lot, I noticed one of my tires was nearly flat. I really didn't want to be bothered with that; I wasn't very familiar with the town, and wasn't sure if I would be able to find an air pump. I got in the car and drove to the gas station; lucky for me they had an air pump, and it actually worked! I put a little air in the tire and thought: "problem solved." I got back in the car, drove away, and it was only like 10 minutes later when the low-pressure tire light came on in the car again. I wasn't interested in getting stuck in the middle of nowhere with a flat tire; so instead of heading directly to the falls, I went back to the airport to get another car.

The budget car rental place was apologetic to me, said they would get the tire checked-out, and gave me another car. My new rental car was a little more scratched and dinged-up than my old rental car. I took a bunch of photos of the scratches and dings so they wouldn't try to charge me for them. It was already time for lunch, I didn't eat breakfast, and I was hungry. Before I started-out on the road again to go to the falls, I needed to get some food in me, but I wanted to stop someplace that was kinda on the way to the falls.

I remember my sister saying something about Middlebury, like it was a place that I would like. I didn't know if that was going to work-out for me, so I did a quick search online for: "raw-organic-Middlebury," and saw that they had a food co-op. I'm a co-op person, and wanted to see what my sister was talking about, so I drove to the co-op in Middlebury.

The Middlebury Natural Foods Co-Op is awesome! It is a very well put together store with standard packaged health food store stuff in the middle, a deli counter, an open-air cooler filled with freshly prepared organic foods, a bulk food section, and another open-air cooler with growlers so you can buy kombucha on tap! Right away I filled-up a couple kombucha growlers. My suite at the inn had a mini-fridge. I figured buying food here would save me money, would be of much higher quality than the food at most restaurants, and would be good to eat on-the-road. So I grabbed a few baggies of nuts, picked-out a few prepared entrées, and ordered a wrap at the deli counter. When I went up-front to the cashier to pay, I was happy to see they had empty shipping boxes to reuse instead of bags. I put all the stuff I bought into one of the large boxes, and walked over to their little indoor seating area to eat my wrap.

There wasn't much room between the tables, so I put my box of food in the middle of the only open table and sat down. I casually looked around as I started eating my deli wrap. There was group of college students at one table, a couple people on their lunch break, a mother and daughter drinking smoothies, and a kindly old man sitting by himself reading a book near me.

I don't read much or often, and I was curious about what he was reading, so I asked him about his book. He seemed to welcome the interruption, because my quick little question turned into a conversation. He was a very nice, very smart man, retired from a white-collar profession. He was a widower, was sensitive to electromagnetic frequencies (EMF), and was reading a book about EMF.

When our conversation had run its course, I grabbed my box of groceries, and headed to the door. The sprinkling rain from earlier in the day had turned into heavy rain. Waiting-the-storm-out didn't seem like a realistic option, so I did a light run out to the car, trying not to get wet.

Perked-up by my conversation with the kindly old man, I selected techno to listen to, and began driving to Warren Falls. Even though it was raining, I enjoyed seeing the greenery, streams, and mountains. As I drove, I wasn't really sure I was going the right way, and got a little nervous that the area might not seem familiar to me. But as I turned, and started driving on highway 100, my uneasiness gradually subsided.

Along highway 100 I recognized a little spot between the river and the road. I pulled-over into a parking area near the spot, and walked the 50' down to the river. At the river was a mostly-level rocky bank. I remembered visiting my sister Sue in the summer, a few weeks before I went into the military. We both love lying in the sun. She took me there one afternoon so we could get some sun our skin. We were still getting to know each other, so it was pretty cool doing something together that we both enjoyed.

Of course, there was no sun this day, but I still wanted to take-in the experience. I walked to where there was a deep pool in the river, I crouched at the pool, and splashed some of the cold mountain water onto my face. I ran my wet hands through my hair, walked back to the car, and started down the road again.

It only took a few minutes, and I was pulling into the parking lot at Warren Falls. It was still drizzling rain, but not bad enough for me to not get out and walk around. The nice thing about the weather and time of year was that nobody else was at the falls. I liked that I had the place to myself, so I could find my way, and walk around the falls at my leisure.

I started with the most obvious place, I went down to the big boulders at the river's edge. I reminisced jumping off the boulders into cold flowing river as I stood on the boulders. I took a few photos, and continued exploring the area because I knew that wasn't where my niece spread my sister's ashes. I walked up and around a hill, still at the river's edge, and found a little secluded area. I instantly recognized it from my niece's Facebook photos as the place where she spread my sister's ashes. I stood there for a few minutes, reflected, and took a few more photos. Starting to drizzle rain a little more heavily, I walked down the trail back to the car.

As I walked down the trail, I realized I needed more. I wanted to relive some of the closeness I had with my sister. To do that, I decided I had to revisit all of the places I remembered my sister Sue taking me to. I only visited Sue in Vermont a few times, so the list of places I needed to go to wasn't extensive.

After the falls, I went to Montpelier. One summer we had lunch at a vegetarian restaurant downtown Montpelier. She liked the idea of vegetarianism, but didn't try too hard to make it a priority in her life.

From Montpelier, I drove by her old house in Berlin, across the street from a cemetery. The summer I went into the military, she bought me a bottle of red wine, and she had a party at her house. That night we played volleyball in her backyard, and toward the end of the evening there was a circle of us in her living room, listening to her play guitar and singing for us. She was a passionate singer; her style reminded me of Janis Joplin, she even looked like Janis Joplin a little. While I visited Sue that summer, I had a loop that I ran, so I drove my old running loop too.

From Berlin, I went to Northfield. Sue earned her undergraduate degree from Norwich University in Northfield. On one of our phone calls after I was out of the military, we joked about how we both had some connection to the military, even though we were both idealists.

After driving around the University I drove to and through another town she used to live in, Barre, and headed back to the hotel in Stowe. Even though it was a gloomy day with light rain off and on, I definitely felt like my Vermont tour helped me reinforce the bond I had with my sister. I also enjoyed seeing again the covered bridges, and ski club shacks nestled in nature along the way.

Back in my hotel room, I enjoyed eating the natural foods I bought at the co-op, and contentedly relaxed in my Jacuzzi tub. I slept a little better that night, and in the morning, it wasn't raining! I had a little time to kill before I needed to checkout, so I checked my checking account online.

I just received a relocation payment from my company to pay for my move from South Dakota to North Dakota. But I live meagerly, so I didn't have much to move. Also, I didn't need the money for down-payments or security deposits, because I already had more than enough money for all of that. Instead, I used that money to make another payment on my debt.

I still owed SoFi $11,972.65. After doing a little figuring, I saw I had enough money to pay-off SoFi, and still had money left over to get settled into a new place. So May 8, 2017, seated at my little work table in room 738, I finished paying-off my 10-year SoFi loan serviced by Mohela. It only took me a year-and-a-half to pay-off that 10-year loan, and I was very proud of the progress that I was making on paying-off all of my student loan debt. All I had left to pay was the loan that started it all, $22,650.61 at Nelnet.

My trip to Vermont was bittersweet; the sweet part was paying-off a loan, the bitter was the part about my family. I went to Vermont to reconnect with people I considered to be family, but I didn't get to see anyone else while I was there. It seems they were only cool with me back in the day to be supportive of my sister; who was just trying to learn more about her biological father, and develop a connection with him. It was cool that they did that for her, but I felt a little naïve for not recognizing that sooner. After that trip, I flew back to South Dakota to prepare myself for my move to North Dakota.

16
North Dakota

Song Suggestions:
Tricky—Overcome
Portishead—Cowboys

While I was running my route for my pumper job in North Dakota, I sometimes considered that I should be using one of my degrees, instead of driving a pickup truck and looking at wellheads all day. I often thought when I completed my doctorate, I would have been in the oil business for a few years, so I would finally have the industry specific experience companies wanted from me, and I could easily move into a white collar position within the company considering my education and experience. Then I dropped out of the DBA program, and that changed. But an MBA should still be marketable, right?

Thinking about stuff like that made me angry, because I was doing really good in my job, and I didn't want to sabotage myself or the progress I was making paying my student loans. I remembered when I was broke, trying to sell real estate, that I often looked back at my time in the Air Force. I was economically comfortable in the Air Force, but I let my feelings get in the way, and I had to separate from the military. I struggled soo much when I got out of the Air Force, I often thought I should have kept my personal convictions to myself, and just did my job. So when I was in another stable job that paid well, I really didn't want to make the same mistake again.

When my oil field company decided to get rid of the rotator program, it was a huge change because they were asking us to commit to the company in North Dakota, and they were significantly reducing our compensation. To help us work through the change, a human resources representative from the company came to Watford City, and made herself available to us. I saw this positive meeting with a human resources representative as an opportunity.

I thought it would be an ideal time for me to introduce myself to human resources in a good way, so I made an appointment to meet with her. I hoped she would know of a job in the company that would be an appropriate use of my work experience, and all or one of my degrees. But when I met with her, she was surprised someone so highly educated was doing the job I was doing, and really didn't know what to do with me.

Dan, who was also going through the same experience, saw the huge slash to our benefits coming months in advance. So when they formally made the announcement, and gave us the opportunity to leave with severance, Dan was already executing his North Dakota exit strategy. For him, meeting with the human resources lady was just a formality, blessing the plan he had already put into play. And, a few days later, he was moving to Texas to do the same job down there.

I wasn't interested to do the same job in Texas, the cost of the transition wasn't worth-it to me. And, I didn't want to try using one of my degrees to find a white collar job at some other company because our local managers hired me when nobody else would. I was really grateful our interviewer took a chance on me, so I was rewarding the company with my loyalty.

But I couldn't get that idea out of my head; to try to use my degrees to get a better paying job, so I searched open positions online at our company website. As before, I looked, found, applied, got interviews, and my interviewers called me back saying I was a strong candidate, and should reapply when they have another job opening. The whole experience actually kinda messed with my head a bit.

The bad thing was, I didn't get either of the jobs that I applied and interview for. The great thing was, I finally got that inclination that I should be using one of my degrees out of my head. Also, I decided that I really didn't want to go through the trouble of learning a new job all over again. It took me years to become proficient at my job. I wasn't willing to put myself in the weak position of not knowing how to handle work scenarios unless the job change was going to net me significantly more time off, or more money.

To help keep myself in a positive mindset and be content in my current job role, I reminded myself that I have what everybody wants, a job that gives me time and money. A lot of people earn great salaries, but don't get enough time off-of-work to enjoy the money they are earning. Other people have lots of free-time, and no money to go anywhere. My pumper job gave me a decent salary, and six days off. I wasn't able to use any of my degrees, but I got to keep the highest paying job I've ever had in my life.

While we were living in the corporate apartments, Ed decided he needed a girlfriend. Ed's girlfriend was a cosmetologist in Rapid City, but she thought she could do more with herself, so she was working on a bachelor degree. When she completed her bachelor degree, Ed thought the best place for her to get the most money with her degree was in the Watford City area. So, she moved into Ed's corporate apartment with Ed, and started looking for work. Like me, she applied-for a lot of jobs, was sometimes interviewed, and always rejected. She was finally able to get a job in a flower shop, but she was earning less money than she did cutting hair, so it really wasn't a win. After a few months of that, she moved back to Rapid City. When Ed's girlfriend moved back to Rapid City, Ed moved into Prairie View RV Park. Prairie View RV Park was one of those original places where the investors bought land, moved a bunch of camper trailers onto the land, and rented-out the campers.

When I made the decision to move to North Dakota to keep my job, I had to let all of my employers in Rapid City know that I couldn't work for them anymore. All of my employers appreciated what I did for them, and were disappointed when I told them that I had to leave. I probably could have kept all of my jobs and drove back and forth, but I really didn't want to pay rent in two cities, plus the gas to travel back and forth, and the wear-and-tear on my Jetta. My car was running great; but I was trying not to drive the car any more than I needed to, because I really didn't want to replace it when it broke down. So, I rented a storage unit in Rapid City, moved most of my stuff into the storage unit, and moved into the camper trailer with Ed at Prairie View RV Park.

Living in a camper is an authentic Bakken experience. Up until that point, I never even camped in a camper. Given the opportunity for that experience, I couldn't miss-out on it.

The camper was kinda nice. It had a bunk bed setup at one end of the camper, and a queen bed at the other end of the camper with the kitchen, living room, couch, and dining area sandwiched in the middle. There was only one parking space next to the camper, and Ed didn't want to advertise that he was breaking his lease, so I kept my work truck and personal car in the parking lot at the office. It was only four-and-a-half miles to the office from the camper, so I rode my pedal bike to the office. Like I did at Williston State College, I slept on the bottom bunk of the bunk bed, and used the top bunk as storage for a few of my totes.

After work, I ate dinner in the camper. My dinner was usually raw broccoli and mixed nuts in-shell. I only ate mixed-nuts in their shells because it was a way for me to practice portion control. It's a lot harder to eat a lot of nuts when I have to break open every shell.

I was trying not to spend any more money than I needed to, so I bought the nuts in bulk, and I didn't buy a nut cracker. Instead of using a nut cracker, I found a couple big pieces of red scoria rock outside of the camper, and used those to smash open the shells of my mixed nuts. After a few weeks of smashing my nut shells, I was looking through the cupboards in the camper one day, and I got lucky! In one of the top cupboards, I found a hammer! So instead of using a scoria rock to smash open a shell on top of another scoria rock, I used my hammer to smash open the shell on top of the rock. My shell smashing was soo much easier with my hammer! The only other fun I had in the camper was laundry day.

The camper park had two coin operated laundry buildings. Ed's camper was only about a block away from one of the laundry buildings, so it was a short walk to do laundry. But all of the roads in the park were gravel, and the park was busy, so I usually had a few automobiles pass me during my laundry walks that covered me in a dust cloud no matter what time I went to do my laundry. And my reward for arriving alive to the laundry building was the stench from two gigantic dumpsters that were usually filled with rotting garbage. The dust filled laundry building had a couple couches, televisions, and a treadmill.

The treadmill was unplugged and dusty; but I thought getting-in a run while I was doing my laundry would be a good idea, so I plugged it in, and hit quick start. That quick start button was no joke. The treadmill went from zero to full speed right away, I could feel it abruptly move, and I caught myself on the handles. I could see why the machine was unplugged, but I didn't know why anyone hadn't thrown it in one of those dumpsters yet.

I loved riding my bicycle to and from work. There were four pubs along my bike route from the office to our camper. I often considered stopping at one, or all of them, and having a beer on my way back to the camper. There were only two major roads going into and out of Watford City. Police regularly patrolled those roads; and it didn't take much to get pulled over, so I knew having a beer and driving my car home was a bad idea. I felt safe on my bicycle, and thought drinking and riding my bicycle home was a responsible choice.

After a couple months of living in the camper and bicycle commuting, Ed's lease was ending, so I was looking for an apartment for us. To make everyone's share of the rent a little lower, Mat was switching shifts again, and moving back to Watford City, so he was also going to move into the apartment. Mat recently closed out of his corporate apartment in Dickinson, so he moved into the camper with Ed and I until I could find a place for us. A few days after Mat moved in, I found an apartment for us on the edge of town. Mat slept on the couch in our camper, but he wasn't nearly as excited as me to live in the camper, so he usually numbed his camper pains at the nearby hotel bar.

Our last night in the camper, Mat invited me and a few of our other coworkers to join him at the hotel bar. The hotel bar, Teddy's Lounge, was just under a mile from Prairie View RV Park (later hit by a tornado). I was looking forward to having a few drinks with my friends, but it was the end of my work week, and I had a few things to take care of before I could meet-up with them.

I like to exercise, so after work I did my normal weights and cardio routine in the office gym. Wearing my black sweat suit, I put my phones, wallet, and keys in my black backpack, and loaded my bicycle into the bed of my work truck. My work truck needed maintenance; so I dropped it off at the mechanic, to work on it for me during my days off. After I dropped-off my truck and key, I rode my bicycle straight to the bar. I was really looking forward to a night out with the guys.

The hotel bar was on my way to the camper. It didn't make sense for me to go to the camper first to change, so I just wore my black sweat suit. After a few hours of drinking, and several drinks, it was time to go home.

Mat and Ed needed a break from the camper, so they decided to spend the night in the hotel we were drinking at. I didn't want to miss-out on any of my camper experience, so I decided to ride my bicycle back to the camper. But I was kinda drunk, and really wanted a bag of Gardetto's to snack-on, so I chose to go to the gas station convenience store first.

There was gas station right next to the hotel, but I didn't have a rewards card with them. I didn't want to cheat myself of any point earning opportunities, so I rode my bicycle a half-mile in the opposite direction past the close gas station, so I could use my rewards card and earn points at the Kum & Go. It was a little inconvenient, but I was in good shape, so the ride wasn't a big deal. I had fun riding to the gas station, and made it safely to the convenience store. I couldn't find the original style of Gardetto's I was looking for, so I ended up buying a bag of the mustard flavored Gardetto's. I swiped my rewards card, got my points, and went out to my bicycle.

There was a little bit of a slope in the parking lot, and instead of moving my bicycle so I could easily get onto my bike, I just tried to fight the slope and hop onto my bicycle. I ended-up losing my balance, and falling onto my hip. By the grace of God I have relatively healthy bones, so my fall to the pavement didn't break anything. I picked myself up, picked-up my bicycle, and opened my bag of Gardetto's. I was still really disappointed I couldn't find the original flavor, but the fact that I was snacking at all made me happy.

At the Kum & Go, I was so close to our new apartment, I considered riding straight to the apartment since I just got the key that afternoon. But, there were a few problems with that idea: we didn't have any furniture in the apartment; so I didn't have anything to sleep on, I didn't have any beer in that refrigerator, and I still didn't want to miss-out on any of my Bakken camper experience. It was a simple decision to make.

With one hand on my handle bars, and the other on my bag of Gardetto's, I started riding my bicycle back to the camper. It was a very nice summer evening, close to midnight, very quiet, and nobody was on the roads in the small town. As I was steering the bicycle with one hand, I was pouring Gardetto's into my mouth with my other hand. They were doing some road construction at a nearby intersection, so I couldn't ride my bicycle on the bike path like I wanted to, and ended-up riding on the road through the intersection under-construction. That part of the road wasn't lit by street lamps, and I was still wearing my black tracksuit and black backpack. My bicycle didn't even have any lights or reflectors on it, but somehow I still caught the attention of the local police.

Just as I passed the unlit intersection, and was about to get onto the bike path, their flashing red and blue lights lit-up all of the area around me like a carnival without any music. It was soo weird, so I pulled over to the side of the road to see what was going on. I hoped the car would just keep driving past me, but when I stopped, the police stopped behind me too. I looked back, and through the dense fog of lights from the police car, I could see an officer walking toward me. I was soo confused. I really didn't know what was going on; so I just stood there with my bicycle, and then I saw his patrol buddy walking up to me too.

The first guy said he saw me swerving on my bicycle, and asked me if it was okay that he made sure I was able to make it home safe. I was thinking to myself; "okay, big f-ing deal I was swerving, I'm on my bicycle." I was also thinking that if this guy was really concerned about my safety, he would just follow me home, make me walk my bicycle home, or give me a ride home. Those were the sensible, care about me solutions, but that's not the direction these guys wanted to go. I really didn't want to agree with his request, because I could already see where this was going, but I thought I would go ahead and play along.

I reluctantly agreed to his ploy, and optimistically wondered what silly little questions he was going to ask me to make sure I was able to make it home safely. Then he started demonstrating the roadside sobriety tests. I thought to myself: "I can do this, no problem." After a couple failed tests, he stopped testing me, and started searching my backpack. I didn't have anything in my backpack except my wallet, keys, personal phone, and work phone, so there was no problem there, but they still arrested me. The DUI complaint card he was filling-out asked for the model of the vehicle, so he wrote on the card Diamond Back. It seemed that these guys were just practicing a DUI arrest with me; it was soo surreal, I was sure they weren't doing the right thing at all.

Up until that evening, it had been 10 years since I had been to court, and 13 years since I had been to jail. I couldn't believe the situation I was in. I was very disappointed in myself. I was doing good for soo long, everything was going great for me! And now I was handcuffed in the back of a police car, on my way to jail again.

On our way to jail, the guy in the passenger seat asked me if I had been arrested before, and I rattled-off all of my past offences. The officer searched their database as I was telling him all of my crimes, and he couldn't find anything about me because my crimes were soo old. When we walked into jail, I was happy to see that they were wheeling my bicycle along with us.

The jail was nice, it was clean and spacious, and there wasn't any clutter at all. They finished building the place only three months earlier. I got to sleep in my own little room with a stainless steel toilet, stainless steel sink, and a thick vinyl mattress with a pillow built into-it. I slept okay, and was up early in the morning, so I stood at my door and looked out my vertical-slit-window into the windowless booking area. They were just starting to deliver breakfast trays to us, but I wasn't hungry, so I rejected my breakfast tray.

After breakfast, they began sobriety tests. The great thing was, I was first in line. The bad thing was, my blood alcohol level had to be below the legal limit before they could release me. I hadn't drank any water all night. I wanted to drink water when I woke up, but I didn't have a cup. I didn't think it was that imperative to drink water, otherwise I would have drank directly from the sink. True to my nature of poor performance on standardized tests, I failed my breathalyzer test, and got to watch everyone else get booked-in.

Watching everyone else going through the booking process was nerve wracking for me. I had plenty of time to think, and thought it was odd that they were booking me before releasing me. When I went to jail in Florida and South Dakota, they booked me first, and then they took me to my cell. After I exhausted all of my thoughts about their administration, all I could think about was my consequences: "I'm going to lose my job," "I'm moving back to Michigan to move-in with my mother," "I didn't even get to pay my student loans off," "All I have left to pay is $22,000 and it's going to take me years to finish paying-off my student loans."

While I was standing at the door, watching people get booked-in,

I heard my personal phone ringing a few times. What a relief! I was soo happy to hear my phone ringing, it made me think that it would make it harder for the police officers to forget about me in my little solitary cell. I also thought the police officers would think that I'm someone people actually care about, and they should move a little quicker to get me out of there.

After they booked-in a few people, they retested me, and I finally passed. At-last, it was my turn to book-in before release. They handcuffed me to the bench, and the police officer in front of me typed all of my information into the computer. One of the police ladies passing behind the desk, working on something else, asked me why I was there. I told her I was arrested for DUI, on my bicycle. She shook her head in dismay and walked away. That was vindicating for me, but it was still a really bad situation.

When they finished booking-me-in, and out-processing me, they gave me my backpack and my bicycle back. As I pushed my bicycle out to the lobby area and looked outside, I saw it was raining, hard. I hung out in the lobby, waited for it to stop raining, and I checked my phone for my missed calls.

Ed and Mat were the people that were calling me. They said they had gone to the camper, and didn't see me there, and wondered where I was at. Then, I had the unfortunate obligation to tell them that I was in jail, and the story of how I ended-up in jail. They were as in-shock about the situation as I was. Distraught, we ended our calls, and I asked them to please not disclose to anyone the extremely unfortunate predicament I had put myself in.

As I was standing in the lobby, I took a minute to sort through my stuff, and make sure that everything I had before I was arrested was still there. The only thing I saw I was missing was the keys to my work truck. I left my work clothes in the gym locker at work, so I figured I just left my truck keys in my pants pocket. The only other thing that was different was my money.

When I was arrested, I had a little over $100 in cash in my wallet, but the officer didn't give me my cash back. Instead, they put my money on a visa debit card. As I was waiting for the rain to subside, I saw an Automated Teller Machine (ATM) in the public area of the jail. I wanted to turn the credits on the card into cash in my hand, so I tried to withdraw my money. I put my card in the ATM, but they wanted three-dollars for a service fee to give me my cash! I wasn't going to give those guys any more money; so I declined to pay the fee, and chose to use the card to buy groceries instead. That annoyed me too because I liked paying for everything with my Delta American Express card to earn miles, so using my jail debit card was gypping myself of miles.

I wanted to go back to the camper, and start moving into our new apartment, but I needed to find my truck key. I was tired of waiting for the rain to stop, so I just got on my bicycle, and started pedaling away from the jail in the rain. It was soo bizarre, I was in a small town, but I wasn't sure where I was because of all the new infrastructure. Perplexed, I kept pedaling down the new street until it took me someplace that looked familiar.

As I was pedaling down the road, in the rain, police officers were driving past me in the opposite direction. I couldn't help but to think they were going to stop and arrest me for something else. After pedaling for about 10 minutes, I could see the lights from the airport. I finally had a general idea where I was, but I wasn't even close to where I originally thought I was. I found the main road I knew, and then I started pedaling to the office.

As I was pedaling toward the office, the rain cloud passed, so now it was just the wind against me. After ten more minutes, I was tired of fighting the wind, so I stopped for a couple minutes at a bicycle tunnel that crossed underneath the city street. While I was standing in the tunnel, I saw little rain clouds pass over other parts of the city. It was nice to be out of the wind and rain for a few minutes, but standing in the tunnel gave me an uncomfortable amount of time to think. I was really upset about my situation, and was starting to feel hung-over. My thoughts weren't productive, so I continued to the office.

When I got to the office, I went straight to my locker in the men's room. I unlocked my locker, opened my locker door, and immediately darted my hand into my jeans pocket searching for my truck keys. The keys weren't in the right front pocket where I normally kept them, so I frantically shoved my hand into the left front pocket. My keys weren't in that pocket either. I started rummaging through all of the pockets on my pants, shirt, and took everything out of my locker, still not finding my truck keys. Then I thought; the police regularly used our training rooms for their own training, so I figured we had a special arrangement with them. I thought the managers had it worked-out so that if someone in our company was arrested, that the police would confiscate their truck keys, and give the keys to the supervisors in the office.

I really didn't see any way of getting out of this now, and decided to get it over-with. I planned to walk to my supervisor's office, and start the conversation with him about my keys. There weren't many people in the office, and when I went to my supervisor's office, he wasn't even there. I saw someone in the office I knew, asked him where my supervisor was, and he told me he was in Dickinson. Of course I'm thinking the worst, that they were having a meeting about me, and discussing what they were going to do with me now. I wanted to get this resolved, so I unlocked my phone to call my supervisor.

When I unlocked my phone, I saw the last number I called was the mechanic. I thought that was unusual, and wondered why I called the mechanic. That's when I remembered I dropped-off my truck for maintenance, and that's where my key was. I was soo relieved by that, and started to feel a glint of hope that I might be able to save my job.

With my renewed sense of optimism, I started thinking about who I could talk to for a referral to an attorney that could help me. I needed to make copies of the apartment key for Mat and Ed, so I rode my bicycle to the hardware store. I figured someone in the small town hardware store either had experience with an attorney, or knew someone who had experience with an attorney.

When I walked into the hardware store, I asked the first person I saw if she knew a DUI attorney. She said she didn't, but she knew someone else who worked there who did. She went in the back to track the guy down, and as she was doing that, I made copies of my key.

While I was getting my key copied, I asked the guy and girl behind the counter the same question. As I was asking them, I noticed a sheriff sitting in his patrol SUV outside. The guy and the girl behind the counter didn't know of anyone, but they knew the sheriff sitting outside, and thought I would get a good referral from him. The guy actually went outside, asked the sheriff for me, and gave me a name. He told me the sheriff was reputable, and wouldn't steer me wrong. But, I wasn't too excited to explore that option, especially since it was a sheriff that helped me get myself into this situation in the first place. The first woman I asked found the guy she was thinking of, and brought him to where I was.

I asked him what I asked everyone else at the store, and he was very forthcoming. His scenario was similar to mine; he told me he already had a couple DUIs, and he was arrested for his third. He said that his attorney used to be the state's attorney, and she helped him keep his driver's license, and stay out of jail. He looked-up her name and number for me, wrote it down on a piece of paper, and gave it to me. I was soo grateful! A former state's attorney helped me solve my DUI problem before, so I felt like I held the answer to my problems in my hand. I left the hardware store with my apartment keys, and a little spring in my step.

As soon as I was outside, I called the attorney's office. The phone rang, but nobody answered, so I left a message on the answering machine. A few days passed, and I hadn't heard anything from anyone. I wasn't confident that anyone actually heard the message I left on the machine, so I called once more. Again, nobody answered, so I left another message. When I called my South Dakota former state's attorney, he answered my first call. I thought about calling him for a referral to an attorney in North Dakota because my next court appearance was rapidly approaching, and I was starting to get really nervous about my situation.

Two days later, a young lady from the attorney's office finally called me back. She seemed a little disorganized, and generally uninterested in me. I mentioned I was a referral from a past client, but that did little to coax any enthusiasm from her. She took some preliminary information from me, and setup a time for me to have a conference call with her and the attorney. It was a really cold call, I wasn't convinced I was going to get a callback.

A few days later, I was pleasantly surprised the young lady from the attorney's office called me back for our conference call. After she had me on the phone, then she added the attorney to the line. As the attorney and I spoke, the young lady updated their client file with details from the call. As my first former state's attorney did, this former state's attorney explained the worst case scenario of how much time and money a conviction would cost me.

I told her I just wanted the charge to go away. She explained to me that the charge couldn't go away, but she may be able to negotiate the charge down. I told her that I needed my driver's license for work, and that if the charge couldn't go away, I needed any other conviction that wouldn't affect my driving privilege. She said she understood, and then we discussed her fees.

She needed $3,250; $3,000 to represent me in court, and $250 for the driver's license administrative hearing. I was happy I had the money to pay her, but I was unhappy that I had to spend my money like that, instead of toward my student loans. Regardless, I mailed a check to her via certified mail, and she started working for me.

I was really angry about the whole situation, but I was determined to turn my negative situation into a positive one. I decided I was going to publish my doctoral study proposal before my next court date. Afterall, my committee chairperson wanted to work with me when I dropped-out of the program, and told me I had a good book. Also, by chance, I met a former Walden University professor who had similar frustrations with the University, and she too told me I had a good book. So I decided I was not going to let the three years I spent writing the proposal, and the $150,000 I spent for six years tuition in the business administration doctoral program go to waste.

I used the anger I had for the Watford City police to critically review my proposal, make some minor edits, and start the publishing process for my book on Amazon. It was the first book I tried to publish, so the process was a little more time consuming than it should have been, but I completed the process. I was soo pleased with myself for my accomplishment that I bought myself a bouquet of flowers, and put the flowers in a vase to celebrate.

I wasn't expecting any sales from the book, because I wrote it mostly academically, and wrote it to the University rubric. The proposal is soo cold and impersonal, the general population isn't going to have any interest in it at all, so I didn't want to do any marketing for it. Some students might like to have a copy of my book as a general reference, and some managers might like to use it as a springboard for ideas, but that is about it. Regardless, a year and seven months after I dropped out of the doctoral study program, Amazon approved the work I submitted, and my proposal was finally published. I even published it before my court date!

I didn't have to meet with my attorney in-person at all. All of our exchanges were via phone, email, or certified mail. A few times I had to get my signature notarized on some forms. Although my attorney's office was in a town smaller than Watford City and two hours away, the notary at the county finance office knew her, and was happy to notarize my forms for me.

My attorney had a couple more follow-up calls with me about my driver's license, and about my conviction. Regarding my driver's license, usually there is a separate administrative hearing to determine to what extent the conviction will affect the offender's driver's license. Fortunately for me, the officers didn't file that paperwork, so we didn't have to participate in an administrative hearing, and my attorney mailed me a check for $250. The last follow-up call was about the terms of my conviction. My attorney offered to the prosecutor disorderly conduct. The prosecutor accepted my attorney's offer in conjunction with an alcohol evaluation, paying court fees, and six months unsupervised probation. I agreed to those terms, and it was done.

I completed my alcohol evaluation, and paid my $750 court bill right away. During my alcohol evaluation, the lady gave me good advice to manage my drinking: one drink per hour, maximum four drinks. I actually followed her advice for a while, and enjoyed drinking responsibly. All I had left to do was not break any laws the next six months.

The best way for me to stay out of trouble is to work all of the time. I needed to stay out of trouble, but I also needed the money to pay-off the rest of my student loans. The drama of my arrest, defense, and criminal conviction caused me a lot of stress, but also cost me close to $4,000. That was money I couldn't pay toward my student loans, so I had a lot of catching-up to do.

Lucky for me, a couple months after my conviction, my route partner hurt his arm, wasn't able to work, and we didn't have anyone else to cover for him. So, I worked all of his workdays, all of my workdays, and I kept doing that for weeks. My supervisor regularly asked me to take time off, and I assured him I would when I needed time off. But I never took any time off. Taking time off was like short-changing myself out of money, I wasn't interested in doing that at all. It was such a rare opportunity to be able to work and earn soo much overtime, I wanted to work as much as possible as long as I could. But after a couple months of working both of our shifts, my supervisor assertively told me to take a day off, so I did. That bought me some time; and again, we did the day-off dance. Every week he reminded me to take time off, and I told him I would, but didn't.

After three months of working every day except one, I finally saved-up enough money to pay-off Nelnet. February 2, 2018 I paid $12,778.08 to Nelnet to settle my debt with them, and be debt free for the first time in my life since I was 15 years old. After I made that final payment, I only had a couple thousand dollars left in my checking account. My route partner still didn't have doctor approval to come back to work, so I got to keep working, and I was soo grateful for every week my route partner was not able to work.

I began to fantasize how much money I would have if I kept working every day for four or six more months. I really didn't want to work that much, but I knew it would be a short-term sacrifice for my long-term economic security. I wasn't planning on doing anything with the money, I just wanted to keep building-up my checking account. But, my daydreams of working the rest of spring and summer came to an end.

After 4 months of working every day except one, my route partner was finally able to come back to work. As much as I wanted to keep working, I was also looking forward to having time-off to myself again. The month-and-a half more of work was just enough to make me feel economically comfortable.

While I was generally trying to be good and not break the laws, I was still really upset that Watford City police arrested me. I felt like they owed me, and that I had a license to liberally interpret traffic laws. One evening, I was driving home after work in my work truck. I was following somebody through town, but they were driving too slow for me, so I thought I would take the side streets and get home quicker. It was snowing, and there was snowpack on the road. As I turned onto a side street, the rear of my truck slid out. I didn't hit anything, the truck just slid a little. No big deal, right? Wrong. Watford City police were quick to pull me over. All of a sudden I wasn't soo angry anymore, and now I had the senses of: fear of the forthcoming consequences, and regret for my emotional decision making. Again, I was upset with myself for putting myself in the position I did.

The policeman came to my window and asked for my license, registration, and proof of insurance. I gave him my driver's license, and looked for my registration, and proof of insurance. I had the registration, but I didn't have a current copy of my proof of insurance. As the police officer searched for me in his system, another police officer pulled-up behind him. I had mixed emotions about my predicament. I thought, how bad can this really be? I felt like these guys were overreacting considering the weather; but, sitting there as he looked-me-up in the system was making me nervous.

When the police officer came back, I was surprised to hear him say my record was clean. He said driving without proof of insurance is a $250 fine, but he let me go with a stern warning that he would fine me next time. As I was putting my papers away, I was unpleasantly surprised to see his patrol buddy lurking at my passenger side window, which was really creepy in the dark. Regardless, I was grateful the policeman let me go with a warning, and I changed my mind that Watford City police owed me. Instead, I started thinking that they were just helping me become a better version of me. Had I been patient downtown behind the slow driver, I would not have slid on the side street, and would not have been pulled over. And of course, the next day I made it a point to get a copy of my up-to-date insurance, and put it in my glove compartment.

Without further incident, I completed my probation in March, 2018. There wasn't much of a celebration, because only Mat and Ed knew about it. Instead, I decided to celebrate my liberation from debt and probation by visiting my family members overseas. I wanted to visit them for many years; but I either didn't have the money, or I didn't have the time. Now, I have both.

17
Australia

Song Suggestions:
L_DG—Sunset Gaze
Drumlinezz—Just When We Thought It Was Over

Having just finished working all but one day for the last four months, I needed a little rest, and I needed time to continue to write this book. Jedediah was living and working on a farm in the Black Hills of South Dakota called Tobias Garden, and he invited me down for a visit. Tobias Garden is near a Seventh Day Adventist wellness center called Black Hills Health and Education Center (BHHEC). BHHEC had a room available, so I booked a room there for a few days.

Nestled in the Black Hills, I had a room with a view of trees, rock ledges, a little grass, and there was even a family of turkeys that passed by my room every morning. I wrote while Jedediah worked, and when he finished work, we hiked around the property and lifted weights in the gym. I really liked the cool fresh air in my lungs, and seeing the greenery was relaxing for my eyes. I also liked having my vegan meals prepared for me.

One day we drove to Rapid City in my car, and rode our skateboards around Canyon Lake Park. Another day we hiked Mt. Baldy with massage school students and BHHEC staff, and sung Seventh Day Adventist songs around a campfire on campus in the evening. I even went to church with them. Toward the end of the trip, I got a massage from one of the massage school students. It was really good to get away, a much needed break for me.

Back in North Dakota, I started planning my next trips. A couple of my mother's sisters moved from Macedonia to Melbourne, Australia, and started families there, so I had family from my mother's side in Australia too. I hadn't seen my family in Melbourne in twenty years, and the weather was good there, so it made sense for me to go there first.

It was late winter in North Dakota; and in Australia, it was early fall. Early fall in Australia is still great weather compared to any time of winter in North Dakota. I called my aunt and cousins, bought a plane ticket, arranged vacation, and told them I was coming for a visit. My cousin Elizabeth and her husband even took vacation for me. Everything was setup, until the night before, when I tried to check-in online for my flight.

I got a notification on my phone from the airline 24 hours in advance that I need to check-in for my flight. When I tried to check-in, the airline wouldn't let me check-in, and directed me to the ticketing agent. I was really nervous about this, and wondered what was going on, but didn't know what else to do but wait and see the ticketing agent.

The next day when I went to the airport, I didn't even arrive early like I should have, considering I potentially had a problem. I walked up to the counter, handed my passport to the ticketing agent, and tried to check my bag like nothing was wrong. When she punched my information into the computer, some code popped-up on her screen telling her I couldn't board the flight. She didn't know why the code was there, so she had to make a call to someone else at the airline to figure out what was going on. After about five minutes, they figured it out, and wrote down a website for me to go to.

I stood at the ticket counter with my bags, and went to the website on my phone. It was an application for an Electronic Travel Authority, a visa for permission to visit the country. This was a new requirement for travel to Australia, they only started the visa requirement four months before I was planning to take the trip. I've filled out lots of applications before, so I wasn't too worried about it. There was a $20 application fee; I paid the fee, and I started filling-out the form.

I wanted to sit down, pull my computer out of my bag, and

complete the application on my computer. But I was short on time, and needed to fill-out the application as quick as I could. Filling-out the application on my phone turned out to be painstaking; I was really regretting not taking the three minutes it would have taken me to open and start my computer. Regardless, I was making my way through the application, until I got to the criminal question.

There was a question on the application asking me if I had any criminal convictions. Right away I started thinking: "what do they mean by that," "what do they consider to be criminal convictions?" I tried to look around the application to get more information so I could appropriately answer the question. But because I was filling-out the application on my phone, I couldn't see anything anywhere that could help me answer my questions. Having just gotten-off of probation, my criminal convictions were fresh in my mind, and my guilty conscience wouldn't allow me to answer anything but "yes." As I was marking "yes" on the form, I could feel it in my body that marking yes was going to cause my application to be rejected.

But, I also kinda thought that some caring Australian person would see the only reason my application was rejected, pick-up the phone right away, and call me to discuss why I marked the question the way I did. Then, in my imaginary conversation with the caring Australian person, she would realize I was not a threat to Australia, and would approve my visa application immediately so I could board my flight to go see my family in Melbourne. And this was all supposed to happen in the five minutes I had before the gate agent needed to close the boarding door.

But that was my idealistic fantasy, and in reality, nobody called. Instead, I failed the vetting process in the automated system, the computer rejected my application, and I didn't get my visa. So, I wasn't allowed to board the plane.

I felt soo dejected. I called my cousin Elizabeth, and tried to explain to her what happened. She was understanding, really nice to me, and told me not to worry about it. Not worrying was easier said than done. However, the ticketing agent did try to make things a little easier for me. She gave me the phone number to customer service at the airline, and told me to ask for a credit so I wouldn't have to spend another $2,400 for a ticket to Australia. So, that was my next call.

The guy at United Airlines was actually nice to me. He put a note in my file, and gave me credit for the same amount I originally paid for the flight. I was relieved that I got the credit, but I was really disappointed in myself for unnecessarily getting banned from a country, again!

I'm not really a criminal. I've made some very poor choices, but I'm not criminally minded. When I finally pulled-up the visa application on my computer, I learned criminal in Australia means a combined prison sentence of 12 months or more. All of the time I spent in jail barely tallied-up to 12 days never mind 12 months. I was soo mad at myself, and determined to turn a bad thing into a good thing. I stayed-up most of the night writing, and finally let myself go to sleep around four-in-the-morning. I really screwed this trip-up, but I was determined to fix it.

In the morning, nine-eastern time, I called the Australian embassy, and explained to them what happened. I was hoping she could just edit the code on my passport to grant me a visa to go to Australia. But she said since my online application was rejected, I had to now submit a paper application for manual review by immigration authorities, complete with results from my state and federal criminal background checks.

Also, for every one of my offences, I had to include a narrative of what happened and why. So in one fell-swoop, I turned a five-minute, two-page, $20 travel visa application into a five-hour, twenty-two-page, $120 application. Determined to get to Australia, I did what they told me, and resubmitted my application with all of the documents they asked for, including my FBI background check.

I called my sister Kathy to let her know what happened; she was sympathetic to me, and invited me to her new place. I liked that idea, and it inspired me. She was in the process of moving from New Jersey to Myrtle Beach, so we negotiated a date, and I bought a ticket to go see her. I was soo upset about my failed Australia trip, and soo uplifted by my conversation with my sister, I started calling more family and friends.

I called my buddy Paul in San Diego, had a similar conversation, and bought a ticket to go visit him. I called my cousin Mike in New Jersey, and bought a ticket to visit him. All of these calls were helping me improve my mood, yet at the same time, I was starting to feel sick.

Mat was on-shift, and he had been sick for several days. I was around him for all of those days he was sick, and didn't get sick, until my visa was rejected. I had soo much stress from the situation, my immune system was vulnerable, and I ended-up being bed-ridden sick for all of my days off that I was supposed to be enjoying myself with my family in Australia. I even had to take a sick-day the day I had to come back to work because I still wasn't well enough to even minimally function. Taking a sick-day is huge for me; I'm not a sick day person, it's like once a decade I get soo sick that I can't go to work. My one sick day was just enough time off-of-work for me. I went to work the next day, and was able to finish the rest of my work week.

While I was waiting for the results from the Australian immigration authorities, I went to Las Vegas. Back in December, Mat's family and I were planning a trip to celebrate Mat's April birthday, my April birthday, and our five-year anniversary of working in the oil field. April was here, so Mat and I flew to Las Vegas to meet his family, and our friends.

We stayed at Mandalay Bay just six months after the shooting. I was a little creeped-out that Mat's parents rented a room on the 35th floor. It was the same side, and only a few floors above the shooter's room. Jason and I stayed in another room that felt like it was in a separate hotel, and Paul and Mat shared a room on some other floor.

One of the days we were there we rented one of the beach cabanas at the pool with a television, refrigerator, tables, chairs, and couches. It was like sitting in a living room; except this living room had food and drink servers, and a pool. We drank most of the day, played Cornhole, and listened to Morgan Page perform at the next pool over. As the sun was setting, we moved the party from the pool to Mat's parent's shooter-side suite.

Even walking down the hallway to the suite felt a little strange. The suite itself was very nice, with a couple bedrooms, and a living room. Awestruck, we all took turns walking up to the window, and looking down-and-out at the Luxor, the airport, and the area in-between. We drank, swapped DUI stories, and the moral of the stories was to never be self-incriminating with law enforcement. I learned a lot from our little knowledge sharing session, and fortunately haven't had to use what I learned, yet.

That night, we had dinner at Gordon Ramsay's Hell's Kitchen. Jason introduced us to flaming Spanish coffee, and we got a photo with Season 17 winner Michelle Tribble. After dinner, Jason, Paul, and I went to Omnia, and everyone else went back to the hotel.

We had dinner another night at Red Square Restaurant & Vodka Lounge. I really enjoyed the food there, it was similar to the Macedonian food I like to eat. I had a good time in Las Vegas, but I didn't have too good of a time, because I was a little uneasy about my Australian visa application.

Before I even heard back from the embassy, it was already time for me to go to Macedonia. It was a little hard to believe it had already been eight years since I last went to Macedonia to see my family. Of the four flights I had to take, I liked flying Austrian Airlines the best, because they gave us stainless steel silverware to use with our meals. I don't think I was supposed to, but I kept the silverware they gave me.

Food, drink, and hospitality are a few of the things I love about my Macedonian culture. Most of the cities and villages have a farmer's market at least one day a week, and most of the food seems un-messed-around-with. A couple of my favorite foods are the crumbly white brine cheese, and the red pepper dip called Ajvar that I love to smear on white bread. Also, everyone makes their own wine and Rakija, or pays someone to make wine and Rakija for them. Rakija is alcohol distilled from what is left over after they make wine from the fruit. Rakija and salad are traditional for hosts to serve when people come to visit their home. I can see where my passion for food comes from, it is definitely in my blood. I did a lot of eating, drinking, socializing, and did a little hiking and running too!

Re-connecting with all of my aunts, uncles, cousins, nieces, nephews and friends in Macedonia was great; I am very proud of my family and friends there. To express my appreciation and affection, I gave an orchid to each of my aunts. Despite a little bit of a language barrier, we enjoyed seeing each other, and everyone welcomed me back.

A couple weeks later, I received an online notification my visa was approved, and I rebooked my flight to Australia. It was nice that part was out of the way, but I still had to get there. This time, when I got the check-in alert from the airline the night before, I was actually able to check-in! That was a step in the right direction, but I had a long way to go.

I arrived at the airport a little early just in-case there was a problem, and I was able to check my bag normally, just like any other flight. When we were able to board the plane, and I was sitting on the plane, I sent a text message to my cousin Elizabeth to let her know there weren't any problems, and I was actually on the plane. Domestic flights went well, and I was able to board the international flight. As we were preparing to land in Melbourne, they gave us an immigration form to complete.

Again they asked their criminal question, but this time, I knew how to appropriately answer the question. I put the form in my pocket, deplaned, and continued to walk toward baggage claim. Before baggage claim, I had to submit my form, and go through another security checkpoint where they asked me the criminal question a third time. Even if I was able to board the plane the first time, I can't help to think my guilty conscience would have gotten me on either the second or third time they asked me the same question. Nevertheless, I answered the question appropriately, and was able to get my bag and enter the country.

My cousin Elizabeth and her husband Sean picked me up at the airport. We hung out at her place, went to lunch with my cousin Steven, niece Makayla and nephew Tristan. On the walk to and from the restaurant, I saw some Australian crows that looked and acted like American crows, but I was surprised to hear they had a different accent. We went for a hike in the bush too, and got to see more interesting birds, and other wildlife. Of course, one of my favorite places we went was the Yarra Valley Dairy. At the dairy, I thoroughly enjoyed their marinated cheeses, and drinking some of their locally produced red wine.

One of my days in Australia, I hung-out with my cousin Ilka, her husband Zoran, son Dylan, and daughter Cassandra. Our day started-out with watching her son Dylan play soccer in the morning. We had an espresso while we watched the game, and after the game, they asked me what I wanted for lunch.

I was in the mood for a crispy thin crust pizza, and my cousin Ilka said she knew just the place. I thought it was going to be in the neighborhood, right around the corner. Instead, we went on a bit of a drive, and ended up in center city Melbourne. We went to a high-end Italian restaurant downtown, had a little red wine with our lunch, and proceeded to tour the city.

After lunch we did some touristy stuff that was a lot of fun! We went on a carriage ride to see some historical places in Melbourne. Then, we went to the Skydeck on the 88th floor of Eureka tower, and I did their Edge Experience. On our way back to the car, we stopped at Ponyfish Island, mostly for the novelty of it. Ponyfish Island is a pub, on an island, in the middle of the Yarra River. Finally home, we had a Mortal Kombat tournament.

I enjoyed myself bouncing on their trampoline, until I tried to do a back-flip. My back-flip attempt failed, and I landed on the bridge of my nose. I was grateful I didn't break my nose, but it did leave a little wound in-between my eyes.

I spent the night at my Aunt Vesela's house, and saw my cousin Constantine. In the morning, my Aunt made zelnik for me. Zelnik is a spinach pie, held together with dough, a little thicker than an average slice of pizza. My Aunt Vesela and I had a shot of rakija with our zelnik, and I dabbed some Rakija on my wound, thinking that would be a good idea. Shortly thereafter, my cousin Julie came over. I told her what I did with the rakija on my wound, and she reminded me my wound was a burn, and aloe is best for burns. So, I screwed that up too. After breakfast, Julie took me around for the day.

We started with deserts and espresso in the morning at LaManna, and in the afternoon we went shirt shopping for me. I was surprised to find some French-cuff shirts that fit me perfectly. I was looking for a nice fitting shirt for months. They fit soo well my cousin Julie bought two shirts for me, and I bought a couple shirts too. After shirt shopping, we picked-up her children William and Charlotte from the International School. We bounced on their trampoline, and I landed a back-flip without skinning-up my face! In the evening, I met her husband Anthony, and we went to dinner at a local restaurant.

Rounding-out my trip, the next evening I saw my cousins Dare and Jordan, their wives Nadia and Faye, and my nieces and nephews. Like in Macedonia, my family in Australia was very welcoming, gracious hosts, and looked forward to seeing me again. I left the next day with a lot of photos, and a lot of fond memories. While I was at the airport, getting ready to leave Australia, Jedediah called me and wanted to do a camping-hiking-road trip with me. We made plans for our trip while I waited in line, and then I boarded the plane.

Back in the United States, it was time for my trip to San Diego to visit my buddy Paul. Neither of us surfed before, but we decided to rent some foam boards, and try surfing at Solana Beach. The surf pummeled us as we tried to get past the breaks, because we didn't know how to duck dive or turtle roll. With our tenacity, we finally made it out to the calm. I waited there, lying on my board, looking at the shore. The waves rolled past me, and I heard them crash on shore. I didn't know what to expect. Then, my first wave caught me! All of a sudden, I was on the wave, and it was carrying me in. The feeling was amazing! It was such an interesting sensation to feel and hear the wave as it propelled me to the shore. I wanted to try to stand up, but I really didn't want the experience to end, so I just hung-onto the board. It was such hard work to get out past the breaks, but it was soo satisfying to catch a wave. Paul and I were hooked. We developed a good routine of breakfast and coffee, lifting weights, post workout smoothies, surfing in the afternoon, and indie films in the evening. One of the other beaches we tried surfing at was La Jolla, but went back to Solana the next day. To keep-up on our nutrition, we went to Whole Foods Market for some produce.

On the way into the market, I saw a woman sitting on the sidewalk, coloring a page in a coloring book. She had a few pages that she already colored on-display in front of her, and I thought she was just showing-off her work. Then I realized she was homeless, and was trying to earn some money from her work. I thought about giving her some money, but decided not to. We walked into the market, bought red beets, garlic, ginger, turmeric, and some greens. On the way out, I saw the lady again, and stopped to look at the pages she had on display in sheet protectors.

One of the pages she colored was line art of a boxcar on railroad tracks; and on the boxcar was line art of a great white shark bearing its teeth. She did a nice job coloring the pages, and even signed her work. I liked that she was doing something for her money, and didn't just sit there with a sign asking for handouts. I happily gave her money for the shark on the boxcar; and wanted to give her the sheet protector back, but she wanted me to keep it to protect the art I just bought. I wasn't going to argue with her, so I took the sheet protector too.

The whole experience made her happy. As I was walking away, she referred to the shark on boxcar, smiled and said: "That's California man!" then she raised her hand like a claw, growled at me, and laughed. It was a fun encounter, and I liked that she wasn't down on herself.

Back at Paul's apartment, Paul recounted how the year before he saw a woman, probably the same woman, sitting around that area. He said he saw a lady and her daughter stop, and give the woman a coloring book and crayons. Paul said he didn't give it much thought until we started talking about it, and loved that he was able to see the full cycle from broke, to enabled, to making money from her work. When I got back to North Dakota, I framed it, and hung it on the wall in my apartment.

Having just had a great time trying to surf in the Pacific Ocean, I was looking forward to trying to surf in the Atlantic Ocean when I went to visit my sister Kathy at Myrtle Beach. We walked on the boardwalks, and I looked for my opportunity, but I didn't see anyone else surfing. They had the red windsocks on the beach, and there were warnings in the news about high levels of bacteria in the water. I was a little freaked-out by all that, so I didn't even touch the water. Instead of surfing, we ate and drank at places that looked interesting to us. We also played put-put golf, and then played checkers at a grocery store.

After Myrtle Beach, I went to New Jersey. I like visiting my family in New Jersey, and usually stay at my sister's place. But, since she moved, I didn't have a place to stay. I ended-up renting a room at an Airbnb in Montclair, New Jersey. I did my usual routine of weights and cardio in the morning, and then it was time for lunch.

I went to Crooks Ave in South Paterson for lunch because I like Middle Eastern food. I ordered much more food than I could eat, so I got a carry-out box. I was waiting for my cousin Mike to finish work, and I didn't have anything else better to do, so I went for a walk.

I went back to Main Street, and started walking toward downtown Paterson. I passed a few Muslim people on the sidewalk as I walked, and saw a lot of Muslim shops and restaurants I was interested to stop and see, but I kept walking. A little under three miles into my walk, I had room in my belly, so I went to the Lou Costello Memorial Park to finish my food.

At the time, the park was covered in garbage, which was a little disappointing. But I picked-up an empty milk crate next to a park bench, cleared off a spot on the park bench, and put my milk crate down on the bench to use as a table. I sat there, and ate the rest of my lunch as I saw some homeless people drag their feet past me. I was tempted to leave my garbage on the park bench. Instead, I walked around the park, and put my waste in an empty garbage can. Then, I went back to Main Street.

I kept walking on Main Street until I got to my favorite place in Paterson. There is a two-story green awning connecting the buildings over Fair Street at Main Street. It's only a block off of Broadway, but it is soo clean and peaceful there. As a child, my mother held my little hand as we approached Fair Street, and we walked under the awning to buy fresh produce at the market. At the end of that block on Fair Street, there is still a market that sells fresh produce, and has fruit and vegetable stands setup outside along the street.

When I got to the market, I sat down on a chair they had against the building amongst the produce stands, and called my mother to tell her where I was at. After my call with my mother, Mike called me to see what I was doing. I wasn't doing anything, so I hailed a cab, and went to Little Falls.

Mike was hanging out at the gazebo in the park. Mike likes drinking Budweiser, had a 30-pack of it, so I helped him drink a few cans while he told me stories about my father. My father was a few years older than Mike, and used to babysit Mike. One story Mike told me was about them going to their neighbor's pool. My father was a confident, fashionable guy, and he was wearing a small tight-fitting swimsuit as they were walking down the street to their friend's pool. While Mike swam and played with one of his friends, my father was lying in the sun at the side of the pool, eating grapes he plucked off a neighbor's vine. It's a simple story, but it gave me a little insight to my father, and helps me feel a little closer to him. A few minutes later, Mike's brother Johnny showed-up to the gazebo, and started hanging out with us. I hadn't ever seen where my grandparents and great-grandparents were buried, but Johnny said he would take me there.

The next day, Johnny drove me to Laurel Grove Cemetery in Totowa. We visited his brother Jerry's headstone, and our grandparents, and great-grandparents headstones. The experience meant a lot to me, it was something I wanted to do for years. My uncle said he would take me there, but he ended up dying before he could do that. I was starting to run out of people, so it was really nice my cousin Johnny could take me there.

I asked my cousin Mike to look for an Abbott and Costello tee shirt for me that I wore as a child in Michigan. The tee shirt was baby blue, and had caricatures of Costello saying to Abbott: "Hey Abbott, Paterson has Everything!" The tee shirt was important to me as a child; because I was uncomfortable in Michigan, and it was my connection to a place where I wanted to be.

Lou Costello supported a boxing gym in Paterson to help give youths something else to do with their time other than run the streets. So my cousin Mike thought by contacting the managers of the gym, he would be able to find the tee shirt for me. The guy Mike spoke with said he had a tee shirt, and that he would set one aside for me. After Johnny and I left the cemetery, I called the guy, and he gave me the address of the gym.

We drove to Paterson, and Johnny waited in the car out-front while I went to the gym. I was greeted by a large old pit bull that was just happy to be alive. I patted the dog on his head as I walked into the gym. The gym was hot, and wasn't well lit, but it was busy. I told the first guy I saw why I was there, and he had no idea what I was talking about. He called the guy I spoke to earlier, and after a brief discussion, they found where he left the shirt for me. I gave the man $20, he gave me the tee shirt, and I was on my way. It wasn't the tee shirt I was looking for; instead, it was a tee shirt promoting the gym. I didn't mind too much, I like supporting honest people working toward a greater good.

When I got back to North Dakota, the supervisors were talking about team building exercises. Our interviewer saw me in the hall, told me he brought his flyboard to ride with his team, and invited me to join them. I had never been hydroflying before, so after work, I went out to the lake at Tobacco Gardens. Most of the guys had already been on the flyboard by the time I got there, and one guy was finishing up his flight, so I chit-chatted on-shore for a couple minutes. When it was my turn, I got in the water, and strapped on the boots.

Our interviewer controlled how high I flew, and I controlled the direction I flew. I was good at keeping my balance on it, but I was terrible at turning, and going forward or backward, so I just stood most of the time. Standing, our interviewer propelled me about 30' above the water. I was fascinated by the water jet below my feet pushing me above the water, it was soo interesting! It was such a cool experience, it was like being in a helicopter. I thanked our interviewer for letting me fly with him, and look forward to doing that again.

At the end of that work rotation, I was driving to South Dakota, and I got a call from my boss that Matt died. Matt used to be a drug addict before our pumper job. He quit the drugs a year before he got his pumper job, but he drank a lot of alcohol to take their place.

One night our group of friends was out drinking before we got our pumper jobs; he was about to leave, and I told him to give me his keys. He told me not to worry about it, kissed me on top of my head, grinned at me, and walked away. I was like, what am I going to do now? I wasn't drinking, so we got in our car, followed him, and watched as he drifted in and out of his lane. We made it home safe, but it was still a tense moment.

Matt's drinking was a lifestyle to him, which is cool, but he didn't do anything to balance-out the abuse to his body. So, I wasn't too surprised when a few weeks earlier I learned he was in the hospital with sepsis. And again, I wasn't shocked when he died. Even-though he was an ass to me toward the end, his death was still sad, especially for the people who care about him.

I was driving down to South Dakota because it was time for my camping-hiking-road trip with Jedediah. When I arrived at Tobias Garden to pick-up Jedediah, he was soo excited for our road trip! Before we left, we went to the garden, and picked some fresh basil and tomatoes. We put his produce and loaf of bread in the cooler with my fruit salad and beet-pesto dip, and started driving.

After a few hours of driving we passed Buffalo, Wyoming, stopped at a scenic overlook, and pulled-out the cooler to have a snack. I took a slice of Jedediah's bread, spread some of my beet pesto on the bread, put a few basil leaves on top of the spread, and topped-it-off with a slice of tomato. The basil in combination with the other flavors on the bread was wonderful! Eating the garden-fresh food in the fresh air of Wyoming was rejuvenating! Energized, we began driving again.

We drove for a few more hours, and it was starting to get dark. We were supposed to camp that night, but there were dark clouds above the mountains, and it seemed a little late to get a camping spot. I was a little intimidated about camping; I camped only once before in my life, 18 years ago. As we were driving, Jedediah was looking online for places for us to couch-surf. I wasn't about to force the camping issue at all; I suggested we stay at a hotel to get refreshed, and Jedediah went along with me after a couple failed couch surfing requests. So, we stayed the night in Cody, Wyoming. We had drinks and appetizers at Juniper, and I met a nice lady at the bar that worked for Microsoft.

In the morning, we drove to Red Lodge, and from there we turned onto Beartooth Highway. Beartooth Highway is a fun, and beautiful drive. At the top of the mountain, we stopped at a scenic lookout. We were ready for lunch, but it was busy up there.

We pulled-out the cooler, walked down the path, and climbed up a part of the mountain that was off the trail. At the top of that part of the mountain we opened-up the cooler and had lunch. It was such a long drive to get there, it felt like an accomplishment just to be there. After lunch, we packed-up our stuff, and headed back to the car.

As we were about to load the cooler into the car, I saw this big red truck pull-up. I couldn't believe who I saw get out of the truck; it was one of my coworkers, Jimmy. I didn't tell him or anyone at the office where I was going when I left on days off; yet, we ended-up in the same parking lot at the top of a mountain in Wyoming at the same time!

After our cool little meeting, we continued going our separate ways. Jedediah and I drove a down the road, and we were amazed to see soo much snow in late summer. One of our goals for our camping-hiking-road trip was to go alpine swimming.

We considered a lake at or above the tree-line to be an alpine lake. The tree-line is at high elevations where trees don't grow. We didn't have to drive far at the top of the Wyoming mountain to find our alpine lake, Gardner Lake. Excitedly, we got out of the car, and headed down the trail to the lake.

It was a windy day, and cold, but we weren't going to miss-out on this experience. It was about a mile hike down to the lake, and we were almost warm when we got to the lake. Prepared for the swim, I had swimming trunks on underneath my athletic gear. I pulled off all of my other clothes, and very slowly immersed myself into the alpine lake.

The water was numbing as it touched my skin. I actually had to get out of the water, get pumped-up again, and slowly start walking a little deeper into the lake. By the time I was waist deep, Jedediah was already jumping off of a boulder into the lake. I decided I was in far enough, and began swimming. The water was soo cold, but it was soo exhilarating! I splashed and swam around just enough to say I swam in an alpine lake, got out, and dried myself off.

While I was drying myself off, Jedediah had gotten out of the water, and jumped back into the water. I considered going back in, but my body was numb, and I really wanted to warm it up. So he swam around for a couple more minutes, and then we headed back up the trail to the car.

After our hike up the trail, we got back in the car, and started driving again. We stopped in Cooke City, Montana to pick-up a few more supplies. Cooke City is a busy town in the summer, and we met a couple from Europe. We had a coffee with them, topped-off my gas tank, and took-off.

Shortly thereafter, we were in Yellowstone National Park, and it was time for dinner. We saw a 20' high bolder in the river, and a little pull-off area next to it, so we decided to have dinner there. People already had a rock pile built-up the side of the boulder to make it easier to climb to the top of it. I reinforced the pile to make it a little safer to climb.

Jedediah climbed-up first, I handed him our food cooler, and then I climbed-up. It was pretty cool eating on top of the boulder in the middle of nature. While we were eating our dinner, a predatory bird flew down the middle of the river with a fish that it caught. When we finished our food, we packed our trash into the cooler, and began to climb down from the boulder. Jedediah, a little taller than me, climbed down first. I handed him the cooler, and then he helped guide my feet down the boulder to the little rock pile.

Safely off the boulder, we continued through Yellowstone. It was late in the day, and we still needed a camping spot, so we became speed tourists. The first part of Yellowstone we saw was the upper falls. We ran to the falls, snapped a few photos, then we ran back to the car. We rushed to Old Faithful, and were surprised to get a parking spot right away.

We were even more surprised when we only saw a mother and her daughter sitting at the geyser. We sat in the middle front row next to them, and started talking to them. They were from a state in the Northeast, and were making their way to the Northwest. The mother was dropping-off her daughter at a college with the car, and then she was going to fly back home. They were fun to talk to while we waited for Old Faithful to erupt.

As we were waiting, we saw a small crowd of people around another geyser not too far from us. We didn't think much of it, until it erupted. The eruption was soo cool; we stood on our benches to get a better view, and it was really fun to watch. When that geyser finished, a park ranger and a film crew from National Geographic setup next to us.

We started talking to them, and learned that we just missed the last Old Faithful eruption, and the other eruption we saw was from the Beehive Geyser. While we were talking to them, slowly, all of the rows of benches around the Old Faithful geyser began filling with people. Just as the sun was setting, we saw the Old Faithful eruption. It was cool, but I didn't think it was nearly as cool as the Beehive eruption. When Old Faithful finished, we got up, and began walking to the car.

There was a mass of people walking out to the parking lot. We needed a camping spot, and knew we needed to get out of there fast to get a spot, so we ran to the car. We were one of the first few people to get to the parking lot and start to leave.

We headed down the highway, and went to the closest campground. It was dark by the time we got there, and they only had two spots left. There was a guy next to us registering for one of the sites, and Jeddiah and I got the last one. We were soo lucky to get a camp site; while we were registering for the spot, a line of people formed behind us who were also trying to get a camping spot. We left the registration booth, and setup camp for the night. At our camp site we made a camp fire, and Jedediah strummed his acoustic guitar. One of the songs he played was Daft Punk—Get Lucky. While he strummed the song, I danced, and we had a lot of fun!

Jedediah had two sleeping bags, one alpine sleeping bag, and one summer sleeping bag. He didn't think it would be very cold at night, so he let me use his alpine sleeping bag, and I used my sleeping bag as a mattress. I was perfectly comfortable in shorts and a tee shirt in the alpine sleeping bag, and I slept soundly in the cold mountain air. Jedediah on the other hand got cold, and didn't sleep as well as me, so that wasn't a good start to our day.

After we packed-up our camp site, the next thing we did was try to find a camping spot at another campground. We went to a campground about twenty minutes away. They told us to fill-out a form, drive around until we found an open spot, hang our form on the sign, and then pay the fee. It was kinda busy, but we found a couple that were just getting out of their tent. We asked them about their spot, they said they were leaving, so we hung-up our reservation notice. The tricky thing about camping is you need to setup your campsite so that someone doesn't just throw away your campsite registration card, and steal the space you thought you had reserved. Jedediah and I loitered in the area, and when they left, we setup our tent.

That day we hiked up a mountain, and I got to go alpine swimming again. The lake was surrounded by mountain peaks, and there was a wide band of snowpack that came down from one of the mountain peaks toward the middle of the lake. There were several people hanging around the edge of the lake, talking amongst themselves, enjoying the satisfaction of a long hike-up. I looked at the lake as I took my clothes off, preparing myself for a swim. This lake had large jagged rocks the size of basketballs unevenly scattered along the shoreline. With my swim shorts on, I checked the balance of a rock, and then I stepped onto it. I saw a patch of sand in-between the rocks, so I stepped there next. There were a couple rocks a little deeper in the water, so I worked my way over to them, and balanced myself on them. All-the-while I was taking quick deep breaths because the water was soo cold. And because it was soo treacherous to get to where I was in the water, it was too difficult to get out of the water, warm-up a little, and catch my breath. The water was about at the middle of my thighs, so I took a deep breath, and dove-in the rest of the way. I yelped a little, and some people took photos of me as I swam. It was soo exhilarating swimming in that cold water, but after a couple minutes, I started swimming back to the rocky shore before my body stopped working. Near the shoreline, I crawled over the rocks on my hands and feet, trying not to fall onto the rocks. I made it safely out of the water, quickly dried myself off, and put my pants and sweatshirt on.

On our way down the mountain we talked to some local backcountry campers, and when we got to the parking lot we met another backcountry camper from Germany. The camper from Germany was a medical doctor, and was spending her vacation in our

American National Parks. She needed a ride to Jackson Hole; we were going to Jackson Hole too, so we gave her a ride.

After we dropped her off, Jedediah and I wanted some fresh food, so we stopped at Albertsons. We made salads from their salad bar, and ate them outside of the liquor store on their stone picnic tables. After our dinner, we bought a couple six-packs of local beer, and drove back to our campground. Jedediah made a campfire, we drank one of our six-packs, and ate some chips next to the fire.

After our drinks and snack, we prepared ourselves for sleep. Since Jedediah was soo cold the night before, he wanted to use his alpine sleeping bag. So, he did what I did. He used his summer sleeping bag as a mattress, and slept in his alpine sleeping bag. I knew I was going to be cold, so I brought an old set of my insulated fire resistant pants and jacket to wear as I slept in my 30-year old no-rating Winnebago sleeping bag my father gave me. Needless to say, I was cold and uncomfortable, and I didn't sleep well as I repositioned myself throughout the night on the hard ground. Naturally, I was in a sour mood in the morning.

Jedediah found another trail for us to climb, so we drove to the trailhead. Well, we tried to drive to the trailhead. The dirt road had a lot of potholes that I was able to negotiate my way through, but as we kept driving, the potholes became far too deep for my little VW Jetta to safely pass-through. So, we went as far as we could, and parked the car. We weren't the only hikers in a car that couldn't drive any further.

As we were having breakfast before our hike, a French family drove-up, and parked next to us. Jedediah speaks French, so he made friends with them quick. When the family was ready for their hike, they started walking down the road to the trailhead, and Jedediah and I finished our breakfast. I didn't have any ice in my cooler, so the fruit salad I brought with me at the start of the trip was starting to ferment. I didn't want to get sick from my fruit, so I threw the rest of my fruit salad in the woods for something else to eat. Then, we walked the half-mile to the trail head.

The trail we were hiking went up a rock-filled gorge. There was a stream in the middle of the gorge, and the trail mostly followed the stream. Three-quarters of the way up the gorge, we met the French family on the trail. They were really tired, and wanted to quit. But Jedediah encouraged them to continue the hike, so they did. When we got to the top of the gorge I was really tired from the hike. Jedediah wanted to see more, so he hiked-on, while I tip-toed into the river for an alpine river swim.

When he came back, he told me he found a beautiful flower filled meadow, and wanted me to go and see it. I had enough hiking, and kept entertaining myself by dunking myself under the water at a deep spot next to a boulder in the river. The French family finally caught-up with us, and went with Jedediah to the meadow. In the meadow, the French family were finally able to relax, and Jedediah took a nice photo that he later sent to them. Jedediah left the family, and came back to the river to swim with me. Of course it was very cold, and we didn't swim long, but it was another exhilarating experience.

When we hiked back down the gorge, we wanted to see more of the park, so we drove. There was a forest fire the next state over, so most of the sites we wanted to see were hazy from the smoke. We stopped at the Snake River overlook, pulled-out the cooler, and had lunch there.

We met a couple from California, and they were thrilled to see the North Dakota license plates on my car. They said seeing a car with North Dakota plates outside of North Dakota was as rare as seeing a car with plates from Hawaii. We talked about National Parks, and they said they were interested to go to the Theodore Roosevelt National Park. I lived in North Dakota five years, had never been to the park, and this couple from California wanted to make a special trip to come see the park. Theodore Roosevelt National Park is only 20 minutes south of Watford City, so they inspired me to go there. After our dinner, we drove some more, and saw a scenic overlook near our campground.

At the overlook, we met a vegetarian hippie girl who lived in her van. A couple nights earlier we saw her van parked in a pull-off next to the road. It was neat meeting her, and we had fun talking to her for a little while. As we were leaving, some deer were hanging around the parking lot, so Jedediah took some photos of them.

When we got back to the campground, Jedediah wanted wifi, so we went to the campground bar. At the bar, we met a mother and daughter who were in-town for the funeral of one of the mother's old camp counselor friends. In addition to the funeral, they were having a camp counselor reunion party. I had a lot of fun listening to the mother's coming-of-age stories as a camp counselor at the park.

She was raised in a small town in the mid-west. For that reason, it was a life changing experience for her to meet other camp counselors from around the nation, so she came back as a camp counselor every year for a few years thereafter. The mother and daughter left the bar, and invited us to their camp site. Jedediah wanted more photos, so he went to the lake to take photos of the Tetons. When he came back, I got a beer to go, and we drove to the mother and daughter's campsite. I liked drinking and driving to the campsite, and when we found their campsite, we found them playing some card game. Jedediah and I joined them in the card game for a little while until the mother said she was ready for sleep. It was a good idea, so we left, and went to our campsite for sleep.

In the morning, Jedediah and I started-out on our long drive home. We broke-up the drive by stopping in Thermopolis, and playing in the Hot Spring pools. After that, we stopped in Casper for fuel.

I don't know why, but I have a thing with gas station bathrooms. While I was fueling-up my car, I needed to go inside and use their restroom. I asked the lady where their restroom was, and she told me they didn't have one for public use. I told her: "I'm fueling-up my car," and she said: "I can't let you use it." My jaw dropped as I turned away, shocked, and frustrated. My bladder had been full for hours! I really needed to use the restroom, she had one, but she couldn't let me use it! That put me in a really bad mood. Jedediah picked-up on that quick, and my anger and frustration put him on edge, creating a contentious atmosphere in my car. Needing a pick-me-up, we went downtown, and stopped for coffee.

I ordered a black coffee with a scoop of ice, asked her if she had a restroom I could use, and a chorus of angles sang as she said: "yes." Doubled-over in pain, I shuffled my feet toward the men's room. When I came out of the restroom, I was finally relieved, but I was still miffed about my gas station bathroom experience. In addition to all of that, we needed food.

We drove to the Natural Grocers. That is another health food store that is well managed. We bought some food to eat now and later, and went outside to eat our now-food. It was a really hot day, so we ate our food in the shade of the building. That night, we were back in South Dakota. I dropped-off Jedediah in Hermosa, spent the night in Rapid City, and continued to North Dakota the next day.

On the drive to North Dakota, the rest areas I saw with picnic tables and benches finally made sense to me. Our predominant culture when they were building the interstates was to pack our own food on road trips, and stop at those rest stops to eat lunch. Of course, they didn't have huge travel centers then like we do now, but I still think it is unfortunate that we have given-up that part of our culture. It's gotten soo bad that states are defunding the travel centers, and tearing them down, because most of those picnic areas at the rest stops are almost always empty. I didn't stop at any travel centers or rest stops on the way to North Dakota; I try not to drink anything, and usually only eat snacks that I pre-packed before the drive.

Back in North Dakota, I actually followed-through, and went hiking in Theodore Roosevelt National Park. I met a girl on the trail who was a Quaker, and she taught at the Friends School in Germantown where I used to work in Philadelphia. We ended-up hiking together, and talking about our similar experiences. Along the way, we met Ranger Jeff, and he gave her a hug and a sticker for bringing water with her on the trail.

Ranger Jeff was grateful she was prepared for her hike. The week before he had to rescue a guy who went off the trail, and collapsed from the heat because he didn't have enough water with him. I didn't get a hug or sticker because I didn't bring water like I should have, and almost got heat stroke. The heat radiating off the rocks was cooking me. Toward the end of the hike I was getting dizzy, and had to stop and drink some of my Germantown Quaker friend's water. Nevertheless, the ranger did invite me to a guided off-trail hike during the week.

I was late for the start of that hike, but caught-up to the group quick, and even had water with me! On the hike we saw Bison and the Little Missouri River. I finished another work week, and began another adventure on my days off.

I really liked the scenic cooler lunches that Jedediah and I had on our camping-hiking-road trip, and wanted that experience again. With my cooler packed, and my car loaded, I started driving. I was heading down to Colorado to see my cousin Tracy, who I hadn't seen since our great aunt's birthday party in Connecticut nine years earlier.

There were two legs to my journey; the first was Watford City to Rapid City, and the second was Rapid City to Littleton, Colorado. I ate before I left, so I didn't stop anywhere during my drive to Rapid City. But when I got ten-minutes South of Rapid City, and was in the country again, I started thinking that I had six more hours to drive. I was dreading that idea; and that was 12 hours of my life that I wouldn't be writing, or spending time with people I care about. I had enough.

I turned around, and looked for a flight on my phone on my way to the airport. That afternoon, there was an earlier flight, and a later flight, from Rapid City to Denver. I was about 20 minutes too late for the earlier flight, so I booked the later flight. Since I had time to spare, I bought a large bag of ice on my way to the airport, and filled my cooler to preserve my food.

When I got to the airport, I knew I was late for the earlier flight, but I still asked my United Airlines ticketing agent about the possibility of getting onto the earlier flight. She told me the flight already left, but was coming back to the airport for maintenance. The flight was full, but she said she would try to get me onto the flight. I really didn't think it was going to work-out in my favor, but I thanked her, and continued through security. Waiting for the late flight didn't bother me; my gate was peaceful, so it was easy for me to continue to write this book.

As I was writing, I noticed the earlier flight did come back, and all of the passengers got off of the plane. When I got up to get a drink from the water fountain, I saw most of the passengers loitering at their gate, waiting for the maintenance issue to be fixed on their airplane. I continued writing, and after about 45 minutes, I heard they were boarding the plane again. They boarded all of the zones and made the final boarding call. After another minute, I was surprised to hear the gate agent calling my name! I quickly put my computer in my backpack, zipped-it-up, and rushed to the gate.

The gate agent was looking down the terminal to see if anyone was walking to her gate. She saw me and asked me if I was Richard, I told her yes, and she let me board the early flight! I was really appreciative of what the United Airlines agents did for me, and I liked that I got to write more on the plane. I even had a little time to write while I was in Littleton.

I stayed at an Airbnb while I was visiting Tracy because she didn't have any room in her place, and her daughter Allissa just moved into a new house with her husband Marcus, so they didn't have anything setup for guests yet. My Airbnb host was trying to payoff her townhouse, so she rented-out her bedrooms on Airbnb, and slept in her garage. I love hearing stories like that; of people doing things differently to get out of debt, and working toward sustainable economic security. Other than working on my book, and talking to my Airbnb host, I exercised!

Every morning I took a Lyft to Snap Fitness in Roxborough Park because it was the closest 24-hour gym to my Airbnb. The idea was I would continue to write during my gym commute, but I ended-up talking to most of my Lyft drivers, and didn't get much writing done. After my workouts, I hung-out with Tracy and Allissa.

Most of our get-togethers were food-centered-socializing. One day we went to downtown Denver for the Taste of Colorado food festival. They didn't have any of the foods that I prefer to eat, but I did enjoy the handmade skin salves, and honey on the comb. Another day we had a barbecue at Allissa's place, where she did have food for me to eat, because her brother Josh brought-over some veggie dogs. The next day we had breakfast at Tracy's place, where I ate most of her ice cream, and then I went to the airport for my flight to Rapid City.

When I got back to Rapid City, I found the ice melted in my cooler. I expected that, but I didn't expect my cooler to leak. After sitting in the sun, closed-up for a few days, my car smelled mildewie. To get the smell out of my car, I kept the windows cracked as I drove. And when I left the car parked in North Dakota, I left the windows cracked so my car could heat-up in the sun, and allow the bad air to vent out of my car.

For my next work week, I went to Billings, Montana. I worked most of the time, but had a Saturday off, so I went downtown. Billings has a profuse independent movie culture, so I went to the Art House Cinema and Pub.

There aren't any independent movie theaters in Western North Dakota, so I had to seize the opportunity while I could. At Art House Cinema and Pub, I saw signs for donating to the theater for Phase 2, so I donated, and became an Art House Cinema Member. I was visiting right in the middle of their MINT film festival; they were soo appreciative of my donation, they welcomed me to their after-party at the Petroleum Club.

I had a little time before the after-party, so I had a few more beers at Carter's, and saw an indie boxing movie at the Babcock Theater. After the movie, a few of the people involved with making the movie answered questions from the audience at the stage, below the screen of the theater. Then I walked to the party at the Petroleum Club, had fun meeting a few independent movie makers, and did a little dancing. The next day, it was back to work for me.

Around this time, Eric moved into the apartment. So it was like the old days for us again, four of us living in a two-bedroom apartment. Unlike the old days, rents are now half of what they used to be, because they built soo many apartment complexes to meet Watford City's housing needs. It's really great that the four of us can split the rent and utilities, if it wasn't for that, it would be really tough to save money and get ahead.

My next trip was to Portugal. My niece in Macedonia said she was going there, and invited me to meet her there. It was a great opportunity for me; I had never been to Portugal, and wanted to go for years. I was only going to see her one day while I was there, so I reserved several Airbnb experiences to fill the rest of my time. As soon as the plane landed in Lisbon, my Airbnb host's friend picked me up from the airport. She took me to my room to check-in at Ericeira, and then my host dropped me off at the beach.

There was a World Surf League competition at the beach, so I watched the competition for a few minutes, and checked-out the vendors. In a rocky area next to the beach they were having surf lessons, and a lot of people were just hanging out on the rocks or swimming. I walked along the rocks looking for a place to safely get into the ocean, but the waves crashing against the rocks made that a little challenging for me.

One of the local girls saw where I was trying to get into the water, and warned me that the waves could throw me against the rocks. I was definitely getting that impression. She showed me a safe place to jump off of the rocks into the ocean, so I did! I was really appreciative of her help, and wanted to talk to her a little more, but she swam away. To occupy my time, I just kept climbing up the rocks, and jumping into the ocean.

That night, I toured the estate I was staying at, and ate figs fresh from the tree! There were many other fruit trees on the property too, but no other fruit was in season. After touring the property, my host led me in a private yoga class until the sun set. I enjoyed the fresh country air, and the cool ocean breeze, I could even see the ocean from my room.

In the morning, my host took me to the beach for a surf lesson. There were three other students with me, and we practiced surfing in the same rock area I was swimming-in the day before. I stood-up on the foam board several times, but the waves were small, and every wave I caught was coach assisted, so I wasn't that proud of my accomplishments. After my surf lesson, I had breakfast at a café on a cobblestone side-street in Ericeira, and my host's friend picked me up to take me to my next Airbnb apartment in Lisbon.

After I checked-in at my apartment in Lisbon, my Airbnb experience host picked me up, and took me to the ocean for another surf lesson. I wanted to accomplish two things. One, I wanted to learn how to get past the breaks. And two, I wanted to try surfing a board that was not a foam board. My surf coach gave me a plastic surfboard that wasn't very buoyant, and taught me how to duck dive to get past the breaks. I was surprised how quickly I caught-on to the duck dive, and how well it worked for me. I was doing great getting past the breaks, and there were great waves in the ocean, but I was only able to body board one wave to the shore. I made the very poor choice of not wearing a wetsuit, so I was really cold, and couldn't stay in the water nearly as long as I wanted to. That night, I met my cousin at her friend Vasco's apartment in Lisbon.

We got warmed up with a beer and a shot of rakija in his apartment, and then we went to a bar called Tokyo. I recognized the music as soon as we walked in, classic eurodance! It's not very popular in the United States, but it's music that I know and love, and it felt soo good to be in a room full of people who knew and loved the same songs as me! Adding another level of cool to the experience, the band, Sultão Veneno, was playing funk covers of the classic eurodance songs! I had an amazing time dancing and singing along with everyone in the bar. When the band finished their show, Vasco took us to dance at Club Lux, and we stayed there until about five in the morning.

When we left the club, Vasco and I needed food, so we went to McDonalds. In that restaurant, they had a McVeggie, a vegetarian sandwich. At the time, they weren't selling the McVeggie sandwiches in the United States, so it was a rare opportunity to eat a vegetarian sandwich from McDonalds. After our breakfast, I tried to take an

Uber back to my apartment.

Somehow my Uber driver screwed-up, and dropped me off in the wrong neighborhood. Even my host's friend from Ericeira, who knew the city, got lost trying to find my apartment when she was dropping me off. The good thing was, my host's friend from Ericeira had to drive around the blocks several times as she was trying to find the apartment, so that helped me get to know the area. So when my Uber driver left me at wrong apartment, I started walking until I saw some familiar landmarks, and then I knew where to go from there. It took me about an hour, but I did make it back to the apartment.

My flight for Porto was leaving at eight in the morning. I thought about going straight to the airport, but I was really tired, and wanted to sleep for an hour before I left. I set three alarms, but I slept through all of the alarms, and woke up to the sound of a car exhaust echoing off the buildings as it was driving by the apartment at eleven in the morning. I felt great after my sleep, but I missed my flight, so I had to get to the airport to get a seat on another flight.

I had to pay a $200 re-booking fee, but I got a seat on another flight at five p.m. It was great that I got another seat, but I missed my afternoon surf lesson and rickshaw tour in Porto. Also, I was supposed to meet my Airbnb host Diogo to drop my bags off at his apartment, but missed that appointment too, so he gave me his father José's phone number to make arrangements with him when I arrived. Adding insult to injury, my flight was delayed, so I was late for my chef hosted dinner in Porto.

Nevertheless, my chef host Hélder welcomed me, and still took good care of me. As I was about to leave, I noticed I was missing my backpack. I was soo confused, I thought I just misplaced it in the house. But when I talked to the other people in my Airbnb experience group, they said I only walked-in with one bag. Somehow I remembered to get my duffel-bag out of the trunk, but forgot my backpack in the backseat. I tried to contact my Uber driver, but he only spoke Portuguese. So I ordered another Uber, and he dropped me off at my Airbnb apartment where José let me in.

José was amazing! He spoke English, so he contacted the Uber driver, and got the address where the driver left my backpack. José told me traffic was crazy in the morning, so I needed to be up and leave early. It was important for me to get there early, because I was supposed to do the Taste Authentic Duoro day trip, and we were meeting at 8:30 in the morning at Starbucks. But, the Uber office didn't open until 8:30. So I did my part, and made it a point to get to the Uber office early.

In the morning, my Uber driver dropped me off at a massive industrial park, and I was actually 45 minutes early! As I was walking up to the side of the largest building on the property looking for the Uber suite, I saw a couple tour busses parked in the building with the garage doors open. I was thinking that might have been part of the Uber operation, but kept walking to the front of the building. When I got to the front of the building, I noticed the doors to the building were open, and the facilities services lady was setting-up, and cleaning the front area. I asked her about the Uber office, and she showed me where it was.

The lights were off inside the office, the door was locked, and I didn't see my backpack. That was a little discouraging for me. Since I was soo early, I sat on a couch in the lobby. I didn't have a data package for my phone, so I asked the facility services lady for the wifi password. She went to a back office, wrote it down on a piece of paper, and gave it to me! I thanked her, and she continued doing her building prep.

While I waited for the guy to come to the Uber office, I contacted Manuel of Taste Authentic Douro, and told him I was waiting for my bag. I asked if I could meet him later, and he asked me how much time I needed. Timing was important, because we were meeting guys at the boats for a Duoro river tour. 8:30 came and went, and I still didn't see anyone go to the Uber office. I'm usually late, so I figured this was just karma. I told Manuel he could leave without me, because I still didn't have my bag. Then Manuel replied to me asking where I was at, so I sent him the address. After ten more minutes, I finally called the Uber guy. He answered, and explained to me he wasn't at the office, he was at the back of the property behind the building.

I thought he meant at the back of the building I was in, so I walked back down to where I saw the busses, and asked the guy there if he was Uber. He just shook his head at me, so I kept walking. The area was starting to look a little uninviting, but I reluctantly kept walking. I saw an operations guy outside in the middle of some maintenance work, talked to him, and he directed me inside.

A short old man greeted me inside. I asked him about my

backpack, he raised his index finger to say one minute, and went around a corner behind a wall. He came back a few seconds later holding one of the straps in his hand, dangling my backpack a foot off the ground like he was holding-up a mischievous child. He set it down in front of me, and I began frantically rummaging through it.

The two most important things to me were in there; my computer, and my car key. I held up my car key to show the guy, and he shook his head down and away from me empathetically as well as grateful it wasn't him. I thanked him, and walked out of there quickly.

I was soo relieved to have my backpack, and was hopeful there was a chance I could still go on the Douro tour. I needed to go all the way back to the front lobby where I was sitting to get wifi, and see if Manuel messaged me. When I got back to the front of the building, I quickly logged-in to check my messages. Manuel sent me four messages saying he could pick me up in 10 minutes, asked me if I was ready, and then told me he needed feedback. I quickly replied to him: "I am ready" and didn't even wait for a response, I just walked back to the gate where I first entered.

I nervously waited at the street, staring at the driver of every car that drove-by on the side-street, looking to see if anyone recognized me or was looking for me. I waited for a while, and wasn't really sure if Manuel was even going to pick me up. I would have been okay with that, I would have just spent the rest of the day writing. I started to think losing my computer wouldn't have been a big deal if I would have had a backup of my book. I originally had this backed-up on Dropbox. But my computer is soo old, Dropbox doesn't support Vista anymore, so my files don't backup to Dropbox like they used to.

As I continued to reflect and plan my day, a black luxury car pulled-up, and stopped in front of me. The passenger side window rolled down, and the flashy guy inside said: "Richard?" with a European accent and in a questioning tone. I excitedly said: "Yes!" He put the car in park, walked around, and opened the trunk for me to put my bag in.

Manuel broke all of the speed limit laws on the way to boat, but, we were exactly on time. That guy's customer service is way over the top. If you ever have the chance to go to Porto, and like to drink wine, do his Taste Authentic Douro day trip. I'm glad he went out of his way to include me on the tour.

241

The river-tour part of the day trip was a great way to start the day. There were eight of us on the tour, and we went down the river in a little motor boat while the driver's assistant talked to us about the vineyards. I liked that I got to see the vineyards of big Port brands such as Warre, Sandeman, and Croft. On our way back to the dock we drank a cocktail, and had hors d'oeuvres. A lady from New York sitting next to me in our group actually complained about drinking alcohol so early in the morning. I told her I would be happy to help her finish her drink, and she was happy to give me her drink.

We had lunch and a wine tasting at a restaurant in a village overlooking the Douro Valley. The lady from New York sat next to me, and was a little overwhelmed by all of the wine we were drinking at lunch. I came to her rescue again, and helped her finish her glass of wine. After lunch, we had an exclusive tour of a local winery.

One of my favorite parts of the winery tour was eating grapes, with seeds, straight off of the vine. The grapes tasted just like the Vintage Port wines I like to drink. An interesting thing I learned is the locals are proud of their wine varietals, but they say Port and Vintage Port are for tourists. While I was at the winery they had wine for sale, but they didn't have any Vintage Port, not even hidden in the back somewhere. We sampled a lot of wine at the winery, and on the car ride back to the city, I took a well-deserved nap.

When we got back to Porto, we were right on time for my next Airbnb experience, a Fado dinner and city tour with Bernardo. My host took me to a park overlooking a river. It was a Monday, and I was surprised to see the park was filled with people. Some people were playing guitars, some were smoking weed, some were drinking, dogs were running around, families were there, children were playing, single people, couples, groups of friends…everybody was there. It was like an event; but they were just hanging out, watching the sun set. My host got me a beer, and we stayed in the park too, watching the sun set. It was soo interesting to me. I've watched the sun set before, and I've seen other people watching the sun set, but there it was something really special.

The Fado dinner was singers dressed-up, passionately singing traditional Portuguese songs. The singers reminded me a lot of our traditional music and dress in Macedonia. As soon as the dinner was finished, and I had my two glasses of wine, I looked for my host. I found him talking to a couple of his friends back at the park. We walked a little from there, and found a girl sitting with her friend, strumming a Portishead song on her guitar. We toured the city a little more after that, listened to more traditional music in his car, and Bernardo dropped me off at my apartment.

I was in bed before midnight because I was flying back to America the next day. This time I woke up early, my Uber driver promptly picked me up, and I didn't leave anything in his car! My flight was on-time to Lisbon, and my flight from Lisbon to America was also on-time.

My next trip was to Salt Lake City to visit Jason. Jason is always an excellent host. When the plane landed, he picked me up in front of the airport, and had a cold beer ready for me. We drove downtown to meet with his Meetup beer-drinkers group. After that, we went to a nightclub called Sky SLC for Therapy Thursday. Our disc jockey (DJ) Tchami, wore a traditional black priest uniform, including the clerical collar, and he called his set Confession. His music was euphoric for me, I felt the music, and it took me to another level as I danced for hours! The light board behind him was entertaining too. Tchami's underground music helped me have the best time ever at a night club! Adieu is a good song to get warmed-up to Tchami.

The next day we drove to Moab. Moab is a little touristy, but I was delighted that we stayed at the completely solar powered Adventure Inn. During the day, we hiked, and saw a couple arches. At night, we did the windows hike, and I was just speed-walking up the trail. But Jason suddenly stopped, so I stopped to see what he was doing, and he told me to look up. At the angle we were at, all I could see was stars through the large window arch that framed the night sky. It almost looked like stepping through the window would take me to another dimension. It was really amazing to see that! We admired the view for a while, and explored the arch for a few minutes before heading back to our solar powered motel.

The next day we began making our way to Las Vegas, but we took the scenic route. We started by driving down to the four corners; the spot in the United States where Utah, Colorado, New Mexico, and Arizona meet. I was surprised the monument is on Native American reservation land. Being there was humbling, and everyone we saw there was quiet and respectful. We snapped photos at the monument, ate Navajo Tacos, and continued driving. Our next stop was the Sunset Crater Volcano National Monument in Arizona. Well, we drove into the park, and went to the visitor center anyway. We were there too late in the day, and the crater was too far away for us to go see. After that, we drove through Flagstaff, and continued through to Las Vegas.

In Las Vegas, we stayed at The Stratosphere (The Strat). I've been to Las Vegas a couple times before, but never did the thrill rides at The Strat. Now was the time for me. I started with the Sky Jump. Sky Jump is an 829' decelerator decent. There are soo many safety checks leading up to the jump off-of-the-building that I was not at all concerned about my safety. The scariest part was standing outside, at the top of the building, holding onto the hand rail as the guy switched cables from standing to jumping. For a couple seconds, the only safety device I had was my hands holding onto the railing, 108 floors above the ground. I really liked the exhilaration of the risk standing there in the gusty wind, and seeing the city out of the corner of my eye. After he put my jump-cable on, he did a quick countdown, and I jumped. It was a nice little ride. Most of the ride I was just preparing myself for the landing, so I didn't get to enjoy much of the view. Jason was awesome, and got a video of me cabling down to the landing pad. Jason wasn't interested in the Sky Jump, but he did ride the Big Shot, and X-Scream with me.

Big Shot wasn't at all what I expected. I thought they were going to raise me up, and then drop me for a freefall. Instead, they launched me from the bottom, and then pulled me down from the top. When the ride took off, I didn't even know what happened to me. I thought I had died; because for a second, I felt like I wasn't even in the rollercoaster anymore. I felt like nobody else was there; it was just me, floating over the city. While I was floating there, I realized I wasn't dead, and I started to wonder how the heck I was going to get to the ground safely. As soon as I finished that thought, the ride started pulling me back down. That is when I remembered what I was doing. I gripped my safety bars tightly as the ride pulled me down. During the ride, I was giggling with fear and delight as it stopped at the bottom, and then shot me back up again. That moment at the top where I felt like I was floating was soo scary, it was such an intense experience. The guy sitting next to me bought the three-ride package, and was staying on for his third ride. I completely understood why he wanted to ride it multiple times.

From there, Jason and I went to X-scream. The roller coaster pushing and pulling us over the edge of the building felt pretty cool, but it was nothing in comparison to the exhilaration I felt at the top of the Big Shot.

The next day, we drove back to Salt Lake City. That loop we did was close to a 20-hour drive. I normally don't like to be in the car that long, but Jason's car had an electrical outlet for me to plug my computer into, so I wrote most of the time. Trapped in the car with no wifi; I did a lot of writing, so those 1,300 miles passed relatively quickly for me. Jason on the other hand was bored out of his skull, and suggested we fly to Las Vegas next time. Flying is my preferred mode of travel anyway, so I was perfectly okay with that suggestion.

After my next work week, I went to Michigan to visit my mother. My mother is very thoughtful; she doesn't expect me to visit her on any holiday, she just wants me to come help her with some yard work in the fall. So that is what I do. Late October I go to her house in Michigan, help her turn the soil in the garden, put the fountains away, and help her do a few other little things around the house. She is very appreciative for my help, and I am appreciative that she is reasonable. Weather was starting to get really cold in North Dakota, and I wasn't ready for winter, so I made arrangements to visit Pam in California on my next set of days off.

I flew to California, and Pam picked me up at the Ontario International Airport. From there, we drove to Temecula. I loved the 80°F weather there, sitting in the sun, and running my five-mile loop in the desert hills above her subdivision. While I was there, I took a Lyft to San Diego to visit Paul, and we went bar-hopping in the Gaslamp Quarter for a night. We had dinner at an Italian restaurant, drank a bottle of Chianti there, and signed the bottle's grass skirt. We hung the bottle from one of the rafters in the restaurant, along with all of the other signed Chianti bottles from their guests. I spent the night at his place, and took a Lyft back to Temecula in the morning. Again, the little downtime I had I spent writing.

Traveling is really unpredictable in the winter, so most of the rest of the winter I didn't go anywhere, until Chris called me in February. He was really excited, he just bought a boat, and told me to come down to South Florida to visit him. I hadn't seen him in six years, so I quickly booked a flight to see him my next set of days off. He was working most of the time I was there. That was cool with me, because you know I spent most of my time working on this book. Saturday morning he didn't have to work, and I suggested we go surfing.

Chris's buddy Gian was a surf instructor at Island Water Sports, so Chris took me there to get a surf lesson. I'm still a little arrogant, and was thinking I knew enough already about surfing, so I wasn't too interested in another surf lesson. But, I agreed to go anyway. It was just a free surf lesson that Island Water Sports does regularly, and there were a lot of people there. I thought it was going to be like every other surf lesson I had, a little disappointing. But, the staff there were high energy! I had a lot of fun, and learned a lot!

What I liked best was that Gian explained riptides to me. Everybody I talked to before this class always referred to riptides like they were the boogie-man. Gian told me how to recognize a riptide, told me not to panic, and told me to swim parallel to the shore until I was out of the riptide. With his simple explanations, he took the mystery and fear out of riptides for me. The other great thing about the class is that the instructors were available for me in the water if I wanted to use them. Otherwise, I was free to try to surf on my own, and I really loved that autonomy.

I was able to catch the first wave I saw as soon as I got into the water, and Chris recorded a video of me doing it! But; it was like my first time riding a bicycle, I quickly lost my balance and fell. Still, I learned, and had more fun in that free class than in any of the classes I paid for.

Back in North Dakota, around this time last year I got sick from my apartment-mate Mat when I screwed-up my Australian travel visa. This year, Eric was sick. Anyone sick in the apartment makes me nervous, but I was determined to not get sick, again. In an effort to take care of my microbiome, so that my microbiome took care of me, every morning I had a spinach and spring mix salad with leek, half an avocado, a half-cup of my eight bean mix, and sprinkled four crushed sheets of seaweed wrap onto the salad. I made my own creamy dressing for the salad by putting into my magic bullet a half-cup of bean juice that I saved from when I cooked the beans, four fresh garlic cloves, ¾ teaspoon ginger, ½ teaspoon turmeric, ¼ teaspoon of cayenne pepper, 1 teaspoon of nutritional yeast, the other half of the avocado, and a splash of apple cider vinegar. I prefer to use fresh spices, but I only had dried spices at the time. Regardless, after a week of being around sick Eric, I didn't get sick! Another reason I didn't get sick was that I wasn't stressed-out about anything; I had a little stress about trying to finish this book, but that was relatively manageable.

After a year of saving money, living mostly frugally except for all of the money I spent on traveling, I was able to save $50,000. What's amazing, is that my current living expenses are actually lower than a couple years ago when I was trying soo hard to reduce my monthly expenses. I was able to do that thanks to Eric moving into the apartment with us to help spread our expenses evenly, and I don't drive 300 miles a week to go to my part time jobs in South Dakota. It feels good to have $50,000 cash, but now that I'm here, I'm looking forward to saving $100,000. Again, my mother said I need to be smart with my money and invest it, but I'm not ready for that. I haven't had any cash for most of my life; I'm still getting used to the feeling, and don't even feel comfortable moving my money into my savings account.

At Coldwell Banker and at Sky Ranch, I worked with a couple guys who had most of their money in investments. As they were getting ready to retire, the market crashed. One guy lost most of his money in the .com bust, and the other guy lost his money during the market crash at the start of the Great Recession. Those guys lost soo much money after the market crashes they had to go back to work for another decade. Also, I've worked with a few old guys in the oil field, thought they should have retired decades ago, and wondered why they were still there. I don't want to be any of those guys.

I know I'm losing 2% a year from inflation, because my money is sitting in a non-interest bearing checking account, but that is a negligible loss compared to what those guys lost. So, I might just leave my money where it is. Or, I might figure-out something to do with my money, and write a book about it.

I was so wound-up from paying my debts for soo long, I forgot how to be me. It took most of a year, and all of that traveling, for me to regain my character that I subdued. I was soo focused on paying my debts, that almost nothing else mattered to me. My mother mattered to me, my physical and economic health mattered to me, and keeping my boss happy mattered to me, but that was it.

Another surprise for me was the more traveling I did, the more proud I was to be an American. I used to be frustrated with our politics, and thought we were soo unempathetic to the working class. I used to hold on a pedestal the ideologies of more progressive European countries. And then I went there, and found-out they're not any better-off than us. They have the same struggles as us, but they don't have the same freedom as us. It's amazing, the grass is always greener on the other side, until you go there.

Setlist

Corey Hart—Sun Glasses At Night

The Pointer Sisters—I'm So Excited

Social Distortion—I Was Wrong

The Chemical Brothers—Dig Your Own Hole

Underworld—Born Slippy (Nuxx)

Goldie—Inner City Life (Radio Edit)

The Exploited—Alternative

Roni Size & Reprazent—Share The Fall (Full Vocal Mix)

Bad Boy Bill & Richard "Humpty" Vission—House Connection 2

Charge Cheer

Moby—My Weakness

Modest Mouse—Styrofoam Boots/It's All Nice on Ice

Delerium—Heavens Earth (Key South Remix)

Nude Dimensions: Naked Music, Vol. 1—The Petalpusher Session
Mixed by Miguel 'Migs'

Ministry of Sound—The Annual 2002, Disk 1

Carl Cox—Mixed Live: Crobar Night Club, Chicago

D.B. Boulevard—Point of View

BT—R&R Rare & Remixed (CD 2)

The Clientele—My Own Face Inside The Trees

Armin van Buuren—A State Of Trance Year Mix 2007

friskyPodcast138—Miss Disk

When Saints Go Machine—Parix

Why?—Good Friday

Estiva feat. Josie—Better Days

KAASI & TÂCHES—Heartbeats

Jenna G—Rising

Linnea Schössow—Someone Like You

Ry & Frank Wiedemann—Howling (Âme remix)

Nicolas Coronel presents Mestiza Records on FriskyRadio June-10-
2013

Miike Sno—Burial

Grizzly Bear—Two Weeks

Jaded—Made in China

Descendents—Catalina

Rationale—Deliverance

Jbre x Dougie Kent—Stimulation feat. SaneBeats & Margret Kramer
Tricky—Overcome
Portishead—Cowboys
L_DG—Sunset Gaze
Drumlinezz—Just When We Thought It Was Over
Daft Punk—Get Lucky
Tchami—Adieu

ABOUT THE AUTHOR

Richard Holzmuller is passionate about diet and exercise, sustainability, and music. Richard loves learning, and sharing what he learns, with whomever wants to listen. Richard loves people; meeting new people, hearing about their experiences, and learning about their worldview. Richard loves art, artistic expression, authenticity, and experiences.

Made in the USA
Columbia, SC
28 April 2021

36461403R00155